THROUGH

CHINA'S

WALL

Through
CHINA'S
WALL

BY

GRAHAM PECK

With Illustrations by the Author

1940

The Riverside Press Cambridge

HOUGHTON MIFFLIN COMPANY · BOSTON

The Riverside Press
CAMBRIDGE · MASSACHUSETTS
PRINTED IN THE U.S.A.

CONTENTS

PORTRAIT DRAWINGS

I. ROUND-TRIP

I LEFT Peking for the last time on a warm afternoon in mid-October, boarding the train from a station platform which lay freakishly quiet and deserted in the clear autumn sunlight. Two months before, every train to the coast had been frantically jammed with refugees, but that stopped after the fighting began at Shanghai and this train carried practically no Chinese; the cars were empty except for a sprinkling of Japanese officers and traveling salesmen, a guard of live Japanese soldiers, and, in the baggage car, a consignment of dead ones reduced to ashes and packed away in small white-enamel boxes.

On the train I was firmly ushered past a line of empty compartments, into one which smelled faintly of feet and was occupied by a gray Japanese in a derby hat, sitting on his heels with his dagger-shaped European shoes aligned on the plush beside him. He hissed punctiliously at me, then, as the train moved slowly out of the station, he unbuttoned his vest and pants, took off his hat, revealing himself an albino, dug from his suitcase a Japanese movie-magazine and a bottle of pop, and settled down for the journey. Through the swamps and tiny fields of the lower city the train glided with increasing speed, plunged through the outer wall, and rolled on into the wide, dusty country.

It was a splendid day, probably the last really warm one of the decaying year. Beside the track the fields glistened with yellow crops and above them the banked foliage of poplars and willows floated like bronze plumes of seaweed under-water. Nothing more serious than desultory skirmishing had taken place here, and in the few spots where the crops had been mashed or the trees splintered, Nature was already repairing itself. There were no farmers in the fields ripe for the harvest, however, and between the rows of grain grew weeds, the first I had ever noticed in the carefully curried Chinese countryside. Also, where fields of tall kao-liang lay near the track, the fifteen-foot stalks, which offered such excellent shelter to anyone wishing to approach the railway unseen, had been cut prematurely and lay rotting in the sun.

As the train passed down near Nan Yuan and the Peking airdrome, three Japanese bombing-planes roared suddenly up from behind the trees, their swollen bodies and long wings black against the radiant sky. They were so heavily loaded they could only climb slowly, and when they crossed the path of the train the cigar-shaped bombs were to be seen quite clearly, clinging in rows to their bellies. They wheeled and droned away toward the north. When they were only dark specks in the sky, they began to weave back and forth, the sun glinting briefly on their wings as they turned. At that distance the seeds they sowed were invisible and the flowers of smoke which blossomed at their touch were hidden below the tree-tops, but when, in a few minutes, the train slowed at the station of Fengtai, the sound of their planting was faintly audible, as a series of soft reverberations in the warm air. In the station no one paused to listen or look. Already the war could be regarded like the weather; it was to be discussed exhaustively at leisure, of course, but its routine events need not interrupt the day's business.

The train had reached Fengtai in half an hour, but there it waited for more than an hour and a half, between sunbaked platforms piled with gasoline tins, motors and motor parts, hay, cannon, ammunition, bales of posters and pamphlets. At length a squad of soldiers double-timed down the platform, leaning forward and holding their hands over their bottoms to prevent their pistols and knives from flapping too inconveniently. Following more slowly came a badger-faced commander with gold braid hanging from his shoulders, accompanied by other officers with less braid, and three minute Japanese women in figured kimonos. When he mounted the train, it began to move. The soldiers and women remained on the platform and as the cars rolled by, the women bowed low three times in unison, while the soldiers removed their hats and sang a short song.

Beyond Fengtai the train crawled down the sloping plain, halting at every station for ten minutes, twenty minutes, sometimes three quarters of an hour, while it was ascertained that the next section of track was safe. All these country depots were surrounded by walls of sand-bags, barbed wire, and railway ties, and bamboo ladders led to their roofs where improvised crows' nests, also sand-bagged, sheltered sentries watching the fields. The platforms were all piled with military supplies and decorated with a festival number of Japanese flags, including many of souvenir size stuck along the crests of the sand-bags or twisted into the barbed wire. In the dust behind the banners, the chunky warriors who had brought them here lounged uncomfortably in their undershirts, their rifles beside them. There were never any Chinese in or near the stations, though occasionally silent groups of them could be seen in the village streets beyond, shading their eyes against the afternoon light as they gazed down toward the track.

Before the war, the running time from Peking to Tientsin had been little more than three hours, but this train was still miles from the coast when it began to grow dark, six hours out of Peking. When the daylight disappeared, the populous plain across which it rolled was entirely black except for the stars and the faint electric glimmer which bathed the occasional stations, casting lumpish shadows behind the pacing sentries and sprawled barricades.

Toward nine, a rising moon showed clustering hovels beside the track, then, momentarily, a chaos of splintered railway cars, scattered about like toys, and a row of shattered buildings — half-glimpses, lost immediately as the train slid into the glare of the Tientsin Station and halted beside a file of soldiers standing at attention to sing a song of welcome for the important man from Fengtai. Here my compartment-mate folded his magazine, put on his hat and shoes, buttoned his vest and pants, bowed and hissed suddenly at me, and quit the train. In time his place was taken by a plethoric British businessman bound for Mukden and the train was signaled out of the station, veering ponderously north through the city and out over the plain again.

Beyond Tientsin the tracks lay through territory which had been all but conceded to Japan four years earlier, and had consequently fallen that summer without a struggle. Here the stations and bridges were still guarded, but there were no more long stops as a precaution against guerillas. This was the main line from the north, however, and the passenger train was often shunted into sidings while long strings of freight cars full of military material — men and goods — thundered south. At bedtime it was waiting on such a siding near Tangku, the port of Tientsin, above a vast flat landscape which shone curiously pale in the moonlight. Military activity had made proper control of the dikes along North China's silted rivers impossible that summer and these fields were shallowly covered with one of those terrible Chinese floods which drown only the crops, but kill the people later by starvation.

We were to enter Manchukuo sometime next day and, as we prepared to sleep, my fellow traveler mentioned that he had been to Mukden twice recently and, though the border was no longer a frontier, travelers through it were very thoroughly and unpleasantly searched. I was carrying out of the country a number of letters for Chinese friends, so before going to bed I tore them up and threw them into the water below the train. When I opened the window to drop them, a bitter draft blew into the overheated car, and through the moonlit trees outside, standing with their lower trunks submerged, I could hear the first winds of winter whistling down from the desert. It seemed grimly appropriate that I should be here for my last night in China, since it was here, also by moonlight, that I had arrived. That was a very different journey, in a different year.

When I landed in January, 1936, I was a tourist expecting to spend two or three weeks in China as the first step in a trip around the world. From the point of view of a tourist, that arrival was very satisfactory because in the shallows off Tangku the small steamer I was traveling on tangled in an ice-floe, then grounded on a sand-bar. The trip ashore and then inland, hurried and quite out of schedule, gave the country an air of strangeness it could hardly have had under ordinary circumstances.

At dusk we passengers had been put off the listing ship onto an ironclad tug, and as it grew dark we were ferried slowly toward land, through miles of fog-covered floes. The scarred moon was beginning to show through the mist when the ice-breaker crawled up a muddy river and docked at a torchlit pier on the edge of a marsh, beside the neglected corpse of a railway station. Here the faint menace of the Asiatic night crystallized in a horde of giant porters in tattered coats and barbaric fur hats. There was a scuffle of shadows and a volley of hoarse cries as they loaded themselves like beasts with the luggage and shuffled under it to the train waiting on the other side of the station.

Tightly sealed, brightly lit, the interior of the train was a fragment of the familiar world, complete to brass cuspidors, but on the battered benches sat a crowd of strange people in silk robes, and as they chattered in emphatic accents, the electric light glistened on violently unfamiliar contours in their round, bland faces. In the aisles were piled mountains of boxes, baskets, bedding, clocks, potted plants, washbowls, fireworks, and musical instruments. Through all the trip up to Peking the train was a cheerful bedlam; in one com-

partment some soldiers were gambling, in another two
elderly men compared the virtues of the larks they carried
with them in wicker cages, in a third a fat little mother was
suckling two of her younger children, at the same time trying to stop a fight between two of the older ones. There was
constant movement among the seats and up and down the
aisles attendants scurried with tea and hot towels.

Beyond Tientsin the moon freed itself from the mist and
in its gray light the train fled across the frozen plain. At
intervals it stopped in illuminated stations where the multitudes flowed on and off the cars clutching their fantastic
luggage or bickered endlessly on the platforms with vendors
of cigarettes, watermelon seeds, frozen persimmons, and the
varnished carcasses of chickens and ducks.

Suddenly, toward midnight, the dim western horizon
jolted higher and nearer, and was nicked with crenellations.
The train veered over and for a moment ran parallel to the
gray rampart, then turned and flashed through a gap in its
masonry. With screeching brakes it coasted along beneath
a taller wall and crossed before a colossally medieval city-
gate; it slowed and suddenly arrived in the long, iron Chien-
Men Station of Peking.

Under the arc-lights, white vapor billowed up in clouds
from the heated train and emerged in thousands of tiny
puffs from the chattering mouths of the dense crowd on the
platform. There were hundreds of blue-coated people milling about the station — laughing, shouting, gesticulating,
quarreling, eating. It was my first experience of the ever-
swarming hordes of a crowded country, and I thought there
must be some special reason to bring so many people out at
midnight, some crisis or celebration. I was very sleepy and
suffering somewhat from tourist nerves; when I found a
rickshaw and rode out of the station yard, through a deep
gate into the inner city, the abrupt silence of the walled
streets excited me still more. There was no growl of automobiles nor clang of trolleys, nothing but the faint, far-off

beat of bells and drums. It was my first experience of an un-mechanized metropolis, and I thought it an ominous hush, a sign of some trouble in the city. At the corners stood slit-eyed soldiers muffled in huge fur coats and hats, armed like bandits with pistols and curving swords on which the moonlight glittered. Down the center of the empty street the rickshaw sped, no sound but the rapid pad-pad-pad of the coolie's slippered feet.

The hotel I went to was in the Legation Quarter, and next morning I left it early, riding past the ornate entranceways of the Embassies, past the wizened façades of the European shops, banks, and churches, finally through a small iron gate and out into the Chinese city. The wide avenue beyond the walls stretched straight into the distance between lines of irregular Asiatic buildings, bald and pallid under the icy peacock sky. Before the shops, swarms of brown-faced people were moving, some dressed in black, but most in vivid blue. Down the center of the thoroughfare came a small scarlet-lacquer coach, drawn by hairy Mongol ponies and driven by a swarthy groom in a giant fur hat; past it plunged a ramshackle automobile, honking vociferously, its tonneau jammed full of fat men in uniform. Along the gutter stood a line of tufted camels and around their legs charged dozens of huge black swine, grunting ferociously at the cracking of their herders' long whip. Through the tangle a fleet of rickshaws skimmed, like peripatetic telephone booths with their tall winter hoods of quilted black felt. Behind them came three open ones, and in these sat three young girls who, to protect themselves from the dust as they rode, had thrown long chiffon veils over their heads and so turned their faces into floating masks, as the wind sculptured the cloth over their small features and billowed it gracefully in the air behind them. For all I had actually seen the night before, my arrival could have been a blindfolded one, and it was a shock and a delight to be plunged so abruptly into another world, one which seemed doubly strange after a blank month on the Pacific.

For at least four hours I was able to take satisfaction in the novelty of what I saw, but even as I rode back to the hotel for my first lunch, I had to admit to myself that, once arrived at this interesting place, as a tourist I had nothing to do but walk or ride about and look at it. This sterile prospect was not one I had reckoned with in my warm imaginings of the difficulties of Oriental travel.

For several days the weather remained clear and sunny, but it turned abominably cold. Arming myself against it, I left the hotel every morning and set out to see what I should see, riding endlessly past the great red ceremonial barriers down the center of the city, or wandering among the gray walls which lined all streets outside the shopping districts and shut every residence off from public view. From those days of formal sight-seeing I now remember only details: the touchy camel encountered on the way to the Lama Temple, which spat condescendingly on the back of my hat when my rickshaw cut across too close under its nose; the gentle old Tartar who lurked on the sunny side of the great dagoba in the Winter Palace, on the spot recommended to tourists as the best from which to view the Forbidden City, and benignly vended pornographic photographs; the loud convention of ravens croaking and skipping idiotically about on the marble platform of the Imperial Altar of Heaven; the durable Englishwoman sent off by the hotel doorman in the same car with me to inspect the city from Coal Hill. This high pavilion-crested mound was shaped like a breaking wave, with sloping flanks and nearly vertical face. When we reached its enclosure, the daughter of Albion took the lead, and without a word or a moment's hesitation began marching up the steep pathless slope directly before the front gate. When we reached the top, panting, dusty, torn by the thorns we had struggled through, she was not even chagrined to discover stone staircases leading easily to the summit from both sides, staircases covered at that moment with amused Chinese.

At that season the hotel was empty except for a dozen permanent residents and perhaps half as many travelers, and I ate all my meals in chilly magnificence at a large table among dozens of other large tables, nearly all empty — a glacier of virgin table-linen. Along the dining-room walls stood a ridiculous number of liveried Chinese and in one corner huddled the members of a Russian string quartet, chewing their pale mustaches as they sawed out the lugubriously dainty music heard in hotel dining-rooms all over the world. Noon and night, the meal included a platter of small birds like snipe, long necked and long-billed, which, in accord with some Oriental idea of fitness, had been manipulated before cooking so that all lay with their necks twisted around and their bills plunged through their own stomachs in an attitude which gave them the appearance of avian suicides.

It was fortunate that during these first days the train of circumstance which was to allow me to settle in Peking and learn the city in more interesting ways was in motion. I had arrived with one letter of introduction, and when I presented it, it proved the first link in a chain of hospitality which within four days had introduced me to two Americans who suggested that I leave the hotel and move in with them, in their small Chinese house. I had already been appalled at the prospect of the world tour I'd contrived for myself, a journey which was just then beginning to appear in its true nature as a barren succession of trips on boats and trains and other public carriers, punctuated by stays in monotonous hotels. Finding the opportunity to break out of this routine and being immensely attracted by what I'd seen of Peking outside the hotel and the labeled sights, I decided to stay in the city for several weeks, perhaps until spring. Just a week after arriving in China, I settled in.

II. THE CITY ENCLOSED

To MAKE a long story short, it was six months before I left Peking. Without ever really deciding to do so, coming to it only by not deciding not to do so, I stayed from January until June.

China is such a country that even if I'd known I wanted to, I don't think I could have gone into it directly on arrival and traveled with any degree of comfort or success; those months in Peking at least prepared me for subsequent journeys. I learned a smattering of the language, customs, and methods. I began to feel at home in the country, and that gave me a necessary degree of confidence. Also I was able to become physically adapted to the country very gradually; by working into the native way of life slowly, I could build up some resistance to the complaints which frequently trouble the Asiatic traveler and owing chiefly to this, I think, I was never ill in all my time in China.

Nevertheless, as it was brought about by nothing more rational than continued procrastination, that first long sojourn was a foolish time. Thinking always that I should be off again in two weeks or perhaps a month, I took no formal lessons in Chinese, and, as it proved, they would have been of tremendous help later. Ostensibly I had come to Asia to paint, but I made no pictures except a few scrawlings which I destroyed before I left; I explained to myself that Peking was too full of ready-made picturesqueness (red walls and golden tiles, moon-gates and gnarly pines), and actually it was months before any part of the Chinese scene became familiar enough to attract me. Of course the real reason for my inactivity was the same one which caused me to stay on and on — that was the extraordinary pleasantness of life in Peking, which moved with so graceful a languor that doing nothing nicely as an occupation seemed not at all unreal.

When I first arrived, the people with whom I went to live were staying in a tiny but very comfortable middle-class Chinese house. Within a month, however, we had the opportunity of renting an immense place of four courtyards inside the former palace of one of the cousins of the last Emperor; it was available to foreigners at a very low rate because its Chinese landlord had recently learned that a Japanese syndicate hoped to take it and establish a combined girl- and dope-shop in it. In March we moved here and thereafter began living like tipsy mandarins. In Peking the proprieties had stiffened almost into a legal code through the dozens of centuries, and apparently they prescribed that any such move as we had made must entail a change in our entire scale of living. Our servants almost automatically increased from two to six, and they and their children and cousins and brothers, who lived with them in the outer court, kept us busy enough just being attended to.

Furthermore, over the long period when it was the capital, Peking had become an unparalleled accumulation of objects and customs designed for the delectation of its inhabitants; once started, this machinery steadily went on showering its benefits.

Our three inner courts and the giant living-room with its painted rafters — the former throne-room — were kept decorated with potted flowers and bushes, and as soon as these withered, they were changed by a genii-like gardener who appeared twice a week with a supply of fresh plants. To shop for pictures or silks or curiosities, or simply to consider some, it was only necessary for us to send for a shopkeeper who would then come and strew his goods profusely over our rugs. For entertainment on an idle evening, we needed only to send for one of the musicians or story-tellers who wandered in the streets. Whenever there were drinks, we had slices of dried lotus-root instead of pretzels or peanuts, and of them we naturally ate quantities lest the whole mirage vanish. It was a pleasant and ridiculous life, and had nothing whatsoever to do with China.

When I thought of it, it seemed particularly absurd for me, since I'd left America with just two thousand dollars to reach the Orient, to see and do what I could, and return. Still, when I thought that with the favorable exchange then prevailing I could maintain myself in such Oriental luxury for as little as sixty dollars a month, I considered it a bargain. A year later, when I had traveled in the provinces and become accustomed to living on thirty a month, I regretted this comparatively expensive period, but half a year after that, when I had seen Peking fall and its easy days end forever, it seemed a lucky investment to have enjoyed the life of the city before it became a shell.

Once I was established behind one set of Peking's secret gray walls, I began to find my way behind a good many others and at the same time I became familiar with the pattern of the huge Imperial ramparts which divide and enclose the city's various parts; I soon realized that these barriers which had blocked me so during my first days as a tourist were the most important factor in the unique character of Peking. Though the Emperor's Forbidden City was empty and the gigantic avenues radiating from it had been shorn of their sacred significance, Peking's shape was still regulated by the Imperial diagram, and even in small details its structure, both of buildings and customs, was largely in accord with the old plan. To an Occidental like myself, recently arrived from a country where a mechanical civilization has slapped together the most confused cities of history, this carefully plotted and constructed capital of an organic civilization was something to marvel at, analogous only to the mathematic structures of bees or ants.

Like every proper house, tomb, temple, village, and town in China, Peking was originally located and planned in accordance with the rules of Feng-Shui, or geomancy, that ancient science or superstition governing the selection of auspicious locations. Through the centuries the lore of Feng-Shui has accumulated as many prejudices and blind formulae as must boil through the mind of a sparrow deciding between two crotches for its nesting place, but like the instinct of the sparrow, Feng-Shui has almost always resulted in the choice of a superbly suitable location. The Feng-Shui architects of Yung Lo, fifteenth-century founder of modern Peking, wished to place the city where it would enjoy the protection of the five dragons — the subterranean dragon whose corrugated back is seen in the crests of hills and mountains, the earthbound dragon whose twisting tail is seen in the winding courses of rivers, the restless, invisible wind dragon, the rain dragon whose body is made of clouds, the celestial dragon who stares at the world through the

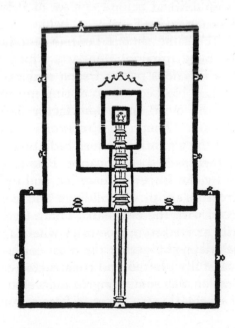

burning disk of the sun. In consequence they located Peking on a plain guarded from the winter winds by mountains in the north and west, irrigated by the waters of a stream which emerges in miraculous quantities at the Jade Fountain, and tempered all year by wonderfully clear and balanced weather.

Feng-Shui also prescribed that cities must stand at the northern ends of plains; the successive invasions of China have always come from the north and cities so situated can best defend the farmlands which feed them. Peking had the logical site for a capital, since it stood at the northern apex of the Great Plain of China which stretched south from there for hundreds of miles, embracing the lower valleys of the Yellow and the Yangtze Rivers, the historic home of the race.

Its location mystically established, the plan of Peking was arranged with the same regard for the occult. Laid out in the days of absolute empire, it was naturally planned less as a city in our sense of the word than as a home for one man, the Emperor, the great Son of Heaven. Its walls were carefully aligned with the outer directions, north, south, east, and west, and in Peking, where the Emperor sat, the fifth or central direction took on a meaning it could have in no other place.

South of the main city was laid out a walled suburb, for the artisans and merchants; then in the center of the main city were erected the walls of an Imperial city for officials and the Emperor's servants. In the center of the Imperial city the moat-encircled walls of a Forbidden City were planned; in this gigantic palace only the Imperial Household could live. And in the center of a hall in the center of the Forbidden City was placed the Dragon Throne where only the Son of Heaven could sit.

Straight south from the throne-room stretched an avenue to the outer gate in the farthest wall. Wherever it passed through one of the concentric walls there were five great gates, one for each of the five ranks in the Central Kingdom. Where it crossed a canal there were five marble bridges. Where it descended an incline there were five carved staircases. Straight south from the throne itself a marble causeway reserved solely for the Emperor led down the center of the wide avenue. The central gates, the central bridges, the central stairs, were for his use alone.

Around the Emperor as a nucleus the city was disposed in a fabric in which the five elements, the five colors, the five ranks, and the five nations were arranged in their proper tributary positions, though of course the first categories of many of these classifications were centered right on the Dragon Throne; it pre-empted the central direction, the color yellow, which was forbidden for non-Imperial use, and so on. Since the Son of Heaven was the kernel of the city's diagram, Peking was furthermore felt to be the center of all things, and every farthest object in the Empire, every creature, every tree, every pebble, contributed to the centripetal pattern radiating out from the city.

This setting for one man's apotheosis had survived its users quite intact, and during those first months in China I never failed to be moved when the orbit of my trivial doings impinged upon one of the grand axes. Bundling across town in a rickshaw, I frequently found myself being drawn down the marble causeway, under the sacerdotal archways and across the consecrated bridges. Even to an Occidental, an outlander whose remote country had no part in its plan, this spine of the city was impressive as the central nerve of an arranged universe. It was not hard to realize what a place of awe the concentric cities must have been to the old Chinese, steeped in the mystic classifications. As for the Emperor himself, however, the hub of the great wheel, the peak of the pyramid, the navel of all creation — even riding down his sacred causeway I could never grasp what he must have felt. It was appalling to think that every time he ascended the Dragon Throne he was conscious that

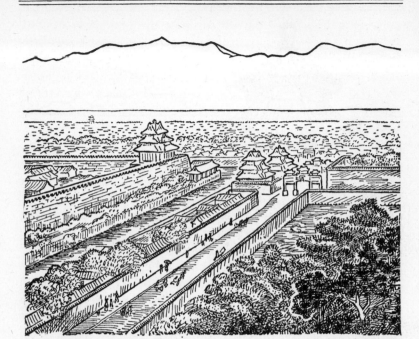

all the world lay about him, in relation to him. Still he
spent a good deal of time on it and the fifth direction could
hardly have been a comfortable seat. Dressed in heavy
brocaded robes of yellow, the color he alone could wear, he
perhaps spent a good part of his mental energy calculating
how he could scratch without being noticed.

Since the downfall of the Empire in 1912, Peking had
slipped from its Imperial austerity, and knowing it only in
the last days of its relaxed period, it was hard for me to
imagine its ever having been so thoroughly dedicated to
inhuman, though impressive, ritual. In 1936 a spirit of
comfortable slackness seemed the essential part of the city's
character. Built as a hieratic setting for one man, it had become a delightful home of many. The ceremonial quarters
were still intact, but their consecrated, forbidding aspect

had gone. The Purple City itself was a public museum; the Lake Palaces were parks full of popular restaurants and tea-houses. The Imperial avenues, once nobly empty except for the banners of tributary processions, had been lined with trees and opened to traffic. Under the Empire an ordinary citizen who wanted to go from one side of the city to the other had had to spend an entire day trudging around outside the walls; more recently trolleys full of the same citizens clanged through the marble courtyards of the Emperor. The bridges and passages once dedicated to the use of the Son of Heaven were open to all comers, and over his own great gate was a clock which democratically told time to all.

Though the Imperial barriers were thus deprived of their most special meaning, they still contributed to Peking's unique character as a city of walls. Inside the massive crenellations of its outer fortifications the city was covered

with a myriad network of smaller ones — first the walls of
the inner cities; then the walls of the Imperial palaces and
their subsidiary avenues and plazas; finally the walls of the
individual residences which filled every space and cut the
entire flat area of the city into thousands and thousands of
courtyards and squares. From an elevation, this city surrounded by benignant dragons had the appearance of a
giant open honeycomb, and in its countless recesses was
secreted the special atmosphere which made it what it was
— an aura of calm or inertia which, like a gas, was best
retained in the most sheltered spots, a static atmosphere in
which the breath of action died and the good life was
vegetable.

Until the city overwhelmed me and made such activity
seem superfluous, I frequently went outside the walls to
walk or bicycle through the near-by countryside, usually
toward the hills in the west. I rode along willow-bordered
canals, through glistening brown fields and into dusty,
sun-baked villages where the dogs barked and children fled
at sight of a white face, but when I thought I was getting
beyond Peking's urbane and favored sphere I was deluding
myself. Obtruding on every rural scene were the sophisticated little villas and tombs of the wealthy Pekinese, also
jeweled pagodas and dagobas and carved marble turtles
which dated from the days when half the plain was walled
and decorated to make a Summer Palace for the Emperor.
Moreover, the high blue hills which bounded the plain on
the west and north — the undulating body of the subterranean dragon — seemed to form the outermost of Peking's
walls and make this sheltered countryside almost a part of
the city. All the plain breathed an air of elegance and
tranquillity; bandits could roam in the hills which bordered
it or floods ravage the plains below it, but it seemed impossible that any sort of catastrophe could touch it.

Perhaps there never has been another locality so perfectly

constructed for man's pleasure. Originally endowed with a balanced proportion of mountains and flatlands, it had, through the many centuries when it was the capital of the Eastern world, been continually groomed and improved by the addition of whatever it naturally lacked. Artificial lakes and hills had been contrived in suitable places and the whole scene had been architecturally upholstered with countless temples, pavilions, and ornamental archways. Even the massive line of the Western Hills had been humanized and brought into scale by a pagoda strategically placed on one of them; to an extraordinary extent this whole landscape gave the effect of a tastefully furnished room.

It was hardly fitting that the natural change of seasons should intrude on such a district, and on my progressively more infrequent jaunts beyond the walls, I was half surprised to find the country nevertheless inexorably slipping from winter to summer.

Despite the harsh weather it was in winter that it seemed most particularly a landscape under glass, sealed under the huge bell of a clear blue sky. In January powdery snows fell, silhouetting the dark willows and emphasizing the strangeness of the curving roofs. February was dry and bright; no life stirred in the country except for the ravens which hopped about on the dun-colored ground or clattered among the branches of the frozen trees. March was a windy but negative month when for days at a time the sky went yellow and the air was full of silently dropping dust.

In April the coarser strains of life began moving, even in this garden valley. Early in the month was celebrated the festival of 'The Stirring of the Creatures,' after which one might expect to find bugs. I was more struck by the uncelebrated stirring of the odors, for as the ground softened rich stinks and strange fragrances floated up in the warming air. The earth reasserted its rule, and every field was full of toiling men and animals; already beginning to sweat in the early sunlight, they drew water, plowed, and planted. In

May the earth began to make its returns; first the fruit trees
exploded into showers of pink and white blooms, then in
a week or ten days the whole countryside was in full leaf.
As rapidly came the heat, tropical and humid. By June
the greenery had grown in a way unknown to the temperate
zone in the West and Peking's Happy Valley was a fecund
jungle.

In the country outside, spring could follow winter and summer follow spring, Nature could unbutton as far as she liked; but inside the walls the changes were hardly recognized. The courtyards of Peking had been warmed by the winter's sun and when the weather grew hotter there was shade to cool them. Exuberant representatives of the vegetable world were allowed inside their ordered precincts only when properly potted; from inside, the carnival of the bursting year could be seen only in miniature, as through the wrong end of a telescope.

Later I came to realize that nothing could really disturb the tranquillity, the divine monotony, of Peking's courtyards and the life they contained. Each one was a unit of complete privacy, a law unto itself, and nothing that happened beyond its limits could really affect it.

Two of the courtyards of the house in which I lived were typical of these enclosures; the other two were out of the usual since the house had been built as a semi-royal palace — the outer court was long and narrow as a setting for ceremonial entries and the small court immediately behind the former throne-room was an ornamental enclosure with red walls cut by windows in the shape of gourds, fans, and vases, roofed over by a thick arbor of wistaria.

Like all proper houses, ours was built in accord with the rules of Feng-Shui. The great gate opened on the street to the south and straight in a line behind it lay the rectangular courtyards, each one aligned with the points of the compass. In each of the two courts around which the living quarters were disposed, the main house stood on the north side, with its court wall a mass of paper-paned windows facing south for a maximum of sun in winter and a maximum of shade in summer. There were smaller houses to the east and west with their windows also facing in, but the south side of the court was a blank wall with an arcade running across it and a gate in its center.

Such a court was a home which fitted man as comfortably

as the cocoon fits the caterpillar or the shell the snail. Though it was a square of perfect living space in all except the coldest months, I think late spring and early summes saw it at its best. When the fine weather came, its walls seemed to change their significance; they were no longer the outer walls of the houses, but became the inner walls of the court, and then the courtyard existed simply as a cube of the marvelously liquid North China air. The floor of the cube was a neatly swept stretch of hard-beaten earth, dappled

with the trembling shade of leaves. Its sides were the cool
gray walls of the buildings, varied by the red-and-white
patterns of the latticed windows. It was garnished by rows
of potted flowers and shrubs, and from the green branches
of the trees and flowering vines, which seemed afloat in its
aerial solidity, cages of singing birds were hung.

After a while it seemed to me that the Peking courtyard
was not only an architectural contrivance; it was also a
state of mind, a private world to be shaped as its owner

inclined. Fancies which could not survive in the open thrived in its recesses; indeed, its complete isolation made such invention not only possible but almost inevitable.

I suppose the idea which most persistently materialized behind its walls was that of the fabulous fragile China of legend, the China of jade, sages, and vermilion pavilions, that faraway azure land which has really existed only on blue plates. In the West this Celestial Never-Never Land has been an enchanting shadow to many generations, and in the East it has been the haven which dynasties of poets, artists, potentates, and prophets have struggled to construct. Never were they able to realize it completely, and seated in a Peking courtyard I think one could come as close to it as any of them.

The quiet walls projected the charm of a dead time and the slight breeze spoke comfortably of remote joys. The trees and flowers would murmur and overhead a flock of doves with whistles on their tails would circle, making a soothing, moaning sound. It could be only a matter of moments before a pink phoenix joined the doves, and a mild-eyed unicorn, so sympathetic that it never stepped on living grass, advanced into the court bearing in its mouth a jade tablet carved with 福 or some other word of auspicious meaning.

When I first arrived, I was inclined to deplore the sporadic evidences of Westernization dotted among Peking's walls — the few shop-fronts, offices, hotels, residences, and banks which might have been in any Occidental city; but after I'd settled in, I recognized them as products of the most interesting part of Peking accessible to me. That was its foreign colony.

Passing through the alleys of Peking, which were completely of the medieval Orient, it was extraordinary to glimpse these foreign buildings over the tiled walls of their compounds or through the red-lacquer portals of their

Chinese gate-houses. Particularly in the sections near the Legation Quarter, the attractive gray uniformity of Chinese architecture was sprinkled with plain-faced American houses, neat fat German ones, fancy French ones, and fantastically Gothic Russian ones of brick and cast-iron; random recollections of Odessa, Dijon, Dresden, or Buffalo. To an American the American houses naturally provided the greatest shock, being islands of the completely familiar in a sea of strangeness. In the big mission and hospital compounds there were whole rows of exact American frame houses, complete with window-boxes and near-colonial door-ways. In some compounds there were even cement side-walks and lawns of imported grass, and beside their walls the fantastic clangor of Chinese street-life was tempered by the supremely homely sounds of lawnmowers and roller skates.

And just as their ordinary houses became strange on a Chinese street, so the Occidental residents of Peking had their peculiarities accentuated by an exotic background. The environment pointed up characteristics which might have been camouflaged by more accustomed surroundings, and in cases where there were no personal idiosyncrasies it emphasized the national ones to the point of caricature. At the same time Peking's special atmosphere tended to cultivate foibles which no setting could have camouflaged, and since many Peking folk had been on the odd side before arriving in the city, its foreign colony was the soil for a truly remarkable flowering of eccentricity.

Through all that first half-year in China my interest was directed more toward the exploration of this group than it was toward learning of the country it lived on. The non-missionary foreign community in Peking numbered little more than a thousand, and as in any small town, a new face was eagerly seized upon; after the American system of social herding which segregates into separate groups those of the same ages, interests, and bank accounts, it was exhilarating to investigate this community which numbered in close association people of all ages and nationalities, nearly every occupation and several sexes. Though some bemoaned the gay days before the Government moved south to Nanking, the city was still the home, temporary or permanent, of a rare collection of diplomats, scholars, journalists, artists, fragments of defunct European and Asiatic aristocracies, traveling celebrities and celebrated travelers, semi-missionaries and ex-missionaries, curio-dealers, adventurers, and so on.

Isolated at the far end of the Orient, their society made a concentrated and rather feverishly colored miniature of the Western world with all its phobias, desires, ambitions, and fallacies. Entertaining was cheap — vodka ten cents a bottle, flowers a penny a bush — and at endless lunches, dinners, picnics, and cocktail parties the Peking foreigners met to rub together their prejudices and peculiarities and exchange fantastic information about their neighbors. In the red-walled hothouse gloom of their elaborate homes in renovated temples or palaces, in the smoky European ballrooms and bars of the two big hotels, or, on hot evenings, at the favored picnic places in the Imperial parks or the Western Hills, Peking gossip grew and flourished like some musky jungle flower.

. . . Nobody noticed what she was doing until she stood up to step out of her dress, but of course the place was thrown in an uproar when the other garments began to go. Someone ran up with a tablecloth, but she was too quick, and in the end they had to turn out the lights while they persuaded her to get into the elevator.

. . . The Frenchwoman was describing her trip out on an Italian boat and the typhoon they ran into just off Shanghai. With effective gestures she was showing how the boat would slide up one wave, then crash down into another, when our mutual friend began jouncing about in his seat. 'I know, I know,' he fluted; 'British boats do just the same thing!'

. . . They should have known better than to take those Mongols to the dance, even though one was a Prince and the other a Grand

Lama. His Highness was immediately fascinated by a girl in a green dress, and no matter whom she was dancing with, he followed her around the floor breathing down her neck like Harpo Marx. His Holiness fortunately remained at the table, but he was impressed with the possibilities of the ballroom as a prayer-hall, and when the music stopped he began bellowing a lama chant to try the acoustics.

... After the time he had in New Guinea you'd think he'd be numb, but every time a waiter came through the kitchen door a fat puff of black smoke came, too, and finally he said, 'Do you mind if we change our table? I simply can't stand the smell of burning meat ever since my wife was eaten.'

... She should have expected it, but when everybody did leave early, she was so exasperated that she took her pistol and shot out all her living-room windows.

But, though a good many Occidentals of violent character had been attracted to the privacy offered by Peking's many walls and the attitude of its Chinese residents who assumed that all outlanders were naturally outlandish, the prevalent tone of the foreign colony was not particularly flamboyant. Eccentricity is demanding work, and the easy-going air of the city which had captured these folk soon made them feel that activity of any sort was not to be encouraged. As their time in Peking lengthened, they sat more continuously in their flower-decked courts behind the high gray walls, listening to the whistling doves and contemplating the wisdom of the old proverb:

In leisure hours the nails grow best,
And the hair grows luxuriant when the mind is at rest.

The only foreigners who seemed to be insensible to the languors of Peking were the Japanese. All during the months of my first stay in the city, they were swarming down upon it in active hordes, putting up a show of great activity, perhaps already aware of the necessity of getting Peking before Peking got them. Though the city was still nominally under Chinese control, a real invasion was in full

swing, and by most observers it was even then conceded
that in event of a showdown this conquest would prove
complete. Since the capture of Jehol in 1933, the Japanese
frontier had advanced within less than a hundred miles of
Peking and by means of the Hopei-Chahar demilitarized
zone their sphere of influence stretched to the walls of the
city; Tungchow, the Japanese-dominated capital of the
zone, was only a few miles from the East Gate, and furthermore, a fortified Japanese barracks overlooked the important railway junction at Fengtai, just south of Peking, controlling communications with Central China and the coast.

Two months before I arrived in China, Japan had suggested that the five North China provinces — Hopei,
Chahar, Suiyuan, Shansi, and Shantung — break away
from the central Government and become autonomous 'as
evidence of sincerity.' The suggestion was, of course, rejected, and as neither side was yet willing to fight about it,
there the matter rested. What preparation the Chinese
were making for the trouble which must end this insecure
peace was only too invisible in Peking, but the Japanese
were taking advantage of the lull to consolidate their position in the city.

Both civilians and military were arriving in large numbers. The civilians, most of them engaged in the campaign
of wholesale smuggling which was then flooding North
China with untaxed Japanese goods, had taken as their
quarter the East City, just inside the Hatamen Gate, and
this district was already overrun with them. There were
ronins — professional rowdies of semi-military status in
riding-breeches and turtle-neck sweaters; also little business
men and commercial travelers in 'klassy-kut,' Western-
style suits, even tourists with lunch-baskets and miniature
cameras. Almost every week saw the opening of a new
Japanese drugstore, lunchstand, or beer-parlor on Hatamen
Street.

Though the Japanese authorities stubbornly claimed that

their Embassy guard was not increasing, in certainly increasing numbers the Japanese soldiers also appeared on the streets. In groups of ten or twenty the duck-bottomed little empire-builders promenaded every day through the shopping districts, grinning like canary-fed cats. In increasing numbers they drilled in the open spaces around the Legations, marching and counter-marching with their officers posting before them like monkeys on the backs of the huge Russian horses they affected.

More unpleasantly the out-of-town troops from Fengtai or Tungchow sometimes came in to demonstrate. In motorcycles or trucks they would smash through the traffic on the big streets, driving at an outrageous speed, and on one occasion they came in a body with a dozen or so tanks and proceeded insolently up the great central avenues to the gate of the Forbidden City, where they took souvenir snapshots of each other.

Despite the lack of organized Chinese resistance, this state of affairs could not help but create tension. This was the period of 'incidents,' which broke out all over China wherever the two nations came in contact. Some 'incidents,' of course, were tragic, culminating in the deaths of Japanese or Chinese, but more were comic, of the sort to be expected from the friction between a humorous race and one with no sense of the ridiculous.

There were 'The Affair of the Pear Seeds,' 'The Affair of the Apple Core,' and other skirmishes which started when Chinese found themselves unable to refrain from commenting with missiles on the sight of Japanese soldiers strutting through their streets. There was 'The Affair of the Horse's Rump' which occurred when the sight of a minute Japanese officer on his immense horse had been too much for some Chinese passer-by. Perhaps unwisely, it was the horse he slapped. The Japanese military command made a formal protest, saying 'an insult has been offered to a Japanese horse.'

As these incidents were made the pretext for minor advances on the part of the Japanese, they went even farther out of their way to find them. In Tientsin occurred 'The Incident of the Embroidered Umbrella' when three Chinese clerks in a drygoods store in the Tientsin Japanese Concession were arrested and charged with spreading anti-Japanese propaganda; their offense had been to sell a batch of shirts embroidered on their trademarks with a picture of a girl standing in the sun under an umbrella. The Rising Sun, explained the Japanese authorities, was a symbol of Japan. The umbrella deflected its rays. A picture of a person using an umbrella was a symbol of anti-Japanese activity, seditious and insincere to the ultimate degree.

In Peking in 1936 the sun of Japan's destiny shone brightest at night. Oddly, the pre-war Japanese advance in all parts of China was most apparent in the fields of entertainment and vice, perhaps a proof that military adventurers are true racketeers at heart. Through their teams of Japanese and Korean ronins, who were given full protection by their soldiers, the Japanese army authorities in North China had embarked on a systematic program of demoralization. Their weapons were opium and heroin from Manchuria, their bait the charms of the squat Korean girls who could be recruited for this work in such large numbers because their own country had for a generation been the victim of the same program. The East City of Peking was honeycombed with their dives, quite openly operated; in some free heroin was even distributed to coolie passers-by to make new customers — once the habit had been started, it could not be stopped without prohibitively expensive treatment.

Besides these establishments exclusively for Chinese, Japan's midnight sun smiled on a growing number of restaurants, dance-halls, and brothels for the Japanese themselves. They were the best gauge of the growth of

Peking's Japanese colony and they multiplied like flies in May. Incongruously built into many Chinese houses of the Hatamen district were Japanese restaurants, complete with paper screens, sliding doors, and matted floors. Strung along Hatamen Street were cafés in frontier imitation of Tokyo hot-spots — they had fake cherry trees nailed to their walls and ceilings and phonographs which bellowed lugubrious Japanese jazz; for dancing partners there were bedraggled geishas with metal teeth or pigeon-toed mogos (modern girls) in décolletées dresses and tortoise-rimmed spectacles. Down the dark alleys to the east were little sex factories where the soldiers from the Japanese Embassy were marched in squads and at the shrill of a whistle were allowed to break ranks for a while. At the sound of another whistle they were ordered back into formation and marched back to the Embassy.

Providing a semi-comic footnote to this dingy tale was the opening in May 1936 of the White Palace, a Japanese-controlled night club aiming to compete with the two homey but dull Russian cabarets which until then had constituted the only night life of Occidental Peking. The establishment was popularly known as the White Pea-Alace because it was advertised first like this:

THE WHITE P

ALACE

A subsequent notice contained this plea:

WANTED

50   Dancing Girls   50

WITH A GRACEFUL FIGURE AND AN ATTRACTIVE
FEATURE

Later advertisements promised drinks and girls of every national mixture, a foreign-style cooling system, and many

more wonders. On the opening night the place was jammed.
There were surprises for all. The foreign-style cooling
system proved to be four buckets of ice, one in each corner
of the dance-floor. The 'graceful' girls were mostly Kore-
ans, black and stubby as chimpanzees. Swathed in showers
of white tulle and orange blossoms, they sat in an uneasy
line on elegant blue-velvet benches, scratching themselves
and picking their noses; with a sublime sense of unfitness
they had all been dressed as brides.

To anyone who has not known the Chinese, it may seem
incredible that the Pekinese could sit by and placidly watch
the preparations for their own conquest. An explanation
might be started with the statement that all Chinese are
easy-going, that the North Chinese are more easy-going
than others, and that the Pekinese are the most easy-going
of North Chinese; certainly prolonged resistance to anything could find no place in the picture of the Celestial
Never-Never Land.

That would be an unkind and superficial explanation,
however. The tendency to apathy on the subject of public
affairs, for centuries very strong all over China, stems from
a quality which has been at the same time the nation's
greatest strength and its greatest weakness. Down to the
last man, woman, and child, every one of the four hundred
million has learned to live as a convinced and practicing
individualist. In matters of war and public peril particularly, they have been loath to endanger their personal interests for the benefit of public ones. They have typically
had a deep distrust of any concerted action, partly due to
their natural hard-headedness, and partly perhaps to the
former state of political chaos which made individual
caution a prime necessity.

An old proverb sums up the attitude nicely:

> *He who learns to swim drowns.*
> *He who learns to shoot will be shot.*

When thoroughly aroused, their anger and determination can reach an hysterical pitch, but in the past they have been weak — I mean from the military point of view only — because their supply of individual sense soon reasserted itself and dispelled the hysteria. I was told that in 1933, when the Japanese were fighting their way through Jehol to the Great Wall, the people of Peking were swept into a frenzy. Crowds congregated to voice their feelings, and individuals rushed into the streets, trembling and shouting, 'The Japanese! The Japanese!' in almost epileptic seizures. In 1936, though, when the Japanese troops were literally at the gates and their agents were seeping continually into the city, there surely was hidden resentment, but on the surface all was indifference. Each man had resigned himself to the fact that he personally could do nothing. Nothing was done.

If I were one to welcome a Japanese conquest of China, I should deplore their present activity. In their former policy of biting off small bits of territory at regular intervals, they made Chinese indifference their greatest weapon against China, and it seemed only a matter of time before they would be able to take over the whole country without very great trouble or expense. Now by forcing matters they have really stepped on the dragon's tail and wakened it. The Chinese people have finally had to face the appalling possibilities which threaten them, and now it does look as if the country will be able to fight to the end of its very considerable resources.

It will be a good thing for the Chinese as a nation if their indifference has really disappeared, but it will be a loss to the world at large. The old attitude could be called a sign of decadence, another indication that China was too old, but by the same standards all other forms of pacifism must be condemned as decadent. It may have been the only really practical form of pacifism. Our own pacifist movements are essentially emotional — their advertising relies on the same appeals that military propaganda uses — and,

as the last year has shown only too clearly, their adherents can be changed to belligerent jingoes without much difficulty. It is a discouraging possibility that true pacifism can only originate in this bald and perhaps ugly form of individual indifference, and consequently can't be attained until a time when no movements are necessary to further it.

I remember one incident in particular which seemed to sum up this whole strangely unresisted invasion. On an afternoon during the Chinese New Year I was riding down the street outside the Legations when I saw a large and happy crowd streaming out of one of the gates of the Forbidden City. My rickshaw boy ran over toward it and I saw

that at its nucleus was a troop of Chinese soldiers. Some of them blew horns and beat drums; some were on stilts; some were made up as clowns; some, dressed as women, were cavorting with exaggerated girlishness. My boy told me that every year on that day it had always been the custom for the soldiers to dress up and amuse the people.

Just at that moment, in an appropriate and perfectly timed entrance, a long line of Japanese army trucks came rolling down the other side of the street. They were covered with mud and dust and had obviously just struggled down the mountain road from the Manchukuan border. They were manned by grim road-worn little Japanese and under their tarpaulins bulked ominous shapes.

The Chinese soldiers went imperturbably on with their fun as the convoy rumbled past and turned in at the entrance of the Japanese Embassy. The laughing crowd hardly glanced at the trucks. They were used to them.

Still, Peking has been conquered before, and each time the quality in the city which made it easy to take disposed of its conquerors in the end. The hardy Mongols ruled their transcontinental empire from the city and in only a few generations were forced to retreat to the steppes again, their spirits debilitated and their nation reduced to a shadow of its former power. The brave and clever rulers of the Ming Dynasty moved up from Central China to Peking and the last of the line faced the crisis which threatened to unseat him by hanging himself with a silken sash from a pine tree, after which the tree was thrown in chains as punishment for its participation. The Manchus succeeded the Mings, and Peking brought that dynasty to a pass where the men of the family could not carry on after their grandmother, the Empress Dowager, died.

Now that new invaders were lodging themselves in the city, one wondered how long it would be before the Japanese commander of Peking district startled the Tokyo War Office with a report beginning —

The lotus are in bloom and yesterday for the first time a butterfly with blue wings flew into my pavilion....

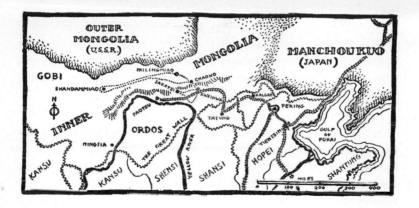

III. THE IRON TORTOISE

WHEN June came and the great heat clamped its moist hand down over Peking, the discomforts of the weather forced on me the conclusion that life in the city was making me lazy and fat. I knew I had had enough, but even though I still considered myself on the first stage of a trip around the world, I hated the thought of leaving China. I was diffident about traveling in the interior alone, and when I found an opportunity to go into Mongolia with a news-reel cameraman planning to make a short film of the country, I seized the chance with pleasure.

The first step of our journey was an overnight trip up the Ping-Sui Railway, north through Nankow Pass and the Great Wall to Kalgan, southwest across the arid, mountain-walled plains of Chahar and Shansi, to Ta Tung, north again through another section of the Wall to Pingtichuan, and then west to the valley of the Yellow River and Kwei-hwa, capital of Chinese Suiyuan. We traveled first class in an elegant compartment lined in green leatherette, next to one occupied by a fat and splendiferous general returning to Suiyuan from a campaign against the Communists in Shansi; he was accompanied by a gaudily uniformed body-guard who spent almost all their time sleeping on the tables in the dining-car, their only duty being to stand at attention outside the w.c. when the general was occupied within. Though the five third-class cars were packed to the baggage-racks, the second-class carriage was empty except for a party of Japanese commercial travelers, mustachioed little fellows in blue serge suits who scandalized the porters by walking about their car in stockinged feet and confounded the peasant waiters in the diner by their ability to write in legible ideographs the names of foods they could not de-scribe in Chinese — literary Japanese, though spoken dif-ferently, is written like the Chinese, from which it is adapted.

These drummers were warriors in Japan's current com-mercial aggression which, as it was based on smuggled goods, had, by that summer of 1936, disrupted most of the foreign trade in North China. Of course, even then there were signs that this conquest was to be supplemented by a more formal one. During the spring it had been persistently reported that Japanese troops from Manchukuo were seep-ing into the Mongol provinces between China and the Russian border. Indeed, our journey to Kweihwa was due to this circumstance, for Japanese pressure at Peking had resulted in a ban on all foreign travel in Mongolia for the summer. The pass above Kalgan, which was the usual entrance to the plateau, was controlled by a band of Japanese-paid mercenaries and was definitely closed, but Kweihwa was as yet too far west to be involved, and in any case the country above it was too empty to be supervised.

Twenty hours after leaving Peking, we arrived at Kwei-hwa in the midst of a minor sandstorm. The city was dramatically situated on a pink plain, surrounded by country as flat as a lake in all directions except the north, where the line of brown and purple mountains marking the edge of the Mongol plateau stretched across the entire horizon. The range was regularly aligned and strangely flat along the top, like a great dam. Up the ridge nearest the city ran a white path, visible for many miles; this was the sheep trail down which for centuries the Mongols had driven their stock to China.

Beyond the station the poplar-shaded streets of Kweihwa were lined with bustling restaurants, tea-houses, groceries, caravanserais, factories, bath-houses, and shops. The Kweihwa hotel was an ungainly gray structure set back in a dusty court in the center of town; it had originally been constructed as a movie theater, but apparently it was built too large for the trade. Subsequently the balcony had been divided by partitions to form a hotel and the boxes walled off to make a restaurant. The pit was still used as a theater, and when we reached it at dusk the building was a fantastic bedlam, with a raucous talkie grinding away at its heart, parties gambling and drinking around its sides, and guests noisily washing and changing their clothes above.

Though the territory around Kweihwa was originally Mongol grazing land and the city itself a Mongol encampment with the charming name of Koko Khoto — the Blue City — China's expanding hordes long ago took its fertile valley, plowed up the grazing lands, and built Kweihwa into a flourishing depot for the rich trade with Central Asia. The Mongols retreated beyond the mountains and in recent years only a few miserable Mongol landowners have remained on the plain to eke out an existence on what rent the Chinese choose to pay them.

In the city, however, we found that visiting Mongols were still common. Hulking creatures with dark, wind-creased faces, dressed in soiled, multi-colored robes, they stood out with a vividly exotic effect against the background of the neat blue-clad Chinese multitudes. Also in Kweihwa lived many Mongol princes from the surrounding mountains and deserts; silly, degenerate nobles reluctant to tear themselves from Kweihwa's tepid fleshpots or from its dim but screeching cinema. In those days the princelings were living on the fat of the land, for though personally ineffectual, their influence among their subjects was still immense, and with an eye to the coming conflict both the Chinese and Japanese authorities were plying them with gifts. They accepted automobiles, cases of whiskey, boxes of cigars, tea-sets, girls, and gramophones from both sides and gave promises in return with complete impartiality. Now their game has been called, but then it was still one of the sights of the town to see the opium-ridden young Prince of Dalat puttering up the street on a motor-bike, or the old Prince of Durbet driving crazily about in a shiny Ford.

Before I left Suiyuan I was to have an audience with this second potentate. I was received in a room upholstered with rose-covered wallpaper and ornamented with expensive gifts from the various political factions. The Prince wore a fine uniform in the foreign manner, but his style was marred by the fact that his pants were entirely unbuttoned. I hoped to do a picture of him, but the astute monarch pointed out that he was so ugly that it was hardly worth while; it's true that his face and hairless dome were unattractively scarred with syphilis. I learned later that this disease had blinded him to a point where his fondness for motoring was dangerous. Not long before he had mistaken a turning in the mountains and driven himself over a small precipice. His major-domo and several high lamas were with him in the car, but luckily they were all wedged in so tightly and so padded with medieval pomp that none of them could jostle about enough to get hurt; though the car was ruined, there were no injuries beyond minor bruises.

On the next day old Durbet had proved that the blood of Genghis Khan was still hot in his veins. He went directly to the Swedish agency, bought a new car and drove it out himself, his myopic eyes glittering in triumph as the dim roadside whirled by with increasing speed.

Sometimes the crowded main street of Kweihwa was threaded by another limousine containing a round-faced fellow in Chinese uniform. This was General Fu Tso Yi, the governor of Suiyuan, by reputation as brave as a wolf and sly as a fox. I was told that when he took over the governorship of the province in 1931, a few years of unsuccessful crops had flooded it with bandits; Fu's initial move was to enlist a large bandit-suppression corps, but the bandits were the first to join the corps, delighted at the chance to double their earnings by working as bandits at night and bandit-suppressors during the day. Since the number of double-dealers was at least equal to that of honest soldiers, Fu was unable to try any punishment for fear that the punished would revolt and overcome the punishers.

Most of the opportunists had come from the plain between Kweihwa and Paotou, so at length Fu ordered the corps divided into nine volunteer companies, one for each of the nine stations on the railway line between the cities. He promised each bandit-suppressor a rifle, unlimited ammunition, and permission to work independently on whatever suppression project he chose.

Faced with this attractive prospect, all the bandits marched to the Kweihwa Station and embarked on the special train of nine cattle cars provided for them. The cars were locked and the train departed. The train crew had orders to proceed to Paotou, dropping one car at each station. Fu then wired ahead to the militia in the nine towns, ordering them to meet the train with machine guns and execute every man in the car which would be left at their station.

All went off on schedule, and in this way were eliminated, in one afternoon, more than five hundred bandits as well as two merchants who had been trying to save train fare by sneaking rides on the military train. I was told that when the car in which one of these merchants was riding arrived at its destination, there was a slight delay during which the traveling man scented what was in the wind and began to protest his innocence. The captain of militia had previously been informed of the number to be in the car and saw that there really was an extra man; apparently it was a situation which appealed to his sense of the theatrical, for he declared that the youngest man in the car was the one to be released. The youngest was found to be a boy of about fifteen. He was freed, while the unhappy merchant paid for his ride with his life.

The bodies of all these men were put on display at the several stations, and as each former bandit-suppressor had boarded the car going to the point nearest his home, they provided a compelling and personal object-lesson to the whole territory. Banditry ceased, and if it hadn't been for the Japanese, Fu's reign might have gone down in Suiyuan history as the years of Great Peace.

Kweihwa was the farthest we could go by purchasing tickets and then doing what we were told. Discounting the train to Paotou there were no established means of travel beyond it except the camel caravans which departed for the oases of Turkestan. My companion had made arrangements with a Swedish resident of Kweihwa, a son of missionaries who had spent most of his life in China and was then making his living trading with the Mongols. He was to drive us up over the plateau and on out into the Gobi in his car, but because of previous commitments, he could not go with us until he had driven to Saratsi, a village sixty miles to the west, to fetch four merino sheep of foreign stock for a client. This he reckoned to be a single day's trip and as the country involved might be interesting and would certainly be new to us, we decided to go with him. As it proved, this was my baptism of fire in the matter of Chinese travel; in Peking I'd naturally pictured the Chinese traveler as smoothly progressing across crystal deserts and through sacred groves, alternately tempted by dancing-girls and baffled by peripatetic sages.

On a hot clear morning we left Kweihwa along the foot of the mountains, following a road which rapidly degenerated from a graveled highway to a boulder-strewn path. The country here was rocky and sandy, but extensive irrigation and the careful labor of the Chinese farmers had produced on it an illusion of richness. By the road thick green fields of corn, wheat, and beans waved in the sunny breezes, and at a respectable distance from Kweihwa there stretched white and mauve acres of opium poppies. Every few miles we threaded through little farm villages of flat-roofed adobe houses standing in groves of rustling poplars and at longer intervals we jolted down the crowded, stone-paved streets of country towns. This populous plain was a finger of arable land stretching along the north bank of the Yellow River between the Mongol deserts of the Ordos and the Gobi; it was originally the home of a tribe of Tungus Tartars, and its population is supposed to have been increased by captives the Mongols brought back with them from various parts of their huge empire. Whenever we stopped in either a village or town, the car was surrounded by a wall of curious faces and in many of the gaping visages it was easy to imagine a trace of Turkish, Hindu, Persian, or even Caucasian blood. Additional settlers had come from all parts of China when the plain was opened to colonization and mixed together here were types common to North, Central, and South China. Many of the country people, men and women, dressed in a curious costume like overalls worn backwards, which I later learned to be the historic costume of the Tungus Tartars; it was the only place I visited in all China where the women habitually left their breasts bare.

Our road was rough and rutted, flooded in places by water from the irrigation ditches, and by mid-afternoon we were still miles from Saratsi. Driving was a dusty business,

and when we passed a Belgian mission on the main street of
one village, we stopped to ask for glasses of cold boiled
water. It proved easier to stop than to start again, however, for the two old Belgian fathers had been months without sight of other foreigners. Their hospitality knew no
limits and it was a full twenty hours later when we finally
managed to get away, still overcome with food and dazed
by home-made brandy.

We were unable to secure the sheep and get them properly
installed in the back seat of the automobile, a rugged old
open Dodge, until well into the middle of the second afternoon. As the road along the mountains had been danger-

ously rocky, we then decided to cut out into the plain toward the town of Tokto, on the Yellow River, whence a better road was said to lead to Kweihwa. At first this scheme seemed wise, for it took us along the bank of a canal, through lush green country dotted like a golf-course with groves. To the north were the jagged mountains of Mongolia and far to the south a pink line along the horizon marked the sand dunes of the Yellow River. The prospect was pleasant and even the sheep in the back of the car stopped fidgeting to stare tolerantly at all the new things.

But soon from a farmer with a harelip, whom we met riding a gray ass down the middle of the road, we learned

that an important bridge ahead was down, and as it was already too late to go back to the mountains before dark, we headed off cross-country, steering by direction and taking whatever paths offered. Comparatively fresh from America and accustomed to pampered, nervous machines, I was surprised and rather shocked at the way the car could be spurred through places where roads had never led. We zigzagged over sandy fields, over fields inches deep in water, and over fields full of crops, crashing through thickets, walls, streams, and groves. We asked directions, variously, from a jolly fat man walking by a brook carrying a gray songbird in a little varnished cage; a clean old woman with a dried-apple face who was riding in a wheelbarrow pushed by an idiot coolie, her bound feet dangling before her in tiny embroidered shoes; a hooting gang of young boys, naked as snakes; a proliferous farm family driving in a little wooden cart hung with a blue awning on which the character for Prosperity was worked in white; a mendicant Taoist magician with his long hair piled in a knot on his scalp and his greasy leather apron painted with mystic symbols. As the going became rougher, the sheep began lurching about the back seat, breathing heavily, their eyes rolling widely with surprise and suspicion.

Soon we drove into territory where automobiles had never been seen before, though oddly enough aeroplanes were a familiar sight; that afternoon one of the semi-weekly scouting planes sent out from the Japanese outposts on the Mongol plateau droned high overhead. As the sound of our motor reached them, whole families of farmers would stop their work in the near-by fields, look wildly into the sky, then at the road, and rush shouting to intercept us. When we passed, they would run alongside for a while with silent, intent faces, then drop back and begin shouting again. When we drove near a village, far ahead we could see the first curious idlers climbing onto the flat roofs to stand with their ears cupped, staring upward for a sight of the plane. When finally one of them chanced to look lower and discovered the metal monster approaching with its belly dragging on the deeply rutted trail, the commotion was always immense. Arms waving, the sentinels would summon the entire population of the village onto the roofs and there they would stand, men, women, and children, like a packed horde of excited chimneys until we had passed out of sight.

Whenever we actually entered a village and stopped for directions, an immense blue crowd would collect and form an interested but cautious circle around the car, with the more timid individuals holding their noses to prevent demons from springing out of the foreign contraption and slipping up their nostrils. Gradually the circle would close in, but a toot from the horn or a growl from the engine could always send them scrambling backwards, yelling with terror and delight. Given time, all would start thumping and scraping at the machine to discover its nature and potentialities.

In one place they decided it was some sort of immature train; in another they thought it was made of turtles. The experts of one village concluded that the vehicle would be more useful if saddles were strapped to its hood so more people could ride. One very old fellow with a red fan examined everything sagely, then tapped a mud-guard and said, 'Isn't it wonderful what things the [Chinese] Republic has thought up.'

As daylight faded, we blundered on from bad roads to worse ones and at dusk reached a settlement where our path was definitely cut by the small river whose bridgeless crossing we had been traveling cross-country to avoid. The muddy stream was nearly fifty feet wide, but by sending our Chinese mechanic wading, we found it was nowhere more than two feet deep. As we made preparations to cross, a crowd of hundreds collected on the sandy pink shores, chattering raucously about the unprecedented event. An old gentleman squatted on an upturned basket and undertook to describe our activities historically as they were actually happening.

'Two ocean men [foreigners] removed garments and walked the river with bundles. One remained in the gas-wagon with four sheep. He was speaking loudly.'

When the Swede had finished promising money to a dozen rather unconvinced coolies if they would run into the river and push should the car show signs of sticking, he backed up the bank and then jounced down it again, his foot on the gas. The car ripped into the stream and miraculously sped across it without a hitch, two graceful wings of spray fanning out from the front wheels, four woolly heads hanging out of the tonneau uttering grunts of rage and mortification.

Darkness found us stranded in a huge field which our headlights revealed to be full of blossoming opium poppies, waiting while the Chinese mechanic chased off after Information in the person of a fleeing farmer. But the farmer was disappearing with the speed which is possible only to men who have just looked into the eyes of a dragon.

At the next little settlement our headlights caused still more consternation, for we could see as we approached that the citizens were taking their ease in the cool fields outside the walls, gossiping, eating, playing handball, and so on. When they saw us coming, they all ran in, slamming their town gates behind them. They mounted the walls to parley, but as they refused to be convinced that we were harmless there was nothing for it but to jolt through the swamp around the walls and find the road again on the other side.

As the hot, moonless night closed in, our journey took on a tinge of nightmare, a lengthy hallucination punctuated by exasperated bleatings and the periodic attempts of our passengers to stampede in a space four feet wide and three deep. We forded another river, were stuck several times and were lost many more, though, strictly speaking, I suppose we were lost all the time. Late in the evening the sheep quieted and made the unfortunate discovery that human sweat is salt and consequently equivalent to a sheep's idea of something tasty; nuzzling their blunt faces into the front seat, they began eating our shirts.

As the dark hours wore past, the dream took on a certain pattern. After every so many miles of road or non-road we would strike a scattered clay village where honking of horn, blinking of the headlights, and persuasive words could bring the villagers out to ply us with misinformation. If pressed on the point, the clustering bumpkins would admit that they had never been more than four miles from their own village, but that never deterred them from giving us detailed directions for the whole fifty miles to Kweihwa. After hearing all opinions we would blunder off and choose whichever path was widest.

At length we found a lean and suspicious farmer who really had been to Kweihwa and seemed to know the road. Even when offered a good sum he was reluctant to come with us, however, saying he might be eaten by a wolf while walking home. After being bitterly assured by his wife, who had an eye to the money, that he was far too unappetizing, he lay on our front mud-guard and for nearly two hours led us over intricate and almost invisible roads. At length, announcing dramatically that he, too, was lost, he jumped off and vanished into the night. It was nearly three in the morning.

A little later we saw a lamp flickering on a hill far to our
left, then another waving in answer through the trees to
the right. The Swede reluctantly admitted that night-
driving in the back country was unwise, as the headlights
could be seen over a wide area, attracting bandits as well
as moths. Almost immediately, however, the steadier light
of dawn flushed above the treetops in the east. We could
see the outlines of the mountains again, and in an hour were
back on the mountain road to the avoidance of which all
our troubles were due. Two hours later we were in Kweihwa,
where we were even more pleased to get out of the car than
the sheep seemed to be.

On an overcast morning three days later we set out for
the northern, purely Mongolian, half of Suiyuan, driving
the old Dodge in which we had fetched the sheep, and a
tiny five horse-power Citroën. Besides the three foreigners
there were two Chinese in our party: Li, a huge, good-
natured oaf who was guide, cook, valet, porter, and all-round
slave, and a wizened and bibulous mechanic named Chou.
The ridge of mountains nearest Kweihwa was the highest
and steepest and its abrupt ascent from the plains, like a
modified 'lost world,' prompted the imagination into
spreading out spectacular landscapes to be viewed from its
summit. As we puffed up the steeps I was forced to picture
the strange plains of Mongolia as they should open out
ahead, but when the top was reached the other side of the
mountain was all that could be seen, that and another
mountain like the first, though smaller. Still the vast,
dusty-pink valley of the Yellow River, stretching to the
horizon behind, was a rewarding sight. Beyond the pass
the road dropped sharply into a valley and proceeded
tortuously along a dry river-bed. This was on the great
caravan route and marching down the valley were hundreds of camels swinging along on the last lap of their two-
thousand-mile trek from Central Asia.

Though satisfactory for camels, the road was not adapted to motor traffic and it was here that we had the first of many breakdowns. The Citroën soon balked, and while Chou invoked the principles of Alchemy and worked strange changes on the car with the tools of the local tinsmith, we had our first taste of what was to be the most consistently recurring experience of the trip. We spent the several hours waiting in a near-by caravanserai, the nucleus of a large and curious crowd.

All the local farmers and their families came to investigate the three ocean men and their two gas-wagons and they stayed as long as we were there, enjoying us thoroughly. The appearance of a foreigner in the interior of China still had much the same effect the appearance of an airplane used to have in America in the early twenties, signaling a general recess for the interchange of comment and opinion.

'They have come in a gas-wagon and now it is stopped.'

'Both gas-wagons have stopped, but only the small one is broken.'

'The last gas-wagon which was here was not either of these.'

Then, when Chou had finished with the Citroën and we were ready to leave, the situation was resonantly summed up by a rheumatic old man:

'Those who ride in gas-wagons know how to fix them.'

As I was beginning to learn, in the tumultuous streets of China anything — a family quarrel, a collision between

wheelbarrows, a beggar in convulsions, the amours of two
oddly matched dogs — could attract the wandering at-
tentions of the community, and in that crowded country
the equivalent of a knot of street-corner gossips rapidly
swelled into a mob of a hundred or more people. Probably
because of this, the public talk had little of the squabbling
give-and-take which pleases Occidental idlers. Rather it
tended to become formalized into a series of pronounce-
ments by the more aggressive members of the crowd. The
Chinese had a natural sense of the theatrical and even in
ordinary conversations enjoyed speaking with dramatic
unction; when they did find themselves before an audience,
even a street-corner one, they would fling themselves into
the situation with gusto and deliver the smallest scraps of
information portentously. Spitting for emphasis, they
would declaim with oratorical pauses and appropriate
gestures. The more sensational the style, the more enchanted the audience. (*'Ah, Ah-h, Ah-h-h-h,'* it would
murmur, nodding sagely.) Oblique remarks were in favor,
also rhetorical questions, magniloquent apostrophes, verbal
posturings of every sort. Most approved were proverbs or
declarations couched in a proverbial manner, succinct and
rich in sound, but curiously shy of meaning.

'One may feel but not see the hair on the back of one's neck,'
remarks the impromptu sage, of a shopkeeper furious because he has just short-changed himself.

'Ha-a-a-a,' says his audience, fanning themselves.

'Shoes for the same foot must be worn by different persons,'
interposes the street-corner Confucius in a shrill conflict
between twin children fighting over a handful of candied
cherries.

'Ah-h-h-h,' says his audience, scratching themselves.

'Can the swallow know the wild goose's intention?' asks the
amateur oracle between the howls of a coolie being beaten
with a broom by his termagant wife.

'Ho-o-o-o,' says his audience, craning their necks to see
the bruises.

'*No!*' he loudly replies to himself as the victim tries to placate her fury. '*Never! It's plainly impossible! It's like a toad trying to prop a bedpost firmly.*'

Late in the afternoon the clouds pressed down on the rocky valley and it began to rain. We struggled along until dusk, but when the motor of the Dodge began faltering we turned in at a mud-walled caravanserai for the night. In the dim light and the hurried activity necessary to fix food and a place to sleep, I hardly noticed what sort of place it was, but next morning we stayed on until noon while Chou tinkered with the car and there was ample opportunity for observing it. I was still only half acclimated to the curious discomforts and curious delights of Chinese travel and at first I found myself objecting to such surroundings.

The inn was a small, one-roomed building set in the center of a stable-yard several inches deep in wet dung. Its dark, smoky interior was nearly filled by two large k'angs — brick beds — and between them ran a narrow space which nominally served as the kitchen since it contained the stove and the water supply, but in addition housed several bedraggled chickens and a small pig, and served as combination garbage pail and spittoon for the guests. It also made a popular toilet for the smaller children. These quarters we shared with twenty or thirty assorted Chinese, some travelers, some local farmers detained by the rain. Most of them were enjoying their leisure by spending the morning in sleep, a condition which approached the status of a recreation among such hard-working people. In one corner, though, was an opium lamp with five or six smokers grouped about it in dismal tableau. One of these was a woman with an infant daughter, and as she lay sucking blissfully at the pipe, the child lay beside her sucking with equal content at her teat. Near her a more conscientious mother sat plucking lice out of her child's head.

These details present a grim picture, but on the fresh green hills outside, the weather was pouring rain in a steady drumming which made it comfortable just to be indoors. Inside, we had a sound roof over our heads and a good smell of wood-smoke to subdue the less agreeable household odors. The landlady busily frying pork and bean-curd in a huge flat iron bowl was pleasant to watch as she made something still nicer to smell. All those who were not asleep were talking, and together they kept up a continuous stream of cheerful and weighty nonsense. It was the opium-smoking mother who in the end made the *mot* of the morning.

'Today is the festival of such-and-such, and it's raining,' she screamed, her eyes popping from her head with wisdom. 'It has not rained on this day since the time when I was very small.'

Enchanted by the thought, she shook off her child, put her breasts back into her shirt, straightened her trousers, and began to comb her hair. Looking like a tired harpy with a head like the tail of a wild horse, she gripped her comb, assumed the immemorial look of vacancy worn in all nations by women combing their back hair, and for nearly a quarter of an hour slicked the frowsy locks to her skull. In one skillfully continuous motion she would rake the comb over her head, flick the lice out of it, and dampen it in her mouth. When her hair was as smooth and shiny as a victrola record, she tied it in back with a scarlet cord, twisted the ends up in an intricate knot, covered it with a black horsehair net, and ended her job looking like a very respectable wife and mother.

I suppose I remember the details of this morning so well because it was my first real contact with ordinary Chinese, my first opportunity to know them as a people who, though they shook their heads for 'yes,' and nodded for 'no,' nevertheless coughed, scratched, gargled, wept, giggled, shook their fingers in reproof and their fists in anger, got drunk, were ticklish, sweated, shivered, and sneezed in en-

tirely familiar ways. Logically enough it was at this inn, six months after landing in China, that I really began drawing. While we waited for the rain to stop, I did drawings of two of the children, first washing their faces for the occasion. Their mother said they had never been photographed before.

At noon we started up the river-bed, but because of the mud our progress was almost imperceptible. Farther up the valley the hills became smaller and smaller, and at length the road emerged into rolling country full of hillocks rounded and abrupt like the backs of whales. All the slopes were thickly grown with grass, as bright in the rain as the cover of a billiard table. The earth was red and the road made a bloody gash across the green. From the higher hills the Mongolian plains were visible in the distance, like an immense blue-green sea.

The fine red road was both sticky and slippery, however, and it took all day to cover the twenty-odd miles to the border. The territory through which we rode had been very recently leased to Chinese farmers by its Mongol owners, but already the Chinese had imposed their pattern on it and made it indistinguishable from any other section of farmland south from there to Indo-China or west from the Pacific to Tibet.

At dusk we drove up a long, low hill toward a summit crowned by a great heap of stones. At the top it was still light enough to see that, while farmlands lay behind, ahead there was nothing but grass. We careened down the hill and into a swamp at its foot. We were stuck, but in Mongolia.

IV. GOBI

AFTER an incredibly long and rainy night spent seated in the cars, the sky paled and we discovered ourselves bogged down in a field of purple iris beside a sandy rivulet meandering across a vast, empty plain. Grouped around the cars was a herd of inquisitive black oxen. On a bluff behind were the crenellated walls of a mud fort and beyond them rose the red-and-white parapets of a temple. On the first slope ahead were three strange structures shaped like squat, inverted teacups. They were mud-splashed and sodden, and in the dim light seemed part of the long rib of earth on which they stood. It was improbable that men, not some huge species of ground-loving bug, should live in such houses. Before long, however, a flap moved on the side of one hive and out came a Mongol from his yurt, resplendent in a blue robe, black boots, and scarlet sash.

Though he looked like a brigand, with a carved mahogany face and an exaggerated squint, he proved to be an amiable fellow, for he walked back to the fort on our behalf and returned with twenty giggling young Mongol and Chinese soldiers in faded gray uniforms. With their help the cars were soon pushed across the swamp. It's ungrateful to mention it, but our progress would have been faster if the idea of aid held by most of the soldiers hadn't been to rush shouting at the cars and show great exertion with the upper parts of their bodies, while all the time their feet were on the running-board.

Before we were entirely out of this difficulty, the clouds began breaking up, and by the time we were on our way again, it was a superb summer's day. The sun shone down out of a warm and windy sky, empty except to the south

where the spent rainclouds were sinking over the edge of the plateau. To crowded, dusty China, the plateau country which stretched ahead was a contrast as complete and refreshing as could be imagined. The high, empty landscape was nothing but earth and sky. All the way to the horizons sloped long shallow hills, rounded and gradual like the great waves of midocean; entirely free of trees and bushes, they had the clean, mysterious look which only summits possess in more ordinary country.

The whole undulating plain was covered with an unbroken carpet of grass, glistening in the sunlight. Thick and green in the valleys, it shaded to silvery gray on the heights, and was everywhere studded with flowers. There were iris and buttercups in the lowlands, tiny blue orchids and fat clusters of white clover on the hills. Riding over one hill, we disturbed a flock of great white bustards, ungainly birds like chickens the size of storks; in the next valley we surprised a herd of antelope who poised for a moment at attention, then bounded across our path and away to the horizon.

Closer at hand scores of prairie dogs scuttled about in the
grass, frightening up clouds of white and yellow butterflies.

Men and their works were dwarfed and nearly lost on the
huge prairie, for until one approached within a few yards of
an object, it was only a dot against the green. Yurts made
white dots — caravans were strings of yellowish ones. The
great herds of half-wild horses clustered in antlike groups
of brown dots while the Mongols themselves were energetic
specks of blue, crimson, or yellow.

We did not linger on this idyllic plateau, for my companion was eager to go far enough into the Gobi to photograph desolate wastes, preferably with camels in them;
though sand dunes are nearly as rare on the gravelly Gobi
as icebergs in the Sahara, he felt he must have a picture of a
caravan crossing one if the men in the home office were to
be convinced that he had been in Mongolia. Our first ob-
jective was the lamasery of Shandanmiao, some three hundred miles to the west, where there were said to be several
patches of sand.

This place was just off the caravan road to Sinkiang, and that was our logical route, but following it we should unfortunately have to go through Pailingmiao, then the seat of the Inner Mongolian Government and a center of pro-Japanese intrigue. As some Manchukuan troops were reported quartered at Pailingmiao, we chose to make a detour to the south, back through the edge of Chinese territory again. After only a few exhilarating hours of open driving, we left the grasslands and for three more tiresome days pulled and pushed the cars through the same sort of territory we had met on the Saratsi plain — rocky fields, fortified adobe villages, a few straggling willow and poplar groves. It was an immense relief when at last the farmlands dropped behind. Then the cars no longer bogged down nor were trapped by ditches. They sped easily over grassy and gravelly plains — no sign of a road and no need of one.

Finally on an afternoon when one sword-shaped white cloud floated high in a parched blue sky, we wound through a range of tiny black-rock mountains scattered on a wide gray-and-pink plain and reached the great caravan route fifty miles west of Pailingmiao. The road which Marco Polo traveled stretched across the deserted plains, straight from one horizon to another like some exaggerated cowpath. Its irregular sandy track was scuffed only by the feet of men and animals; along it innumerable camel bones lay scattered among the withered grasses, bleached white as picnic papers.

Down this trail we drove for nearly two weeks, from the tablelands north of Kweihwa down to the basin of the Gobi, across the Mongol provinces of Darkhen Bel and Mo Mingan to the desert principality of Dunder Gung. The farther west we went, the drier and more desolate the country became, deserted even by the nomadic Mongols. Between horizons of small dark mountains, the landscape resolved itself into barren but dramatic combinations of arid plains and rocky hills, across which on some days cloud-shadows, and on other days mirages, drifted.

Of this trip I have vivid but unconsecutive recollections. All the days on the Gobi, alternating between burning noons and icy nights, have slid into one day. The endless pebbled flats and shimmering hills have all merged into one austere landscape. Only certain details stand out with clarity against the strange and somewhat monotonous background.

I remember a small white temple built at the foot of a cone-shaped hill, passed on a brilliantly sunny noon. Before it was spread the mirage of a lake in which all the details of the temple and the purple hill behind were reflected.

On another glassy morning we entered a wide valley where nearly a thousand antelope were grazing. We shut off the engines of the automobiles and tried to approach them on foot. Except for the peculiar barking of the herd, the silence was intense, when suddenly there was a roar above, like an aeroplane or a falling meteor. A great black object dropped out of the sky, then out of it burst two dark, tent-like wings, and it rose again. It was a Central Asian eagle, a lammergeyer, swooping on some smaller bird and rending the air as it fell.

The most significant parts of any landscape are those animated by the presence of water. This is particularly so in a desert and in the Gobi the rare appearances of water were always dramatic. One noon we passed up from one arid plain to another, through a narrow red sandstone ravine. The gulch was only a few hundred yards long, but flowing down it was a clean and lively little stream, its bed covered with pink sand and its banks tufted with clusters of emerald-green grass. The stream, so to speak, was the secret of the ravine, for its water welled out of the sands at the head of the gully and sank back into them at its foot.

Farther into the desert we reached a river which had quite the shape of a real stream, with banks, a bed, even tributaries, but it failed in one important respect. In rainy weather it may have filled with water, but when we saw it, it was only a river of the greenest grass, dotted at intervals with shallow pools in which minute white water-flowers bloomed.

Far out in the Gobi we reached a river dry even of grass. Its banks were lined with treacherous beds of loose sand, and while we fought the automobiles to its brink, black clouds gathered and we could see that torrential rain was falling in the mountains farther upstream. Suddenly the river filled and became a boiling brown torrent more than a hundred feet wide and two or three feet deep. For an hour the flood hurried past, rolling out to sink into the bone-dry plain. At last the current slackened and the river broke into a chain of sprawling pools. The pools sank slowly into the still-thirsty sand and the river was dry again.

During our first day on the camel road we passed several tents full of tired men and scattered herds of the grotesque beasts lunching boredly on thornbushes. That night we were passed for the first time by a caravan on the march. We had stopped at a Chinese caravanserai and, finding the accommodations insufferably crowded and stuffy, had taken our bedding up onto the flat clay roof. Just before midnight a tiny jangling of bells sounded from the dark western horizon, distant but phenomenally distinct in the empty desert air. For half an hour it increased, until the tone of the individual bells became audible, booming, clanging, tinkling, tolling in rhythmic cacophony; reading their noise our guide, once a camel-driver, informed us that the caravan was a company of a hundred and eighty or two hundred beasts.

Gradually a soft confusion of sounds materialized; the many-footed pounding of camel-pads, the crunch of gravel, the low grunts of the animals, and the sleepy cursing of the camel-men. Suddenly, almost under the eaves of the building on which we lay, the procession of great ungainly ani-

mals began swinging past. There was a hum of voices in the
rooms below and the dogs of the inn ran out to bark shrilly
at the dogs with the caravan. As each group of twenty
camels filed by, the particular tone of its lead animal's bell
took the solo and sounded above the others. For five, ten,
fifteen, twenty minutes the vague shapes loomed and
passed; the line seemed endless.

At length the noises grew less and as abruptly as the first
camel had appeared, the last one passed and vanished.
For a moment the bells all sounded at the same pitch, then
all receded. A tardy dog raced past, growling, and the
night was silent again, except for the slowly diminishing
tune of the bells which for another half-hour faded toward
the eastern horizon.

As long as we stayed on the Sinkiang road we passed east-
bound caravans every day and were passed by more every
night. They were laden chiefly with wool, camel's hair,
sausage-casings, toothbrush bristles, wapiti horns (for
medicine), and the coffins of Chinese who had died in
Turkestan and must journey home for burial. At that season all were heading toward Kweihwa and the near-by
grasslands for a summer of grazing to restore the camels
after their long winter's walk. Actually those we saw were
behind schedule, the caravan business being strictly regulated by the camel's peculiar annual rhythm. As the grazing
season had already begun, they traveled very slowly, with
long rests wherever there was grass. The beasts did look to
be in very bad shape, though I understood it to be their
ordinary spring appearance. Their humps hung slack and
pendulous, emptied by foodless weeks, and their bushy
winter fur was peeling off in tatters, exposing obscene
patches of wrinkled gray flesh — as this thatch fell off, it
was sedulously collected by the drivers and put back on the
beast, into its pay-load of camel's hair.

Besides the caravans we encountered some independent
travelers: Chinese or Turkoman merchants in neat blue

gowns, mounted on tiny long-eared donkeys, or Mongols in soiled robes of rainbow colors, galloping proudly over the plains on black and mahogany-colored ponies. As our road was not only the highway from China to Turkestan, but also the main route from Mongolia to Tibet, we passed groups of pilgrims on their way to and from Lhassa. These were mostly lamas dressed in red or yellow, wearing fantastic hats — high-peaked fur bonnets, wide gilt platters of wickerwork and papier-maché; one even in a black derby of Shanghai make. The holy men traveled mostly on fast-trotting camels or in camel-carts with gigantic wooden wheels, swearing jovially and taking huge quantities of snuff as they drove.

The strangest traveler was a plump little Turkoman merchant we met a few miles behind a big caravan. He wore a green velvet fez, rode a little gray mule, and was quite happily drunk, charmed to stop and gossip. He told us that certain men in the caravan ahead had quarreled the night before and fought until one was killed. This amused him tremendously, and when we left him his round melon face was wreathed with smiles. Later we stopped at the same settlement the caravan had used on the previous night and learned that our friend in the green fez was the killer.

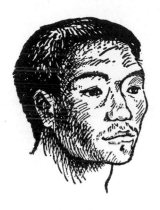

In the far west the driving became difficult again. The country grew sandier and each day resolved itself into a round of skirmishes between the automobiles and the desert. On foot we searched ahead for possible roads; slipping and shoving we pushed the cars through places where there never had been, nor would be, any roads. At last, nearly three weeks after leaving Kweihwa, we arrived at Shandanmiao.

The lamasery was a sprawling heap of white and red buildings in the Tibetan style, scattered up the side of a desolate black ravine. Set among naked rocks under the burnt blue desert sky, the pile of bald-faced temples and dormitories had an unapproachable, inhuman look, as if it were the home of a colony of insects or a settlement of creatures from another planet. Its walls were cut by rows of staring triangular windows, as black as blind eyes against the dazzling white masonry. Around the cornices of the larger buildings were heavy beet-red copings ornamented with bosses of gold. Symbolic brass beasts and wheels and beflagged pitchforks decorated the roofs.

The architecture was of Mars, but with a dash of the Bronx. It was rather irritating to be forced to admit to one's self that some of the angular, many-windowed brick

buildings, though in the heart of the Gobi, nevertheless resembled apartment houses. A few of their windows were even shaded by striped red-and-yellow awnings which, though made of wood and intricately carved with Buddhist symbols, looked very suburban from a distance.

A crowd of unwholesome lamas in red robes swarmed out of the lamasery as we approached. They giggled and chattered softly as they stood about us, plucking at our clothes and furtively pointing, but when faced with a moving-picture camera they became alarmed and suspicious; we were not invited inside any of the buildings and had to be content with wandering through the blank streets of the temple-city, followed by the whispering monks and sniffed at by a pack of black Tibetan mastiffs.

Still we stayed for several days in a settlement of Chinese traders just outside the hills of Shandanmiao, and one morning, when I went to sketch at the lamasery, I found

the brass-bound door of the largest building open. No one forbade me, so I entered. The passage gave on a small paved court lined about with a carved portico painted in peacock colors. There were at least a hundred small neo-phytes in red togas sitting in the court, chanting shrilly and clapping their hands as they learned the Buddhist scrip-tures, while a dignified preceptor strode around the portico in a flowing red robe and a towering hat of yellow fringe. My presence was tolerated until I began drawing, but this upset the discipline of the class and then the preceptor made it clear with a direct gesture that my absence was more desirable than my presence.

Beyond Shandanmiao it was impossible to proceed farther toward the sands in an automobile, so we left the cars at the Chinese settlement, hired what animals we could, and proceeded — more as a traveling zoo than a proper ex-

pedition, for we rode on horseback, donkeyback, and camel-back. All these animals were new to me as means of trans-port; the horse I found the most exhilarating and the don-key the most comfortable once one had the knack of keeping one's feet from dragging on the ground. The camel, with its whims and its motion of a small ship in an angry sea, was the most exasperating.

Indeed, if ever an animal deserved to be called misbe-gotten, the camel is it. Structurally it is outrageous: its neck grows out of its stomach instead of its shoulders, its legs fold up in the wrong directions, and it urinates back-wards. It has no proper camel noise but expresses itself unbecomingly in grunts, whinnies, screams, hisses, and roars. Its body-smell can only be compared favorably with the odor of its breath. Its temperament impels it to kick and bite readily, and worst of all, to spit. For though the camel eats only in summer, it chews all year. Regrettably it chews the same things nearly all year, since the desert provides so little opportunity for finding new forage. In the course of time its cud passes into the extreme stages of decay; a quart or two of such semi-fluid ordure is what the camel spits when crossed. Displaying a hideous personality, it does so with a smug expression of refined contempt. As we fortunately found, however, anyone so drenched need only stand in the sun for a few moments and the loathsome stuff will dry into a green dust which can easily be brushed away.

Out in the sand we moved through a shifting world. The dunes stood in isolated groups on the gravel plain and in the constant desert wind they were all invisibly on the march. Pointing their direction, there trailed from every summit a long pale plume of windblown sand.

Our destination, reached without difficulty, was the oasis of Eylis Nor, a field of brilliant emerald grass attractively dappled with blue iris and set in a circle of pink sand-hills. At one end of it were two shallow salty pools surrounded by mud flats on which quantities of amazingly tame birds squabbled. Here we were to wait until a caravan should pass, and it was fortunate that a sizable one happened to arrive late the next day. It had come all the way from Hami in Turkestan and was a company of very tired men and animals. In the slanting light of afternoon, the camels plodded into the oasis, deployed into a grid of parallel lines, and sank complaining and grunting onto their bellies. As soon as their loads had been removed, they went off to graze, and when the oasis and the dunes around it were dotted with the wandering horde of misshapen animals, it lost all relation to reality; a landscape so inhabited should only appear on a slide, under a microscope.

It was even stranger at dusk when the camels were rounded up and forced to sit down in a tight-packed crowd around the driver's tent. They all sat facing in and it was almost terrifying to stand at the mouth of the tent and confront this crowding audience of furry, chewing faces and derisive animal eyes.

We sat with the caravan-men that evening, watching

them joke and swear over their knitting. Oddly, all the drivers were prodigious knitters — I've even seen them stitching and purling at socks and scarfs as they walked with their camels. That night as they crouched in the shadows around the smoldering fire, the occupation seemed peculiarly out of place. Either their knitting should have been replaced by knife-whetting, or their horny, weather-ruined faces should have been softened to a more apple-cheeked appearance. As it was, they looked like so many wolves pretending to be grandmothers.

For refreshments they gave us raisins and bits of sun-dried melon from Hami. The melons were a Turkestan specialty, for only in the clear air of Central Asia is the heat of the sun sharp enough to dry them in this way, completely evaporating their moisture before the vegetable oils can also disappear and turn them hard and withered. They were of the same consistency as dried figs, but retained the bland flavor of melon. The pieces offered us were like dirty amber, as they had come from Hami in an open pack on the back of a camel, but after the sand and hair had been removed they were delicious. Their unaccustomed taste, delicate but telling, took me the closest I was to come to the life of the secret oases of Central Asia.

In two days, when the caravan had rested sufficiently and packed to go on eastward, we prepared to return with it to Shandanmiao.

When the time for departure came, three of the caravan camels were too exhausted to get to their feet. They sat in stoic scorn while their drivers beat them and tried to prod them up off the ground with sharp sticks. At length two were lifted up bodily and managed to stay shakily erect, but the third would not budge. Its burden was loaded on other beasts and the caravan set off. The doomed camel chewed contentedly on, looking about with a condescending eye, and only when the last active animals were about to leave the oasis did it begin whimpering and scuffling its legs in an effort to get up. It could not move. The last we saw of it, it was silent again, munching its cud as it watched us disappear.

The dying beast pointed up a fact which I had not previously accepted in its full strength — that the country through which we were riding was not just an ordinary stretch of treeless country, perhaps dry and inconveniently sandy in spots, but was indeed the Desert, a place as different from habitable country as is the Ocean. By its nature it was a place in which men could as little live as they can in the sea; they could only pass over it by special adjustments and their only traces in it would be relics of their failure to do so — in the sea fish swim through the barnacled ribs of sunken ships, and on the desert beetles crawl over the dried frame of an abandoned cart, or through the bones of a dead beast of burden. Poetically the desert and sea are alike, with the same silence, the same loneliness, the same hostile immensity. And like the sea, the desert has become a scene for legendary heroics, a background against which even misfortune seems exciting. It has its peculiar hardships — its cruelly sharp mirages, its soft smothering storms.

But to tell of my only taste of the special discomforts of

the desert would be bathetic. I had it in the afternoon of the day we left the oasis, at the moment which was the climax of our trip west, since we were standing on the top of one sand-dune while the caravan filed across another dune before my friend's camera. It was a fine day for photography; the sky was clear except for one fat dust-colored cloud on the eastern horizon. There was a strong east wind, however, and this cloud began to grow with amazing rapidity, rolling up the sky like a gigantic mass of taffy. Its upper billows churned brown and yellow in the sun and, as it moved, it trailed a curious thick shadow. When it reached us it towered above in a solid seething mass; for a moment we still stood in clear sunlight, then a veil slid over the sun and the air was suddenly thick with burning particles.

The sandstorm lasted for nearly an hour. Photographically speaking, it was a great piece of luck because, when the storm struck, the caravan turned in a dramatic retreat to the oasis. While it lasted, however, it was my job to hold two of our horses, both of them anxious to gallop away from the sand. With a halter in each hand I could only lean backward into the wind and try to give as little ground as possible. Fortunately I was not wearing shorts that day, but on my head was an old sun-helmet minus its brim, held by a strap under my chin; soon it was blown to the back of my head and the strap found its place just behind my ears, propping them out like fins. As I backed into the wind they caught the brunt of every stinging blast, but with a horse for each hand I was helpless. I can best suggest how I felt by saying that after the storm we found all the varnish had been sand-blasted from the camera tripod.

When we returned to Shandanmiao, we stayed a few days before pushing on eastward, while Chou, who had apparently been drunk all during our absence, finished preparing the cars for the return trip. Much of this time we

spent at the settlement of the Chinese traders or 'mai-mais.' These men led meager lives in their isolated clay hovels, but their hospitality was a touch of luxury to us. I remember particularly going one day to the chief mai-mais to buy some rock sugar, which we had found very good to suck in place of candy. The trader was a dignified old man, immaculate in blue robe and trousers, white socks and black silk slippers. His washed and shaven face shone as brightly as the crystal spectacles on his bony nose. Sitting on a handsome rug at the back of his round little hut, he conducted the transaction with formality and wrapped my sugar neatly into a paper parcel.

Behind him in the cool gloom his wares were stacked in orderly piles: shining copper kettles and pots; porcelain bowls and spoons; neat jars of vinegar, oil, and soy; scissors, knives, fireworks, whiskey; boots and slippers, bolts of cloth; and so on. After the past weeks in the open, I reveled in the atmosphere of civilization and was not inclined to think of it as alien. It was a shock when I chanced to realize that, except for a few cartons of cigarettes, every object in the store was specifically Chinese. All the familiar-looking necessities — the scissors, the spectacles, the wrapping paper — had been invented in the remote past on the Oriental side of the world and developed under conditions which should have made them impossibly exotic to me.

I had always thought of Europe and America as being, so to speak, the only properly furnished rooms in a house whose other sections were either ruined or unfinished. Now it was graphically demonstrated that in a different wing, at the end of a maze of dark halls, there had always been another brightly lit room with furnishings as comfortable as ours. It was hard to have to admit that these furnishings were perhaps in a more consistent taste and had certainly been kept in good condition for a much longer time.

Since then it has struck me that in this same territory Marco Polo and other early European wanderers got their first taste of the civilization they were approaching. Perhaps even the circumstances were the same; Chinese traders were doing business in the desert outside the Great Wall long before the thirteenth century and their stock in trade has not changed appreciably in the intervening years. The appearance of their neat little stores impressed me sufficiently, returning as I was from only a few days in the sand. What an impact it must have had on those medieval travelers who reached them for the first time after months of deprivation! And after they had cautiously been peeping over every summit before crossing it, to make sure that the next valley was not full of romping gorgons, ten-headed panthers, or scaly men with red-hot teeth. After such precautions, what a shock this solid appearance of domestic comfort must have been! Finally to find themselves, not at the

crumbling edge of the world, but on the threshold of a remote civilization as great or greater than their own. What
a disappointment!

Rather unfortunately, travelers from that day to this
have been reluctant to give up their lurid ideas of what
should exist at the other end of the world. It may only be
that once they've returned, they can't resist the double
temptation of telling the stay-at-homes the kind of thing
they like to hear and building for themselves a pleasantly
exciting reputation, or perhaps it's that in such a remote
matter as the Far East, the Westerner simply refuses to
relinquish the privilege of believing what he wants to —
Marco Polo himself was a hard-headed little Italian who
wrote a good salesman's report of the territory he covered
and would be shocked by what has since happened to his
name.

Whatever it is nourished by, the legend of the 'Mysterious East' certainly flourishes still. When the East was unknown, it was mysterious in the simple sense, but now it
does seem irrelevant to go on thinking of it as a mysterious
place full of mysterious people doing mysterious things.
For too long the typical Chinese has been regarded as a fantastic figure to fear or to ridicule. In popular legend he still
appears too often as John Chinaman, the comic laundryman
who eats eggs a thousand years old, or as the sinister mandarin with slit eyes and long finger-nails who does little but
slink through beaded curtains, sniffing the fumes of incense
and plotting deviltries to be accomplished at the sound of a
gong.

For a more useful picture I would substitute that of an
elderly but plump fellow sitting on a bench which had best
be placed against the sunny side of a garden wall. Under
his trig tailored robes every curve of his figure expresses
well-being. His skin glistens with health. His face is bland
and open, not a bit secret once his expressions are familiar,
nor do his eyes really slant — only a fold in the upper eye-

lid makes them look so. If there should be two of him, both would be talking with great speed and relish, laughing extravagantly. As there is only one, he sits enjoying the sunlight with an almost vegetable content, betimes picking his teeth or performing some other service to his own comfort.

I think the essential mystery of the East, of China at least, is that it admits of absolutely no mystery. It is completely matter-of-fact and in so bald a fashion that the West has been ever unwilling to accept the simple explanation and has enveloped it in a cloud of typically Western mystery. The occult East of gongs and incense is a fantasy in the pure Gothic style.

Some consider that the weather and climate of the racial homeland affect the ideas and character of a nation; they point at the sensible French who live in a clearly lighted, temperate land, at the alternately lazy and violent Italians who live in a country striped by harsh sunlight and languorous shade, at the fogbound English, and so on. The theory comes dangerously close to the romantic way of feeling ideas, but I think it can be helpfully applied to this question. Certainly most of Europe has the climate of a miasmic swamp in comparison with the dry, sparkling airs of China. And in the same way it does seem that many of the ideas of the West have grown up away from the sun of logic. They are full of obscurities — the ideas of swamp-dwellers — and are characterized by a quality of struggle, with its result which is the glorification of victory, and the result of the victorious state of mind which is the tendency to commend excesses as virtues. In contact with the smallest details of environment, the Western aim has been to exceed, not to adapt its obstacles, but to push through them and beyond them, transcend them and in the end demolish them.

The arts make a good basis for comparisons of this sort. Occidental painting, for example, allowed itself to be entirely metamorphosed by the discovery of perspective and the other accessories of realism. Then, having achieved literalism, it pushed out and began imitating the other arts, invading fields still less fitted for pictorial expression. Pictures have been painted in the West which attempted to be flat approximations of the actualities they represented, or on the other hand tried to substitute themselves for stories, songs, fireworks, or psychoanalytic descriptions of the men who made them. The Chinese have never lost sight of the fact that painting is primarily the decoration of a surface.

Our music has found its peculiar extremes. Not satisfied with the fact that music was by nature the freest and most moving of the arts, Western musicians have tried to break its limits and make of their work a story, a picture, a piece of architecture. The Chinese still regard music as an interesting noise.

The glories of Western architecture — the Gothic cathedral, the baroque palace, the skyscraper — are all signal examples of this immoderately pushing, leaping spirit. Chinese architecture has produced no such unnatural forms; it has always remained the art of building adequate homes, whether for men, their gods, or their dead. The abyss which lies between it and its Western equivalent is indicated by the fact that it has had no material change of style in the three or more thousand years since it began.

I think the contrast between the two spirits can be neatly summed up by comparing our Saint George with a Chinese hero also famous for vanquishing dragons. Saint George, who filled himself with righteous anger and fought a dragon to the death, in a swamp, has become the patron saint of Great Britain and a favorite symbol of the belligerent ambitions of the West. The Emperor Yu conquered not one dragon but two, and he did it without rising from a comfortable seat.

As the story goes, he was crossing the Yangtze one day when the beasts — big yellow ones — swam up and took his barge in their mouths. All on board were terrified except the Emperor Yu. He only laughed and remarked, 'To be

born is in the course of nature; to die is by heaven's decree. Why be troubled by the dragons?'

When the dragons heard this they were chagrined and swam away, dragging their tails. It is patent that they soon deflated and died without issue.

The days when the Gobi was important as a link between the East and the West are long past and for centuries its wastes have been as devoid of significance to the world at large as are the valleys of the moon. In these last years, however, particularly since 1936, it has been coming into the scope of world events again as part of the area of the Sino-Japanese conflict and a potential scene for the threatening war between Japan and Russia. Possibly important events are already happening in that wilderness which was so empty three years ago; Shandanmiao is in the center of the territory through which China can best receive supplies from Russia and is consequently of strategic value to Japan. But its isolation is so great that no one can know what results intrigue has already had there, what battles have been fought and what blood shed — a unique situation in this age of highly publicized conflicts, particularly since the ultimate importance of the unknown events cannot be exaggerated.

By climbing the hills behind Shandanmiao we could see a huge section of this arena. In all directions stretched the burnt plains, still as vacant as they looked on the map. Across our southeastern horizon the range of Kara Narin Ula Mountains, which rim the great northern sweep of the Yellow River, bulked in a dark purple line. In the west were wrinkled pink sands, and the barren sea of yellow gravel which led on for hundreds of miles to the scattered oases of Turkestan. All across the north stretched the great basin of the Gobi, shimmering red and gray in the heat. Somewhere on it, probably just short of our horizon, was the forbidden frontier of Soviet Outer Mongolia.

Even at that time the forces now in conflict in this area were moving toward it. From the traders we heard rumors that detachments of the Chinese Communist army, retreating northward on its great trek from Kiangsi, had already reached the Alashan Mountains, the range immediately south of the Kara Narin Ula. It was then believed that they would continue north through the territory where we were traveling and enter Soviet Russia; in those days the Chinese Communists were generally thought of, and in the foreign and Chinese press invariably referred to, as an ordinary bandit army and an unsuccessful one at that, since it looked as if they were about to be driven out of their country. It was the low ebb of their fortunes. Few even expected that they would be able to fight their way south and east into China again and I think that nobody would have ventured to predict their ultimate rise to a position of such importance in their country's scheme of defense.

On the frontier to the north of Shandanmiao the Russians were also alert; we continually heard reports from Mongols and Chinese of Russian scouting trips down into Inner Mongolia, some in armed trucks and tanks. Their own

Outer Mongolian border was guarded with fantastic care. Perhaps so far in the desert they had not yet taken such extreme precautions, but in the more accessible east, guard-houses were maintained at ten-mile intervals along the whole Chinese-Russian frontier and every day a mounted patrol rode over each ten-mile stretch. On the grassy steppe the tracks of any traveler were visible. All who crossed the border were followed up and captured. Anyone entering Outer Mongolia was sent off for imprisonment and in-vestigation at Urga. Anyone leaving the country was shot on the spot.

Of course the Japanese were busy too; it was not without reason that they had forbidden the country to foreigners other than themselves. As it happened, one of their tenta-tive advances was made while we were still in the desert. In the middle of one morning — I think it was the day before we started back from Shandanmiao — the sunny si-lence of the Gobi was marred by an inexplicable droning. It swelled, then jumped to a roar as two khaki-colored trucks flying Japanese flags burst into sight around the side of a sand-hill. They bore down upon our camp and stopped. From the cars a half-dozen Nipponese stared at us with ex-pressions of profound astonishment; they plainly had not expected to meet any foreigners in this area. Our surprise must have been equally evident, since we had had no previous intimation of Japanese designs on territory so far to the west.

Wearing sheepish smiles, and shiny revolvers that seemed too large for them, the six little Japanese got down from their trucks. They approached our camp with the stiff-legged suspicion of terriers on a visit. We received them with the hauteur of visited terriers. No one had anything to say. In silence we walked figurative circles around each other — the atmosphere was so completely one of canine formality that it was perhaps fortunate that the encounter took place in a treeless desert. After an embarrassed interval the Japanese returned to their trucks and drove away.

Afterward we learned that these had been only the chauffeurs and automobile guards for a large party of 'observers'
and 'advisers' on its way to Ninghsia, far up the Yellow
River. When the party had reached an impassable belt of
sand, its more important members had gone ahead on
camels, leaving these six to take the trucks back to Pailingmiao. Subsequently we heard that the main party had
reached Ninghsia and still later the incident was closed
when we heard that the Chinese of Ninghsia, politely but
firmly refusing to tolerate their presence, had run them out
of town.

The first part of our return from Shandanmiao was along
the same route we had followed into the desert, but before
long it became evident that by a miscalculation we lacked
enough gasoline to get both cars back to Kweihwa. The
only possible place to buy more gas in all Mongolia was in
the Chinese settlement at Pailingmiao, though by going
there we ran some risk of being arrested by agents of the
Japanese and never getting either car to Kweihwa. In the
end we decided to attempt Pailingmiao anyway, hoping to
hurry in and out of the place so quickly that no one would
have time to stop us. If worse should come to worst we felt
we could be detained for only a short time and forbidden to
go where we had already been.

This program had immediate advantages, for we traveled
east all the way along the caravan road, avoiding the ex-
ecrable trails we had struggled through on the way out.
We returned into the grasslands during the rainy season,
and after the parching winds and corroding sun of the Gobi
it was delightful to drive smoothly over the dappled green
hills, under a sky checkered with torn and leaking clouds.

On a particularly misty and fragrant morning we approached Pailingmiao. Over the rolling hills on which red
horses and black oxen grazed, a knot of small, crumpled,

blue-and-purple mountains appeared. As we drew nearer, a narrow valley opened in its northern wall. We drove down this, splashed through a shallow river, and drove up a steep bluff on its far side. At the top of the bluff was an elaborately carved and painted dagoba and when we reached it we found that we had suddenly arrived. Ahead was a huge round valley, shallow as a plate and rimmed about by mountains. It was a bright green plate, painted with lush stretches of grass, and on it like food were arranged the buildings of Pailingmiao. On our right was the lamasery, a low mass of cream-and-red temples and dormitories, so closely packed as to seem one huge building. On our left were fifty or sixty round white yurts, the home of the Inner Mongolian Government. On the other side of the valley ahead was the jumbled adobe town of the Chinese mai-mais.

There was no time to admire the tasty prospect. We drove on as fast as the road would allow, across the plate to the trading settlement. A large crowd collected on our arrival, but no one made any hostile moves. With the greatest dispatch we bought gasoline and cigarettes and departed, roaring past a gaping Manchukuan sentry and sizzling up the other side of the valley. After our premonitions it was rather anticlimactic. Behind us there was a certain amount of tardy commotion and a squad of soldiers could even be seen double-timing down from the Government yurts, but by that time we were again on the rim of the valley and, realizing its futility, the pursuit soon slackened its pace and finally sat down.

Beyond Pailingmiao for the first time in a month we were traveling along a road which was reasonably adapted to motor traffic. In that summer of 1936 it was an extraordinarily crowded and busy road for the Gobi, with two or three cars passing over it every week; it was a road of importance as it led from Pailingmiao, the headquarters of the Japanese aggression, to Kweihwa, the capital of Chinese Suiyuan. From the rumors we heard at our stopping-places

along it, it was evident that the country through which this road ran was already peaceful in appearance only. Both Chinese and Japanese were using the road in hurried efforts to improve their positions before trouble should break, while the Mongols were enjoying a last shower of gifts before the time for bribery should pass.

The Chinese had sent out a Famine Relief Commission which was distributing money in all the Mongol principalities. At their disposal was ten thousand dollars for each division. Four thousand of this was given for actual relief, since the previous winter, a severe one, had killed much livestock and precipitated a minor famine. Three more thousand was for the local prince, and the remaining money was distributed among the more influential men in the district.

The Japanese were also plying their prospective allies with presents — Prince Teh, their chief puppet, even had an aeroplane; but the canny islanders were fortifying their position with more than good-will. Most of the traffic on the road consisted of Japanese trucks busily carting military supplies from the railway at Kweihwa to the barracks of

Pailingmiao. It was rather hard to understand the acqui-
escent attitude of the Kweihwa Government which knowingly allowed this state of affairs to continue when it could
have stopped it; but it was not as surprising then as it became later in the summer, for even when the Japanese
launched an attack against this very railway, their supplies
kept arriving by it and were openly trucked upcountry to
their headquarters.

Accustomed to thinking of war as a highly organized
conflict between relentlessly opposed forces, I was becoming
more and more astonished as I learned of the vague, informal nature of this Eastern tangle. Driving south from
Pailingmiao that day, we encountered singular evidence of
it. Crossing a sandy valley, we passed a line of carts loaded
with timber. They all flew small Japanese flags and tacked
to their sides were passes from Japanese headquarters. The
timber, we learned, was to build a Government building for
the Mongolian council at Pailingmiao. This would have
been clear enough if it hadn't been that the timber belonged
to the Chinese Government and it was this faction which
was to pay the costs of construction.

Be that as it may, we were grateful for the smooth road
these tortuous politics had produced. Careening southward at a thirty-mile-an-hour pace, dizzying after our
previous speeds, we reached the verdant grasslands we had
first approached and stopped in a district called Chao-Ho,
or Temple River, in Shabi province about halfway between
Pailingmiao and Kweihwa.

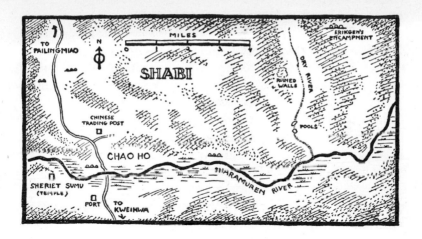

V. THE GREEN GRASSLANDS

HERE we went to rest for a few days at the encampment of a Mongol friend of the Swede with whom we were traveling and here my companion decided to return into China to get more film. He and the rest of the party left for Kweihwa, but because there was only enough gas for one car and it was felt that the trip through the mountains could be made more rapidly with as small a load as possible, I stayed on at Chao-Ho with the Mongols. A week later the others returned for a few days and, when they left for the second time, finding myself with the opportunity to stay and having liked what I'd seen of the place, I remained at Chao-Ho again. Discounting a few short trips, I was there for the rest of the summer.

The encampment where I stopped lay in the center of a flat valley one or two miles wide and about eight miles long, otherwise quite empty. Like all Mongols, the family I stayed with lived in a yurt, or, to be exact, in four yurts.

Set out on the vast green plain, these small round huts looked like nothing so much as a cluster of inverted white salad-bowls. They were typical of the simple Mongol dwellings so much condescended to by non-Mongols unaware that the squat, ground-hugging shape of a yurt is the only one which can survive the fierce Gobi winds without elaborate anchorage. As I later learned, the yurts were also extraordinarily efficient mechanisms for shelter, built of the only materials available on a pastoral steppe — felt, a few slim poles, and horsehair ropes for fastenings. Incidentally a proper yurt was not only a streamlined machine for living, but was also assembled from parts of standard shape and size, making it the first of prefabricated houses.

The first time I approached the hive which was to be my home for some six weeks, I walked around the windowless

walls, stooped awkwardly through the low door on the south
side, and dropped to the ground until my eyes, temporarily
blinded by the change from the brilliant sunlight outside,
could become accustomed enough to the gloom to apprehend
the details of the dome-shaped interior. Gradually there
materialized round latticed walls and a roof supported by
radiating poles stained reddish-brown, making a pleasant
pattern against the white felt of the outer covering. The
floor was completely padded with white mats quilted in
geometrical designs. There was no furniture in our sense of
the word, but around the low walls were stacked great red-
lacquer chests with heavy brass locks and hinges. At one
side were racks holding wide bowls of milk, cream, and
cheese; from the roof-poles hung whips and harnesses, and
by the door were stacked several wooden saddles.

Against the back wall at the left was the family shrine, the God-Box. This was a small red-lacquer case jammed full of little Buddhas, paper ornaments, candles, incense, and stale offerings of meat and whiskey. In the center of the yurt, directly beneath the round skylight, was a square of bare earth on which stood a round wrought-iron grate. Here a fire burned amid chunks of a curious gray matter: this was the infamous 'argol,' dried camel-dung, which has always made such fine fuel for treeless desert countries, being plentiful, portable, highly inflammable, and free. It notably lacked the disadvantage one might expect and on the contrary gave off quantities of pleasant piney-smelling smoke.

In the windowless yurt there could be no cross-draft and the smoke billowed straight up and out the skylight in a well-behaved way. With shafts of sunlight striking obliquely through the bluish clouds, a pot of something good on the fire, and a few furs for the white felt floor, the nestlike interior made a pleasant sight, an extremely cozy definition of the word 'shelter.' The Mongols have developed an extraordinary addiction to this form of house, possibly because the small crowded yurt provides a needed antidote to the vast, featureless rotunda of sky which dwarfs them everywhere on their native plains. Mongol princes and high lamas who possess real palaces built by Chinese masons invariably prefer to do their eating and sleeping in yurts which they have erected in their courtyards or, in some cases, inside their large official rooms.

I think the best way to approach the routine of life in a yurt would be to describe the way a guest was received into the life of a particular yurt. Not my own arrival, though. Mine was not typical because at the time I knew nothing of Mongol etiquette. When I had lived with the Mongols for a while, I began to realize what a disappointment my shambling and inept entrance must have been to my hosts. By observing subsequent guests I learned how much I had left undone.

The plains people led such isolated lives that a visit was an event both to the guest and the host. The welcome was controlled by strict ceremonial and was elaborate to an extreme. The basis of formalities was the exchange of snuff-holders, small stone bottles capped by coral plugs. No Mongol would think of traveling without his snuff-bottle and only once did I see a visitor lacking one; it was a woman, and she saved an embarrassing situation by first slipping into the yurt informally to borrow one of her host's extra bottles, then going out again to return in a proper entry.

When the bottles had changed hands, guest and host would kneel facing each other and plunge into a formal dialogue.

> *How is it?*
> *It is well. How is it?*
> *It is well. How are the herds?*
> *The herds are well. How are the herds?*
> *The herds are well. How is it at the yurts?*
> *It is well at the yurts. How is it at the yurts?*
> *It is well at the yurts. How is it along the road?*

This went on until the cordial feelings of both parties had been satisfied. Then the snuff-bottles were returned and everyone squatted around the fire for a real gossip.

In Mongolia even this spontaneous move was governed by certain rules. The host traditionally sat opposite the door, with his guests on his right, his family on his left. No one was to sit in front of the God-Box. All should sit so that their feet were not pointing toward the inner end of the yurt, toward the fire, or toward the God-Box. If, during the long conversation which followed, anyone found it necessary to spit or dispose of a cigarette butt, a bug, or any other sort of refuse, the matter was to be thrown out the door or into a corner. It was absolutely forbidden to throw anything but fuel into the fire, lest it pollute the beneficent flames. To the foreigner still unused to the Mongol fuel, this convention could seem ironic. And for the foreigner unaccustomed to

squatting on the ground, the sitting regulations were a constant source of embarrassment as cramped limbs would
unconsciously unwind in the impolite directions. The Mongols wisely sat on their feet.

At no matter what time of day a visitor arrived, he was
offered tea. This was quite a substantial meal as the tea
not only contained milk and sugar, but usually salt, butter,
and cheese as well. The guest was expected to provide his
own cup; most Mongols carried beautiful little silver and
birchwood bowls inside their robes and even I had a tin cup.
With his tea the visitor was offered a heaping bowlful of
roast millet seed and the great Mongolian staple — milk —
in two forms.

The first of these, called 'dzokhey,' was simply sour cream
with sugar and roasted millet seed added according to
individual taste. It was excellent, particularly delicious for
breakfast.

The second, called 'urum,' was more complicated. It was

a sort of cake made by keeping milk over a slow fire, just under the boiling point, for twenty-four hours or more. This process formed a thick skin on the surface of the milk, to which all the richness in the liquid rose and adhered. At length chopsticks were slipped under and the skin was lifted off the thin milk. It was folded into a big sandwich — sticky side inside — and sliced into bits. It had a voluptuously mellow flavor, like sweet creamy cheese, and would melt in the mouth like butter. Rather confusingly its outer surfaces had a granulated texture which made it look like bread. Unlike some Mongol delicacies it could be relished by the foreigner at first trial. It was dangerously rich, though, and could prove upsetting in large quantities.

If the traveler signified that he was really hungry, the tea was followed by a full meal. In the old days before Genghis Khan, the Mongols lived entirely from their herds and their hunting; they ate nothing but milk and meat and on this hardy diet made their conquests. With victory, however, came spoils and they soon learned to eat the rich food of their subjects. But they continued to eat such things only as long as they had captive cooks to prepare them, and during the long disintegration of their empire they abandoned one after another of the foreign luxuries. Since the eighteenth century they have been eating even more simply than their pre-conquest ancestors, for their conversion to Buddhism has forbidden game to them.[1] Two cereal products imported from China, macaroni and whiskey, have been the only real innovations. They have been important innovations, however, for in many districts, including the one where I stayed, macaroni had replaced mutton as the backbone of the diet, while the whiskey, called 'bygar,' had almost succeeded in making the Mongols a nation of drunkards.

[1] The Mongols were very serious about Buddha's injunction not to kill. Sheep could be slaughtered if it was done in a special way, but otherwise they were reluctant to harm any living thing. Even in cleaning house, I've seen them carefully catching the bugs alive and taking them outside to release them.

This Mongol macaroni was made either of wheat or oats and a fresh supply of it was prepared every day by the women of the house. For wheat macaroni the cook would mix water and flour into dough, then beat it out into a flat cake. After sprinkling it on both sides with more flour, she would patiently roll it with a stick until it was a great round wafer nearly a yard in diameter and perhaps a quarter of an inch thick. Then she would fold it up and slice it into ribbons, tear the ribbons into bits, and throw the fragments into boiling water.

Preparing oat macaroni was more of a task and took two women to do it properly. One of them would roll out noodles between her palms while the other pinched off bits of dough, pressed them into pancakes on a flat rock held in her lap, and flipped them around her finger to form little cylinders. These were placed together in a wooden tray with a latticed bottom and steamed.

Various sauces were used to dress up the rather monotonous taste of such dough-cakes. The most common were a mixture of onion and roast mutton on the boiled dishes and onion with soy or even sour cream on the steamed ones. Raw carrots pickled in vinegar were sometimes served as a sort of salad, but they were imported from China and I understood that they were enjoyed only by the wealthy. The onions were available to all, for they were raised in the yurts in little earthenware pots, much as flowers are grown in Occidental houses. This was as much farming as a Mongol ever did, since religious and tribal taboos forbade him to break the surface of the earth for more extensive crops.

As this food was fairly liquid, it was served in bowls, usually the same ones used for tea. The Mongols had learned the use of chopsticks from the Chinese, but on occasion would revert to their native tableware — fingers and lips. They observed only two rules of etiquette. The first was always to accept a bowl of food with both hands; this practice was said to date from the days when a guest

with a grievance was not above stabbing his host with one hand while taking food from him with the other. The second rule, sometimes a trial, was to eat everything found in the bowl.

With his meal a guest was usually offered something to drink. The Mongols used three forms of alcohol: arak, kumyss, and bygar. The first two were milk wines. Arak, made of cow's milk, was a sweet and mildly stimulating drink in which a pleasantly milky taste was evident. Kumyss, on the other hand, was a bitter brew of mare's milk which tasted like rotting beer. It did not seem intoxicating and in fact wasn't as long as one remained seated, but it had stealthy tricks and could paralyze the legs without warning the brain. Bygar was a colorless liquor distilled from oats, the rawest and angriest drink devised by man. It was always warmed before serving, and to taste it was to experience the sensation of having swallowed a hot frog. The Mongols doted on it, however, and drank it whenever they could afford to. They also used it as a disinfectant and cathartic, employments to which I personally thought it much more suited.

It's impossible to disguise the fact that the Mongols have

turned into savage drinkers. To say that a Mongol was in the money was almost synonymous with saying that he was in his cups. Unfortunately they tended to be ugly customers when drunk, just how ugly to be gauged from the tradition that it was quite honorable and polite for a host who was visited by a drunken traveler to climb onto the top of his yurt and entertain his guest from there.

Though the Mongols liked to drink strong drinks, they did not keep late hours. Sunset was the national bedtime and before complete darkness arrived, the family and its guests would settle down on the floor-mats for the night. As with the seating arrangements during the day, so for sleeping each person had a traditional place. The head man of the family naturally retained his inmost position. It was the warmest and least disturbed. Beside him on his right slept his wife, then his eldest son and his wife, and so on down. The guests disposed themselves similarly on the other side. All slept with their heads toward the hearth and their feet politely pointed away from the fire, the Gods, and the heart of the home. Sometimes twenty people would be wedged into this design, which was a combination of the herringbone and sunburst patterns. When one sleeper moved, the whole mass would ripple, like a restive jellyfish.

As I've said, the family with whom I lived had not one yurt, but four. There was one for the Gods (empty except for a shrine), one for the guests, one for the family, and one for the servants. This was fortunate for me, as I was not particularly crowded and was not constantly exposed to the risk of committing sacrilege with my feet.

As the possession of so many yurts would indicate, my host was a man of substance. His name was Erikgen, and he was a retired bandit chief, once known and avoided all the way from Tibet to Manchuria. About twenty years ago he had become such a menace that he was offered the governorship of the province in which he was living when

I stayed with him. Accepting the office, he not only gave up banditry, but turned into an ace bandit-suppressor. Soon he was able to drive away all his old colleagues, and settling down with a tidy accumulation of ill-gotten gains, he had embarked on a righteous dotage.

In the years since his reform he had turned into a mellow old reprobate, very fat and lazy. During my stay he spent all his time sitting in his yurt, telling his family how they should act and overseeing every household operation from the branding of horses to the skimming of milk. He scarcely ever moved, and all his conversations, whether with someone seated beside him or someone down at the well, were carried on in the same even bellow. He would have been an intolerable old tyrant if it weren't for the fact that his bitterest tempers were succeeded by increased geniality.

There were two creatures for which the old rascal showed a touching affection. One was his dog, the other his daughter.

The daughter was the child of his old age, born after his reform. She was an autocratic little twelve-year-old beauty named Pagmattra, who could ride like the wind, curse like thunder, and eat like the tide. She was never backward in using over the rest of the family the authority which her father's preference gave her, but was at least a model of consideration and politeness wherever he was concerned.

Like the daughter, the dog was conscious of a superior standing in her master's affections. She was a tiny honey-colored mongrel bitch, probably half Pekinese. Her long tufted fur and button-eyes made her look like a toy, a resemblance emphasized by a harness sewn with small brass bells. Like a fury this mite would attack any dog, cow, or camel presumptuous enough to come too near the yurts. They always retreated, made uneasy by the bells, I thought.

Between forays the dog slept in Erikgen's lap. When he was away, she would sulk, and when he returned, she would lead the welcome. I remember one occasion when Erikgen returned after several days' absence, in a cloudy temper and

unwilling to pay attention to the little dog's greeting. He entered his yurt and sat down with his heavy felt coat billowing out all around him. The dog saw its opportunity and leaping inside the coat, began to race around and around her master's great belly. The old bandit roared his amusement, but even through his howls you could hear the muffled jingle of the small brass bells.

Erikgen's wife was his second; his first had been the companion of his bandit days, a Mongol gun-moll who bore him two sons and conveniently died before he became respectable. When he received the governorship of the province, he had shopped about for a suitable first lady and eventually married a daughter of one of the proudest families of Chahar. She was the mother of Pagmattra and the mistress of his household. Her name was Urjun, and though she must have been over forty she was still a beauty, with serene features and a clear brown complexion. She had something quite rare among Mongols — a real passion for cleanliness. Under her régime Erikgen's yurts were kept in

exemplary order, their hearths tidy and their felts swept
carefully every day. In her person Urjun was just as
scrupulous. She was an extremely impressive figure in her
long purple robe, her face framed by an intricate headdress
of silver, turquoise, and coral. Much of her spare time was
spent in the use of a combination tooth-nose-and-ear set,
a delicately wrought assortment of little silver picks and
scoops which, when not in use, was hung as an ornament on
the front of her dress.

Erikgen's oldest son had an establishment of his own, but
his second son lived at home. He was a solid, good-natured
fellow named Yetenzo, married to a charming girl named
Meutingal, and the father of a lively little daughter named
Uttoval. Yetenzo and Meutingal were my own age and
were consequently delegated to be my active hosts. It was
her job to see that I was fed twice a day and every evening
he sat with me, solemnly examining my possessions and
trying to teach me to speak Mongol.

Besides the family there lived at the yurts three shy but

ribald serving girls called Djeema, Nyeema, and Dunkai, a silent herdsman named Gandjur, and an inquisitive orphan shepherd boy called Torroveh.

The Mongols have always held a tradition of unlimited hospitality; all travelers were supposed to be welcome at all yurts, and generosity was so taken for granted that the Mongol language contained no words of thanks. Theoretically this tradition would have made such a visit as mine possible at any group of yurts, but I doubt whether the welcome would have been so real elsewhere as it was at Erikgen's. Being a very wealthy man and first citizen of his province, it was a suitable addition to his prestige to have a foreign visitor. Most important of all, he was an old friend of the Swede under whose auspices I had arrived.

There was no question of my paying for my stay with money; the offer would have been an insult and as recompense the act would not have been successful, since money had little value in a country where there were no towns or

stores. I did what I could, however, in the way of drawing. I made Erikgen pictures of his wife, his daughter, and his best horses, while for Urjun I decorated two Shell gasoline cases with pictures of flowers — she planned to give them as wedding presents to her nieces. Late in my stay, when I made a trip to Kweihwa, I brought back presents for the whole family: a clock wreathed with tin roses for Erikgen, a lacquer box for Urjun, a harmonica for Pagmattra — it was amusing to see how shy that aggressive little girl was rendered by her gift; she would never blow it where anyone could hear, but she always carried it in her clothes and would ride off on the prairie to use it.

The most successful present was one I had intended for the infant Uttoval — a toy pair of tin roosters which fought when wound up. Uttoval was suspicious of it, so it was appropriated by her grandparents. Laughing with joy, they wound and rewound it for hours until the spirit, or the spring, in the roosters was broken and they would fight no more. Erikgen's clock had much the same fate; it was forced

to strike twelve at least forty times a day, and before long
it was silent. As its tin roses were bright as ever its value
was hardly impaired.

The routine of Mongol life as I saw it was pleasant if
monotonous. The family lived entirely from its herds, and
as there was more than enough grazing land for all — the
nearest neighbors were almost ten miles away — the only
really necessary labor was the protection of the livestock
and its occasional conversion into food and clothing. The
country was so sparsely inhabited that the competitive
element was entirely lacking. Such at least was the happy
state of affairs in the summer; during the long bitter winter
I expect the weather could make a very considerable antag-
onist in the struggle for existence.

The first chore of the day, performed at sunrise, was the
milking of the cows. After a scanty breakfast of Mongol tea
and millet seed had been consumed, the camels and cattle
were watered and sent off to pasture, Torroveh went out
with his sheep, and Erikgen, Yetenzo, or Gandjur rode away
to see the herdsmen who were staying out on the range with
the horses. Then the women cleaned out the yurts and
poured fresh milk into the pans used for making urum and
dzokhey, while one of the serving girls, usually Dunkai, was
detailed to hunt up dry dung for the fire. Beyond this there
was very little to do. The women spent their day mending
clothes or household goods in a desultory way, or else they
simply spent it in talk. The men spent their day repairing
harness or tools, doctoring animals, or else they simply spent
it in talk. There was not even the bother of preparing and
eating a midday meal. A full kettle of fat tea was kept on
the hearth and anyone particularly hungry was expected
to help himself.

At about five o'clock, when the sunlight was slanting and
yellow, the herds returned. Up over the flat hills would
come the camels, the cows, the sheep, the goats, and on

some days even the horses. It was rather like the millennium as these varied herds took their turns at the well and flocked together for the night. The calves were carefully tethered close to the yurts as a protection against wolves, and the cows assembled near them. The sheep and goats were driven into a brushwood pen while the camels grouped themselves aloofly in a circle and sank grunting to the ground. Last of all the cows were milked again and except for the preparation and consumption of the evening meal this was all the day's work.

Until the unfortunate events which ended the summer, excitement disturbed the delightfully placid tenor of such camp-life only twice. One dawn, when even the dogs were asleep, a wolf came calling. It had approached within fifty yards of the yurts and was appraising the smaller calves

when it was discovered by Dunkai, whose job it was to get up first and start the fire. She screamed, and everyone awoke. The dogs ran out to hector the wolf, while Erikgen struggled to assemble his wolf-scaring machine — a gun, home-made of an iron pipe; it would shoot neither straight nor far, but could make a most satisfactory noise. But before any action might be taken, the wolf concluded that he was outnumbered and departed down the valley.

On another morning a slavering, snapping mad dog appeared, racing up the slope toward the encampment. All Erikgen's eight or nine black mastiffs set upon it. Circling it, they whirled among the yurts in a maelstrom of teeth and fur. The whole household took up the chase, armed with whips, kettles, knives, and saddles. At length the possessed animal tried to dig its way through the back of a yurt and Djeema brained it competently with a tent-pole.

Even the temperament of the Mongols, which might have been precipitating violent situations appropriate to an ex-bandit's camp on the edge of the Gobi, did nothing to break the pleasant humdrum of pastoral life. The ideas and emotions of my host and his family, though sometimes expressed in an exaggerated fashion, could always be identified as familiar ones. As an example I remember a passage in a Mongol flirtation I was amused to witness; the serving girls were making macaroni one afternoon when Gandjur lolled in with a roving eye. He chaffered with them all for some time, then singled out Nyeema and said something I couldn't understand, but emphasized it with a gesture that was unmistakable. The young lady pretended to be offended, by which I mean she jumped up laughing, snatched a red-hot poker out of the fire, and with it slapped the fellow across the bottom.

My own routine during those six weeks spent in a felt beehive on a bare plain was necessarily simple. Much of the time I painted, or rather I drew. I had oils with me, but found their use in a yurt inadvisable, since the Gobi winds, whirling in with sand, dust, and shreds of dried grass or dung, always took part in the work, applying texture with a far too lavish hand.

My drawing was also hindered to begin with by the shyness of those I wanted to sketch, for at first the Mongols thought that to be drawn was a painful if not dangerous process. One by one, however, the men bravely submitted to the operation, then the women were sufficiently emboldened, and finally even the children succumbed. At the end of my stay, when it had been generally agreed that the process was not harmful, I even had people come of their own free will and ask to be drawn.

The fact that I was white and made pictures naturally gave me a certain amount of celebrity among the Mongols, but I became notorious because of two other practices: I walked and I bathed.

The Mongols never walked. Mongolian distances are so great that riding had become to them the only possible form of locomotion for man and they would get on horseback to travel a few hundred feet — indeed they used horses the way we use cars. Of course the idea of walking for exercise was a piece of decadent folly they could not possibly have understood.

Still my walks did not cause half the sensation that my baths did. About five miles from Erikgen's yurts was a sparkling shallow river with the liquid name of Sharamuren. On sunny days I used to spend hours in its rapid water or on its sandy banks. I was surprised at it once or twice by wandering shepherds and peddlers, and before long the whole province was alarmed to hear that the foreigner was in the habit of taking off his clothes and lying down in the river.

Deplorably enough the Mongols themselves never bathed. Their desert heredity was so strong that even in places like Chao-Ho, where water was plentiful, they were reluctant to use it externally and habitually went from birth to death unwashed; this gruesome state of affairs is one of the chief reasons which has led the Chinese to classify the Mongols with the Europeans and Americans as outer barbarians. Fortunately, the strong sun and winds of the plateau did marvels for them — I rarely noticed an odor except in a closed yurt where a fire was burning. It can't be understood just how good the open weather was to the Mongols unless it's also mentioned that they not only went unwashed but entirely unwiped. In their original haunts paper was rarer than water and of course there could be no leaves in a desert.

In my frequent walks to and from the river I became accustomed to the bare-looking plains and found that they were far from monotonous. In the pictorial sense the prairie landscapes had no foreground, no bushes, houses, or rocks to obscure and vary the view, but as compensation the backgrounds were colossal. Even in the valleys or on the level one could see for miles and from the deceptively low-looking summits a whole section of green countryside was visible, forty or fifty miles in every direction, a gigantic panorama of folded hills stretching empty to the lines of dark blue mountains on the far horizon.

The sky was more than half of such landscapes and the prospect altered with each change of weather. On clear days the plains seemed flatter, baked gray and featureless under a towering blue dome of sharp sunlight. On days when tufted clouds were floating swiftly across the sky, the contours of the plain were exaggerated by the glancing light and the dark cloud-shadows which undulated as they slipped up hillsides and slid over into valleys.

On some days huge thunderclouds advanced through the empty air, as black and solid as flying locomotives. Here and there they dropped curtains of rain and then with a short flourish of rainbows moved on, leaving a clear sky out of which the sun shone hot enough to dry the grass and drenched clothes in four or five minutes; in the emptier districts it was possible to avoid all discomfort by taking off one's clothes, putting them under a rock and sitting on the rock until the shower was over.

On the rare days when it really rained steadily the country changed most completely. Then the ragged clouds pressed down close to the ground and the rain walled off each valley into a small and intimate landscape. All the grass turned bright green and the flat places were dotted with pale transient pools.

Besides men and their herds which dotted the grass in nearly every valley, these plains were full of wild things. Though I never saw antelope here by the thousand as we had encountered them farther west, there were frequent groups of fifty or a hundred, fairly tame, too, as the Mongols never shot at them. Flocks of lumbering white bustards were common, and in the evening solitary wolves could be seen stalking along the ridges. In the grass lived millions of smaller birds and animals; larks, sparrows, mice, and a kind of prairie dog which the Mongols called 'hauligan.' Sandy places were full of ridiculously scurrying lizards, darting and halting stock-still with their long tails held absolutely vertical. It always amused me to watch these small reptiles, for they would slowly curl and uncurl their erected tails in exactly the manner of those carnival whistles of rolled paper tubing; the ferocious dinosaurs who once terrorized the Gobi must have turned in their fossilized graves every time one of their minute descendants did this.

But I am no naturalist, and I was pleased when my wanderings resulted in the discovery of more unusual things than birds or beasts. Most satisfying was the day I found the walls of a vanished city. I had passed the place every day for weeks, noticing nothing, until late one afternoon when I was walking high on the opposite wall of the valley and the sun lit the grass in such a way that I could see very clearly the square print of four walls, dark against light. Having seen it so, it was easy to recognize a regular alignment in the low mounds I had previously ignored. I spent an entire day searching inside this enclosure in the hope of finding some remnant of the city's past existence. I found nothing, but the grass inside the walls was thick with a variety of bright blue flower, like a forget-me-not, which I never noticed in any other place; it suggested that the city was one of those legendary strongholds destroyed by genii for love of a blue-eyed princess.

On two other occasions I found evidence of the civilizations which have moved and are moving around the desert as tracelessly as ships. One was a carved stone half buried in the earth of a small unfrequented valley. On it were chiseled several Maltese crosses, a design of geese and lotus, and an inscription in Syriac script. It was a relic of the obscure civilization of the Nestorian Christians who built cities in the Gobi between the fifth and fifteenth centuries and have since disappeared completely, that civilization of which rumors reached medieval Europe to build the legend of Prester John, the Christian king reputed to rule in farthest Asia.

My other discovery would hardly rank with this if it weren't so pertinent. It was a product of the civilization over whose ruins the grass had yet to grow and the sand to drift. To me it was particularly interesting, as I found it just behind the hill which overlooked Erikgen's encampment. It was a crumpled package of Japanese cigarettes.

VI. A LOST WORLD

THROUGH the pattern of the effortless nomad routine time slipped very rapidly and I should hardly have realized its passage if it hadn't been for the rapid growth and flowering of the season. Through the hot and thundery weeks the country almost visibly grew greener and richer. The buttercups and iris withered, but were replaced by a quantity of gaudier flowers, pink, magenta, and scarlet. About the first of August the rains ceased and day after day the sun swam across a flawless sky. It was the peak of the year, the short period toward which all the colder months had built; its briefness and beauty were closely linked, as it combined the freshness of spring with the fullness of an early autumn unmarred by the tired time which intervenes in other climates.

Not long after the first of the month, this peaceful scene became alive with ugly rumors. It was reported that the renegade forces of Li Shou Shin, a one-time bandit then employed by the Japanese, were marching down to attack Chinese Suiyuan. Later it was rumored that they had attacked and had been repulsed, but no denial ever came of a report that a bandit army of Mongol and Manchukuan mercenaries under another old brigand, Wang Yin, was marching westward toward the district where I was living.

In the fine weather the fruits of intrigue were ripening along the whole border. In the region north of Paotou an old tribal feud was reported to have revived itself rather mysteriously and a band of Mongols invaded Chinese territory. Chinese soldiers sent out to preserve the peace

easily repulsed the Mongols, but they were astonished when they found among them, and captured, two truckloads of munitions convoyed by six Japanese soldiers. The munitions were confiscated and the soldiers sent under guard to the Japanese consul in Tientsin. As a fine Chinese touch, the trucks were politely returned to the unofficial Japanese headquarters in Pailingmiao, causing a loss of face.

Still Shabi Province where I was staying remained a secure island in the roughening political sea, chiefly because it was such a small province and had no prince to provide an opening for graft. Furthermore the difficulties in other districts made little or no impression on the Shabi Mongols; they were not involved nor was anyone they knew. The impending Midsummer Festival at their provincial temple was much more important to them. The local Living Buddha had recently received permission from Lhassa to return to his home in Tibet for a five-year visit, and as he was to leave with his retinue in early September, the festival

was planned as a farewell for him as well as the annual mid-summer jamboree.

The setting for the celebration was a small but charming temple called Sheriet Sumu, built on a grassy bluff above the river Sharamuren about twelve miles from Erikgen's yurts. Riding to it early on the morning of the festival, I found that an arena had been roped off before its red-and-white walls, and fronting on this space was erected a pavilion of blue cloth painted in white with fantastic clouds and bats. The tent was furnished in the best Arabian Nights manner, with carpets on the grass, cushions, and low tables. In its center stood a high red-lacquer throne, flanked by two gilt tables of exuberant design.

To the Mongols sociability and gossip were a larger part of the festival than the sporting and religious events, and they began assembling hours before the performance was to begin. On horseback, singly and in groups, they converged on the temple. Galloping up from the river and down from the hills they made a proud sight. It is not trite to say that they galloped in from another age because, as Marco Polo's descriptions prove, Mongol ceremonial clothes have changed little or not at all since the thirteenth century. Both men and women strutted about the temple in bulky costumes of purple, blue, beet-red, pink, mahogany, shrill green and dark green, magenta, yellow, scarlet, brown, chartreuse, and black. In extravagantly contrasting colors their garments were cuffed, collared, sashed, slashed, and quilted. On their heads were crowns of black velvet or muff-like fur bonnets, or white cones ornamented with peacock plumes and scarlet fringe. The women glittered from head to knees with profuse cascades of silver, coral, and turquoise; the men wore jeweled daggers at their waists. Except for the massive curved boots in which both sexes clumped awkwardly about, they were all ideally costumed, in the most flamboyant taste, for a fantastic ballet of haughty doings in hidden Asia.

Mixing with this highly colored crowd were a good many Chinese; traders, masons, metal-workers, and others who made a living off the Mongols in less straightforward ways. At that time I still tended to lump the Mongols and Chinese together as yellow races and consequently alike; this was the first time I had seen groups of the two nations together and they made striking evidence of my mistake. In every respect they were products of different civilizations. The Chinese were most obviously marked out by their sober and sophisticated clothes; one Chinese woman came as near as possible to making her Mongol neighbors appear raffish and crudely dressed. She wore trousers and a jacket of immaculate white brocade. On her tiny bound feet were black silk shoes and her hair had been combed and slicked until it shone like a lustrous cap of the same black silk. Behind one ear was her only ornament, a small flower of scarlet crêpe.

As the representative of still another civilization, I made
a poor showing, for my wardrobe had deteriorated to the
point where I had only a shirt, shorts, and shoes. What
with my notoriety as a walker and bather and my attempts
to make drawings of the festival, I rapidly acquired the
immense popularity of a free show. Soon someone made
a discovery that capped the list of my eccentricities. The
Mongols and Chinese have no hair on their arms and legs;
mine is blond, and, as I had been in the sun a great deal, it
was bleached nearly white and was very evident against my
soiled and sunburnt skin. Word spread that the foreigner
had feathers, and after that I knew no peace. Wherever
I sat or stood I attracted a group of investigators who came
to snatch at my legs to see if my plumage were detachable.

Shortly before noon the ceremonies began when the Liv-

ing Buddha appeared in a litter carried by four lamas. He
was a wrinkled and wry old man swathed in robes of sulphurous yellow silk, drooping under the weight of a high
gilded hat. His carved litter was attended by several high
lamas in yellow and followed by a rabble of common lamas
and neophytes dressed in dirty red. To the piercing music
of horns and cymbals the procession circled three times

around the temple and then the Buddha was carried to the
blue pavilion and settled on the high red throne. After some
squabbling among themselves for the best places, the lamas
sat down around him.

Before the pavilion appeared ten or a dozen small scared
boys dressed in coats and drawers of yellow cloth painted
in a pattern of leopard spots and bound about with purple

and red sashes. They were to be jockeys in the horserace, and after a brief blessing they scampered off to their mounts. There was no more formal start to the race and as soon as each child was ready, he galloped away. Since it was to be a twenty-mile race, to and from a shrine on a distant hill, there was no question of watching it.

The wrestling games began immediately. Stripped to the waist, but still wearing their ungainly hooked boots, the contestants advanced pair by pair to the Buddha's pavilion. They approached in a peculiar kicking run, their arms folded high before them, and after a brief benediction they gripped each other by the shoulders and began the struggle. The loser was the one first thrown to the ground. The winner was rewarded with a handful of holy bread which he was expected to throw either into the crowd or onto the roof of the Buddha's tent.

The laity stood in a great intent square around the wrestling-ground, but in the pavilion the lamas sat feasting as they watched, attended by servants with brass bowls full of mutton and trays of unleavened bread. The shaven-headed holy men ate gigantically, spitting out crusts and gristle and throwing the stripped bones over their shoulders. The presence of a Living Buddha was apparently no cause for restraint, for they laughed and shouted as hugely as they ate. From the raucous quality of the mirth and the prominence it gave to six old Buddhist nuns, two of them syphilitically noseless, who were seated in one corner, I concluded that the humor was typically stag.

Still for a foreigner the most unusual aspect of this gathering was to be observed on its outskirts where, as the celebration wore on, the Mongols strolled to relieve themselves. Our variety of privacy in such matters is an unknown luxury to these dwellers on the open plain. On the other hand every Mongol is in a sense his own closet, for by swirling out his robes before squatting he can construct a makeshift tent. By noon the plain was dotted with decorously squatting individuals of every age and both sexes, their occupation betrayed only by the faraway look in their eyes.

Toward the middle of the afternoon the horses returned in a finish that was surprisingly close for so long a race. The winning jockey received a handful of bread and the owner of the winning horse received as his prize the privilege of donating his animal to the Buddha. In a renewed din of the cymbals and horns the Buddha retired and gradually the audience scattered.

The second day of the festival was celebrated with a performance by the lamas of the dance pantomime known to Mongols as the God Dance and to non-Mongols as the Devil Dance. As this was a religious event it was held inside the temple compound. For the occasion the Living Buddha's pavilion had been moved to the stone porch of the largest temple, beside and above the court which was to be used as a stage. In the center of the court was erected a smaller pavilion sheltering an altar.

The day's events were again begun with the appearance of the Buddha, but this time he was preceded by eight lay officials carrying ominous black standards on pronged and tasseled poles. Again he rode in a litter and again he wore yellow, but he crouched under a much larger hat. The band followed after him as before, but it had been augmented by several drums and two huge Tibetan horns at least fifteen feet long, manned by relays of brass-lunged lamas able to keep them zooming mournfully and continuously through the entire day's performance. Behind the band marched the lesser lamas, better dressed and better behaving than on the previous day, and at the end of the procession came four high lamas carrying among them on a tray a towering pyramid of sticks draped with gaudy rags and cut paper.

The Buddha ascended his throne and his attendants seated themselves around him, this time with dignity. The

musicians took their places before the large pavilion. Grouped around the small one stood the banner-bearers. The audience clustered along the walls of the courtyard and fell silent. Last of all, the high lamas placed their curious burden on the altar in the small pavilion. The stage was set.

After these portentous preliminaries the first section of the pantomime was an anticlimax, consisting as it did of a series of ballets by the smaller demons. These parts were taken by the youngest neophytes, boys ten or twelve years old, and they threw themselves into the dance with a gaiety that was far from preternatural. They squatted, leaped, whirled, and waggled, acting in the way any children, anywhere, would to play bogymen. They were masked with grinning white death's heads and wore giddy costumes striped and speckled in pink, blue, and green.

After several of these turns — the effect was very vaudeville — the performance developed a more sinister note. Heralded by a troupe of specters dressed in flags, two figures of really gorgeous maleficence appeared. They wore tower-

ing black-and-gold masks, one in the image of a bull, the
other a stag. Their costumes were of dark brocade, and
hanging from their shoulders and waists were many scarves
of shrill and clashing colors. Through a series of hieratic
postures they danced pompously across the court, brandishing swords and swirling out their multicolored clothes in the
sunlight. The music rose with irregular rhythm and
flowered into a shrill bedlam.

Then the happy company of lesser demons re-entered,
urging along in their midst a very distressed old man. He
was robed in white and the crown of his round, gawking
mask was painted blue as a sign that he was mortal. In his
hand he clutched a wad of blue gauze, the symbol of his
mortal sins. In a lengthy comic skirmish, obviously unre-
hearsed as the actors enjoyed it as much as the audience,
the old man tried repeatedly to escape. Then he implored
clemency from the Buddha. Mercy was refused and with
extravagant gestures of despair he resigned himself to his
fate. A priest took his sins from him, in the form of the blue
gauze, and the two gaudiest demons seized him and hustled
him off to limbo.

An expectant murmur stirred in the crowded audience. The priest who had received the blue gauze advanced and draped it over the tangled pyramid of colored paper and cloth on the altar of the small pavilion, then the four lamas in yellow again took up this contrivance and began to march slowly toward the main gate of the temple. The obese grand lama, next in rank to the Buddha, came and paced behind them in voluminous yellow robes and a mask of black silk fringe. Flanking him were two neophytes carrying bronze censers and behind him walked lamas holding a pink silk canopy. In one hand the grand lama carried a bronze bell, in the other a black scarf, and with each deliberate step he took, he clanged the bell and waved the scarf.

Behind him crowded all the lama musicians, frenziedly blowing, beating, and clashing their instruments. Noise begat noise, and many spectators began unconsciously shouting. As the lamas passed under the central gate, the entire audience pushed and poured through the two side entrances. Like a bowl full of brightly colored marbles they spilled out onto the plain. Some hundred yards from the temple a bonfire had been prepared, and everyone ran to squat in a long single line between it and the advancing procession.

Over the bowed heads of this line the lamas carried their fantastic paper mountain. Already the home of one man's sins, it was considered a natural bait for iniquity, and as it passed overhead, each individual was to feel the evil in his system rising up to lodge in it. The noise-makers following behind were to frighten any spirits from turning back, and when those carrying the fetish had passed down the whole length of the iridescent human serpent their burden should have been a heavy one.

At the bonfire the drums began a furious tattoo. The fat grand lama, sweating and obviously frightened under his black mask, seized the ornate pile of cloth, paper, and sin, and consigned it to the flames.

This was the final event. After It the Mongols slowly began to disperse for another long winter to be spent talking about the last festival, and accumulating sins for the next one.

By the end of August the brief season of heat was over. The grass faded, the summer flowers died, and only a rash of fiery blue gentians kept the land from complete barrenness. The nights grew colder and frequently for days at a time thick clouds hid the sun. The air was full of the doleful cries of birds flying south and often giant formations of honking geese passed overhead on their way from Siberia to the rice-fields of Tonkin.

To the Mongols this melancholy season was a signal for increased activity. An extra well was dug, the sheep were shorn of their summer coats, and Erikgen's great herd of five or six hundred horses was rounded up for branding. On the day this last chore was undertaken, the weather was raw and windy. Close overhead huge gray clouds scudded along the plain. Around the yurts the horses surged in a sea of restless black and brown bodies, clustering and scattering as the herdsmen rode among them with their lasso-poles.

The earth was jarred by the continuous rumble of hoofs, and the air, crisp with the smell of burnt hair and flesh, was rasped by uneasy neighs and shrill whinnies. Dressed in a massive sheepskin coat, Erikgen stood by the glowing brazier and carefully branded each colt himself. The shouting, the violence, the nervousness of the animals, and the ominous turn of weather all helped evoke a very dramatic atmosphere.

To the Mongols the branding was part chore, part celebration, like a husking-bee or harvest-home in America; many neighbors came to help and were later rewarded with a feast. Two sheep were killed for the occasion — slaughtered in the strict Buddhist way, with the butcher ripping open their chests, reaching in and squeezing their hearts. By mid-afternoon the meat was cooked and the herdsmen stopped to eat.

I found that, as the only foreigner present and in a sense the guest of honor, I was to have a special dish consisting entirely of odds and ends which I should have thrown away immediately if I had been cleaning the sheep. From the beaming faces of those around me, though, I could see that my share was thought to contain the greatest delicacies so there was nothing to do but gulp it down. Toward evening I dosed myself with some pills I had brought with me for such emergencies and next day before dawn was up and about, busy as a bird. As soon as it was daylight everyone in the settlement knew what ailed the foreigner, but I got little sympathy. To tell the truth I was joshed about it, in horrifying sign language. Finally in her capacity as hostess Urjun fetched a brass bottle of bygar, heated it on the fire, and made me drink it. Taken so on an emptying stomach, its effects were far-reaching. Long before breakfast I was hopelessly snarled; all morning I sat in the yurt, a miserable vessel of internal turmoil, but by noon my head had cleared enough for me to be astonished that my stomach was also in order.

As the cold weather approached, the number of travelers increased. All business was to be finished, all journeys made, before the winter set in. Nearly every night I shared the guest yurt with other occupants, usually lamas in red and sulphur-colored togas. Having always been specially privileged — though they numbered one third of the country's population the lamas lived completely as parasites — these holy men lacked the politeness and good temper which seemed innate in other Mongols; like monkeys they would stare at me and pry into my belongings. Their presence was concretely disagreeable, as I'd been told that at least ninety per cent of all Mongols harbored venereal complaints, to which the lamas were notoriously well exposed. By far the most disagreeable person I ever had to share the yurt with was a pustulous young one, who spent his time scratching under his robe, then wiping his fingers on the felt floor-mats.

At the other extreme was a charming old one who came

to stay two or three days. I don't think he had ever seen a foreigner before, he spent so much time watching me and chuckling at whatever I did. He wore a beautiful pair of glasses, for dignity not vision, of Central Asian rock crystal with carved brass mountings. I had a pair of cheap green sun-glasses from Peking and as he coveted mine as much as I coveted his, at his suggestion we finally exchanged. It was an ideal transaction, for each of us was certain he had hoodwinked the other.

Two of my other yurt-mates were a Tibetan Buddhist priest and a Chinese Mohammedan trader who came on the same night. At bedtime the priest assumed the cross-legged position of the Gautama, took his rosary in hand and began rumbling through his 'Om-mani-padme-hum's.' The Mohammedan threw himself to his knees with his face toward Mecca and began salaaming furiously. Sandwiched between two such devotees I felt there was no way I could have impressed them short of baptizing myself.

Some non-ecclesiastical travelers passed through, odd ones appropriate to such an out-of-the-way part of the world. There was, for example, a smiling young Tibetan in a Panama hat who had been to study Chinese in Peking and had stopped on his way home to tour Mongolia on a Japanese bicycle. There were also itinerant peddlers, beggars, tinsmiths, carpenters, and musicians. One of these last arrived on the day after the herdsmen had found a dead wolf in the next valley. The animal's pelt was stretched on the roof of a yurt to dry and when the old musician saw it his eyes lit with avarice. He asked if he could have it and, as the skin was so torn that Erikgen had little use for it, he told the man he could have it if he sang well. Leaning against the doorpost and clattering his castanets, the wrinkled old minstrel sang for an hour of the brave and ribald accomplishments of dead heroes and when he was done he hobbled off with the skin — the only thing I've ever seen really bought for a song.

Over the fire on these autumn evenings there was much chatter and sociability, with each guest trying to repay the host by adding to the winter's stock of conversation. Much of the talk seemed to be in the usual style of neighborhood gossip, but, judging from the manner in which they were told and listened to, some of the stories were in the grand tradition of the traveler's tale. One told by an old man from the near-by principality of Darkhan Bel, which I was able to hear translated as my Swedish friend was in Chao-Ho at the time, was indeed astonishing.

It seemed that an unknown lama had appeared in the district and, going to the yurts of a certain wealthy man, demanded hospitality. The master of the house was away, but his wife readily supplied the lama with food, drink, and shelter. These needs satisfied, the lama asked his hostess for generosities of a more special sort. She refused. Laying a curse on her the holy man departed and within a few days the woman was dead. Her two brothers then went to the lama and threatened him, whereupon he replied with another curse; they retreated in fear and soon were dead also. In the next few weeks at least six people crossed the desires of this itinerant bogyman and died mysteriously.

The affair was brought to the attention of the Prince of Darkhan Bel, who declared that the lama should be captured and tried. When the lama heard this, he announced that he would bewitch the Prince, and in a fit of anger and apprehension three of the Prince's henchmen hunted him down and butchered him.

This put the Prince in a dilemma, as he was obliged to punish the murderers in some way, and in the end he settled on a penalty which satisfied both his conscience and his inclinations. He condemned the three men to wander in chains for a year; special bonds no heavier than bracelets were forged for them and when the culprits had been decked with these they were equipped with horses and sent off. As the whole province had heard of, and admired, their

crime, they were in effect condemned to a year of visiting
and entertainment. The events of this medieval fable occurred in the spring of 1936 and I know that when I was in
Mongolia the three men were still in chains.

As another preparation for cold weather, a wedding was
held in the next valley. I attended and found that the
Mongols had reduced the ceremony to its most rudimentary
form; the bride and groom were simply locked in a yurt
while the guests gathered around to stupefy themselves
with food and drink. In the doorway of another yurt three
traveling musicians, two women and a blind man, sat all
day with their faces uplifted as they intoned one haunting
song after another.

All through the summer I had enjoyed the music of the
Mongols as they sang and whistled at their work. Though

they had no system of musical notation, they possessed a huge store of folk-music passed through the generations from mouth to mouth. Some of the songs were charming, such as this picture of a prairie flirt:

> *Oh, you who live in the round felt house,*
> *What right have you to wear red shoes?*

> *Oh, you who wear red shoes,*
> *What right have you to worry your lover's heart?*

This was another, less idyllic, which I understood to have been very popular during the famine of 1932:

> *Only a half-pot of oatmeal left,*
> *Out of it she makes little cakes.*
> *Ya-ma-aah.*

> *Then she's thrashed by her husband,*
> *For she gave all the cakes to her lover.*
> *Ya-ma-aah.*

The ditties had queer fluting melodies and were sung in a most insinuating fashion. The music was always in minor key, repetitive in form, with an indeterminate floating quality as if without real end or beginning. This may have resulted from the fluctuating way it was sung, or rather chanted — in solo, in chorus, then in solo again. At the end the songs did not stop but died away. The effect was poetic, as if the singing had only made audible for a moment a continuous silent melody.

With the vividly evocative powers of music, remembered snatches of such tunes can still create for me pictures brilliant with details I had thought forgotten — on the open steppe under a vast sky full of tumbled clouds a solitary horseman moves, and as his figure is only a speck on the prairie so his plaintive whistling is only a tiny piercing sound in the huge noises of the wind.... In the yurt the women are at work, sitting with unmoving lips; all of them hum and in the close nestlike dwelling the throbbing tune swells mysteriously from a circle of impassive figures.

To me these songs seem the ideal expression of the peculiarly lonely quality of the plateau country and the simple, lyric life of its people. Their charm now has that poignant quality which accumulates about anything departed or lost; with the fighting between China and Japan well established and the conflict between Japan and Russia looming uncomfortably close, it is probable that that summer of 1936 will prove the last in which the old ways of Mongol pastoral life were to be practiced in peace.

Early in September the first snow fell, melting soon in the sunlight but nevertheless definitely marking the finish of a season. On a cloudy afternoon, a few days later, an excited rider galloped to the encampment on an exhausted horse; he was one of Erikgen's men stationed with a herd some distance to the east, and he brought the news that five hundred Manchukuan bandits under the brigand Wang Yin had appeared near-by. He reported that they were still at least ten miles to the east, but were heading in our direction.

Rapidly Erikgen and his family made preparations for flight. They dug up the jewelry and money buried under the floor-mats, loaded an ox-cart with food and bedding, and saddled horses for all. The cows and sheep were driven off to the west and orders were sent to the men with the big herd to stampede the horses if any bandits appeared.

Very luckily my Swedish friend was then at Erikgen's with his car, and in it we promptly set off for Kokohirgen, a walled city on the Chinese border near the edge of the plateau. It was the nearest place of assured safety, distant about thirty-five miles.

As we drove away we saw the usually empty plains of Chao-Ho teeming with activity; the whole countryside was in flight. Under a low-hanging ceiling of clouds, the dun-colored hills and valleys were dotted with horsemen. All were heading for the provincial temple where the community stock of munitions — forty rusty flintlocks — was stored. With these they hoped to defend themselves.

Looking back, our own flight seems comic, but at the time it was difficult to see it so. On the way we had two flat tires and a broken axle, repaired in the expectation of seeing all five hundred bandits ride yelling over the horizon. It was long after dark when we reached Kokohirgen, and as we drove up to the locked and barred gates we could see the city wall faintly outlined against a starlit sky. On it was silhouetted a company of soldiers, their guns trained on us. When at last they had been convinced that we were not bandits and had agreed to open the gates, we could hear, up and down the line, a faint click, click, click, as they uncocked their guns again.

Next day it developed that the alarm had been unjustified. Though it was true that there were bandits on the move, they were still at least thirty miles away and as yet had shown no intention of coming west. I was able to return to Chao-Ho for two more weeks, until cold weather became as threatening as the bandits had been. Nevertheless, my

recollections of the premature departure are far more vivid
and final than those of the day I really left for the last time.
That brief glimpse of the fleeing countryside was prophetic
of what must soon happen, and in fact has since happened.
For me it was only an inconvenient interruption to a
pleasant summer, but for the Mongols it was a grim re-
hearsal of what was bound to occur again in a few weeks or
a few months.

Although I did not know it until I returned into China,
serious fighting between the Chinese and a Japanese-
controlled army of Mongol and Manchukuan mercenaries
had already broken out at Pingtichuan, about one hundred
and fifty miles east of Chao-Ho. It was the opening of the
Suiyuan campaign of 1936–37, precursor of the larger
hostilities to be launched in the following summer. Through
October and November of 1936 the fighting spread westward and in December centered around Pailingmiao. Reports of the hostilities were scanty and I was never able to
hear whether the district I knew had been affected, though
it was almost inevitable that it should have been. In the
same way in the heavier fighting of the next summer and
fall, I could learn that the Japanese had taken Kweihwa
and some of the territory beyond, but I was never able to
find out specifically the fate of the countryside around
Chao-Ho. I still have no way of knowing what has become
of Erikgen, Urjun, Yetenzo, Meutingal, and Uttoval, but
they are fortunate if they have escaped harm. Just as it
appeared to be on that cloudy autumn afternoon, theirs
was a doomed land.

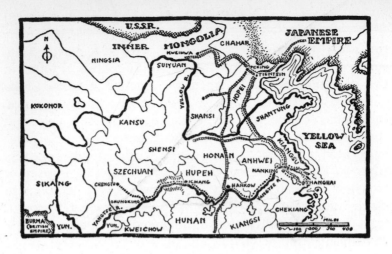

VII. CLUTTER

IT WAS on a late September evening of clear yellow moonlight that I left the plateau for the last time, and descended
through the mountains to Kweihwa. As our car reached the
top of the pass above the valley of the Yellow River, a
small, solid desert thunder-shower crossed the western sky.
Flanked on one side by the huge moon and on the other by
the ghost of a rainbow its brilliant rays had created, we
plunged down the barren slopes and entered a layer of
dusty air so much hotter and more humid that sinking into
it was like sliding into a warm pool. When we reached the
plain, the dark trees and bushes by the moonlit road had
an unaccustomed look to me, clothing the earth with a lush
and complicated fabric full of recesses infinitely mysterious
after the bald plains entirely open to the sky. Whenever
the car slowed, I could sense a new quality in the air, which
here was not cleaned by desert winds but lay protected by

the walls of vegetation, seasoned with the meaty farm smells of late summer and alive with the sounds of water in the irrigation ditches. When we reached Kweihwa, the bannered arclit streets, full of the murmur of many tongues, the shuffle of slippered feet, the clang of brassy music, and the shrill cries of vendors made an indescribably full and variegated contrast to the silent starlit upper country. After so long a time on the bare plateau, this impact of crowded, intricately civilized China was overwhelming; to make a musical simile, it was like hearing a crash of sound from the full orchestra after a prolonged passage for a single instrument, flute or violin.

In a few days I took the slow train down to Peking and through a long afternoon and evening sat swallowing quantities of dust as the engine zigzagged among splintered mountains, over arid golden plains dotted with autumnal trees. Early next morning I was wakened by a shrill hoot from the engine just as the train passed down the mountains by the Great Wall, sliding across the last of the rocky slopes and curving out on the green, densely tree-covered Peking plain. The horizon in the east was already yellow and showed countless tall columns of smoke rising from early fires in the farms and villages beyond the treetops. Trotting methodically over the hard-packed, grassless earth in the groves beside the railway, multitudes of blue-coated farm people were already astir, carrying water, fuel, or vegetables, leading animals, or promenading. After the empty plains, these many people moving unconcernedly among the trees had for me the curious and exciting appearance of animals in a menagerie. Through the open windows of the crawling train, the hot winds of the coastal plain blew with a zoological warmth and richness, making restless the tightly packed sleepers in the long car, and emphasizing for me the fact that my journey from an empty land to an overfull one was complete.

I spent all October in Peking, intending to paint and

sometimes painting from the sketches I had done in Mongolia. Soon the crisp weather came down from the mountains, making the cloudless blue days electric with a hint of cold, turning the leaves red and yellow and floating them into the dusty streets where vendors wheeled carts full of persimmons, pumpkins, apples, and other ruddy autumn fruits. Released from the necessity of struggling against the leaden heat, Peking seemed more than ever the Celestial Never-Never Land.

Early in November I boarded the Shanghai train, regretfully too, as at the time I thought I was leaving Peking for good. Departing in the late afternoon, the crowded string of cars descended to the coast, threaded through the sprawling city of Tientsin in the middle evening, then turned south and labored all night over the flat plains. In the small hours it clicked across the long viaduct over the Yellow River and at dawn passed the red and violet mountains of Shantung. For the rest of that day it rattled across the sea-level plains of Shantung and Kiangsu, where tall junks sailing the numerous lakes and canals mingled astonishingly with the crops and houses on the flat horizon. Even after a month among walls and trees, I was aware here of an increasing luxuriance of foliage and elaboration of architecture, of cluttered towns and farms more tightly packed in the fertile countryside.

Late in the evening the train reached the Yangtze, crossed on a barge, and after a long wait in the huge new cement station at Nanking, proceeded eastward with frequent stops. At dawn next day it crawled through strange suburbs where belching factory chimneys loomed beyond medieval hovels, and the hooked roofs of temples projected above Occidental cigarette advertisements. It wormed past lines of teeming streets cluttered with Chinese banners and festooned with tangled telephone wires, and finally slid into the many-tongued confusion of Shanghai's North Station.

I stayed in Shanghai for a month and more, making the

first slow attempts at writing; but learning little about the city beyond its appearance. After nearly a year in Peking and the unchanged interior, it was fantastic to reach this massive structure of an international metropolis, this jungle of factories, skyscrapers, and apartment houses paradoxically sprouting in a swamp on the southeastern rim of Asia. But of course nowhere else in the world could have existed such a city, with its Oriental river-front of crowded wharves overshadowed by office buildings and battleships; its race track ringed about by skyscrapers; its flimsy alleys and avenues lined with American filling-stations, Chinese temples, German pharmacies, English boarding-houses, Japanese brothels, French restaurants, and Russian garages; its multitudinous shops; its multigenerous cabarets and dance-halls, varying from glossy pavilions upholstered with plush, mirrors, and photo-murals, to tiny dives around whose dance-floors were curtained booths, and in the booths, beds. Nowhere else could have gathered this swarming population of Chinese, Japanese, Russians, Portuguese, North and South Americans, Germans, English, French, Turks, and Hindus. Nowhere else could have lived these pullulating hordes of the doomed Chinese suburbs, or the unlikely denizens of the International Settlement, among whom, to reach at random, were the Chinese politicians living on graft from distant provinces who could be seen gorging themselves on English whiskey and French pastry at the big hotels; the stylish American and European business people who drank cocktails at the country clubs, dressed in elegant riding-clothes, though they'd never been on a horse; the Chinese students who assiduously chattered American slang in the lobbies of the super-cinemas; the tiny Chinese beggar children who stood on street corners cheerfully whining in English, ' No-mama-no-papa-no-chow-no-whiskey-soda.'

I regret that I did not learn more of it now that the blatant, immensely prosperous Shanghai, through which

the wealth of a whole subcontinent funneled, has become a thing of the past. To have seen it just before its downfall has something of the fascination that must accumulate about a visit to any place soon to be violently and permanently changed — analogous, say, to a trip to Petrograd in 1915 or '16. It was already only half a year before that breathless Saturday of August when the planes suddenly appeared, the first explosives fell, and the streets, lined with the pale many-windowed façades of hotels and stores, were tangled with dark crowds blindly fleeing from the terrible corners so thickly buttered with squashed bodies.

During the time when I was in Shanghai, two of the events which were to shape the city's tragedy took place.

In mid-November the fighting in Suiyuan swelled from a provincial skirmish into a campaign of national importance. With the rest of China, Shanghai became alarmed when Japanese forces openly advanced into Chinese territory and after the astonishing Chinese victories at Pailingmiao excitement reached a fever pitch. The newspapers boiled with news of the conflict, the magazines blossomed with feature articles on Suiyuan, and the whole town was deluged with the hysteric odds and ends of war-time publicity. There were drives for aid for the wounded, and widely publicized sales of 'comfort boxes' and gas masks to be purchased by patriots and sent as anonymous gifts to the soldiers. In connection with this last it was pathetically ridiculous that after hundreds of masks had been sent off despite the fact that no gas was being used, it was not only discovered that the masks were so cheaply made as to be useless, but were also made in Japan.

Early in December was effected the kidnaping of General Chiang Kai-Shek at Sian, and from the day of his imprisonment until the time I left Shanghai, the streets were always full of newsboys shouting extras on either this crisis or the Suiyuan war. It was here that I had my first taste of the curious attitude toward events around them which was traditional to foreigners in China, for all this time the foreign population of Shanghai was far more interested in an event on the other side of the world — the boiling-up of the scandal which was to unseat Edward VIII — and month-old American magazines were read more avidly than the day-old local papers.

When I came to Shanghai I rather stupidly persisted in thinking myself on a tour of the world, chiefly because the one intention with which I had set out from America — that of circling the globe — was the only long-range plan I ever made on the trip. When I reached China I had lost sight of the country-to-country schedule in the more realistic fascinations of going from place to place in China, and I had really forgotten my first scheme to such an extent that I neglected to abandon it until I had to test its actual mechanics. From Shanghai I had planned to take a boat south through the Indies to India and on through Suez, but once in Shanghai I was unable to find any boats sufficiently cheap, and with a dwindling purse I was reluctant to venture into any of those countries where I'd been told that it was part of the white man's burden to travel first class. In the end I decided to remain in China until I was left with just the minimum sum to get me back by way of Siberia, Russia, Europe, and the Atlantic. When I had made this decision it was with a great, and previously unsuspected, relief at not leaving China that I engaged passage on a Chinese steamship sailing up the Yangtze.

The *Ming Kuei* was scheduled to sail on the evening of December twenty-fourth, and at nine that night I taxied down through the gaily lit streets of the International Settlement, past pine-decorated stores, past one where a Chinese was unconvincingly disguised as Santa Claus, jolting out through the neglected streets of Frenchtown and on to the black wharves by the Chinese city. Once aboard I found the ship was not yet loaded and spent the night lying in a chilly cabin while two hundred coolies ran chanting up and down the gangplank outside the porthole, intermittently dropping bales and barrels into the hold below. The dirty dawn of December twenty-fifth was just breaking when the small ship finally swung out on the rancid waters of the Whangpoo and churned past Shanghai's cluttered water-front; asleep in her swamp, the Pearl of the Orient was looking her worst. I remember that as the boat came abreast of the Bund of the International Settlement, a clock in one of the fog-shrouded skyscrapers boomed five with sepulchral emphasis. 'Merry Christmas, Merry Christmas,' it seemed not to be saying.

Beyond the sprawling factories of Shanghai's outskirts, the river was lined with marshy farm land almost as flat and dirty as its own water. Soon even these insignificant banks slipped off toward the drizzly horizon; the water became yellower and the currents of a greater river boiled through it in many directions. The boat plowed out to a point from which no shores were visible, turned west, and proceeded inland.

Flowing between horizons smudged with yellow sand-bars, the immense yellow flood was dotted with ramshackle yellow junks hung with yellow varnished sails. Skimming close over the soiled current, even the clouds reflected a yellow taint. On the edge of the jaundiced water the distant shores made only a threadlike rim; the only permanency in

this wide world of molasses was plainly the river, building
and destroying the land as it twisted its course, making life
insecure for men, beasts, and fish. It was not until dusk
that the scene narrowed to more comfortable proportions
and we sighted over the damp sandbanks a few bedraggled
bluffs which must at all times be above water.

In China that Christmas Day of 1936 was notable as the
day on which Chiang Kai-Shek left his captivity at Sian.
The news of this event came in on the ship's radio during
the afternoon; all the Chinese on board were jubilant and an
impromptu banquet was arranged for the evening. I doubt
if these middle- and upper-class travelers would have been
so happy if they had known the meaning of the event as it
was later to be interpreted and they certainly would not
have celebrated if they had realized how soon its effects
would hasten on the war. As it was, it seemed only a personal triumph for Chiang Kai-Shek — it was officially announced that Chang Hsueh Liang had been moved to release him on reading his diary.

When the brown shadows of night fell over the river and
the engines were turned down to a slow, persistent slogging,
the cabin passengers and the officers, talking zestfully in
the tumbling, shapeless Shanghai dialect, congregated in
the dining-salon — a snug room containing three tables,
a small harmonium, and an electric icebox enthroned in
a jungle of tired rubber plants.

The food at the feast ranged from fried octopus to boiled flowers, all of it accompanied by plenty of Chinese whiskey, and after dinner there were entertainments by the passengers. The star performer was a well-known female impersonator on his way to a season in the theaters of Szechwan; he sang with astonishing shrillness, accompanying himself on the huchin, a sort of Chinese violin of a limited but piercing range of tone. Traveling with him was his daughter, a miniature beauty four or five years old who caused much amusement to the audience when she also sang, with precocious aplomb, but caused me more amusement later when she nonchalantly relieved her bladder into a cuspidor in the corner of the room. Another performer was a young lady in tortoise-rimmed spectacles and a green gauze gown who favored us on the harmonium. She knew a number of Chinese wheezes, excruciating when played on an organ, and a single foreign number, 'The Volga Boatman.' Frequently between her Chinese songs she would pause to render this plaint and whenever she did, she and all the others in the salon would turn to smile at me, the only Occidental on board, and I would have to smile and smile and smile, until the last of the mournful chords was struck.

The steamship line on which I sailed, the Ming Sung, was entirely Chinese; financed, managed, and manned without foreign help. Its craft were not so fast, safe, or comfortable as the British and French river boats, but they charged little more than half the fare on the foreign boats. I think the ship I traveled on was actually of foreign manufacture, but its familiar Occidental structure was a background for an assembly of richly Oriental characters.

The captain, Mr. Yueh, was a happy little dandy whose only worry was the fact that he looked like a Japanese; the resemblance was so great that even his inferior officers felt privileged to josh him about it. His nature was so agreeable that he always took it in good part, but I have since speculated as to what a source of tragic embarrassment, if not real danger, his appearance has become. Entering and leaving port the small commander wore a uniform composed of approximately one part serge to four parts gold braid, but for more comfortable occasions he preferred a gown of chocolate-colored silk and a rakish black lambskin hat. His chief interest was his birds, of which he had so great a number that the bridge and wheel-room were as full of cages as a pet shop.

First Officer Wang was more interested in calisthenics and calligraphy. His cabin was decorated with specimens of the handwriting of the sages and mottoes inscribed in the styles of Chien Lung and other of China's great emperors who were pre-eminent for their culture as well as their power. As Wang had a paunch and affected a turtle-neck sweater, his appearance was not aesthetic, but every morning he would appear on deck with a gaily tasseled wooden sword and poised himself at the bow, first on one foot, then the other, as he gracefully propelled his ungainly body through a series of stylized poses.

As the purser, who could speak some English, informed me, these exercises were based on the Taoist theories of the Yin-Yang ☯, being specially calculated to induce the flow through the body of the active Yang principle ☯ and drive out the sluggish Yin ☯. By the inert nature of his physical composition, the purser said, man had naturally a preponderance of idle Yin. The air about him, being quite free of material form, was Yang at its purest. The ideal state was one in which an exact balance of Yin and Yang prevailed, and as man was in the air and the air in man, he could best induce the flow of Yang through him and capture the vital essences by motion. The kinetic Yang principle in the air was concentrated as Ch'i, the cosmic breath, the breath of life, and with some confusion between the fields of poetry and science, this was decreed to be strongest among growing or moving things. This was the reason why First Officer Wang did his exercises at the ship's bow where the spray flying up created an aura of the most active, Yang-impregnated atmosphere aboard; why city dwellers preferred to go into the blossoming groves outside the town walls to practice their calisthenics; indeed, this theory was responsible for the belief that if exercise failed to help, colds and numb feet could be cured by having a growing child blow on one's navel.

With the collaboration of Wang I tried the first simple motions of the Ch'i-inducing calisthenics and regret I hadn't opportunity to learn more; though mild, they were the most far-reaching and refreshing exercises I have ever attempted. There were no mechanical repetitions, as of our 'daily dozens' or setting-up routines. Instead the process was a dance involving the controlled transition of the body from one set attitude to another, some passages to be accomplished very slowly, others at a single bound. The effect was to stretch and limber every muscle without exhausting any. As might be expected of a system of exercise devised in the thought of man as afloat in the vitalizing air, the effect was most closely akin to that of swimming.

First Officer Wang was also an ardent amateur gardener and daily sunned his pots of ferns and flowering vines in the shelter of ventilators and derricks. I believe he considered the lifeboats the best hothouses for more tender growths.

A brisker note was sounded by Purser Dzau, a bony young fellow with brilliantined hair and foreign clothes — highly colored shirts and ties, and a very blue suit double-breasted almost to the point of triplicity. Dzau had been educated at a mission school and had there absorbed some eccentric English and some foreign ideas. Thinking of the strenuous life, he paced the decks for an hour every day with a concentrated look on his face and a hairnet on his slippery locks. He disapproved easily and informed me with confidence that the ills of China were caused by rich people who 'did not make studies but used their money to purchase bad actions,' an accusation made sensational by his way of pronouncing 'bad' as if it rhymed with 'red.' His conversation with me was largely concerned with the comparison of my behavior with that of the only other non-Chinese passenger the boat had carried in recent months, a traveler who I think must have been a lama strayed rather far from his monastery; Dzau referred to him succinctly as 'that Tibetan monkey.'

Up the sliding brown waters of the Yangtze the ship trudged, past Wusih and past Nanking, where the new cement buildings of the growing capital, glinting white in the misty December sunlight, made an attractively modern setting against which I have never been able to picture the atrocious mass brutalities which were to take place there just one year later. The smaller river cities slid by almost indistinguishable from one another; the approach to such a city was aptly described in a saw recited by Purser Dzau, who assured me that it was a very old Chinese saying.

> When the pagoda is seen the town is near,
> And it is close indeed when the gas tanks appear.

It was true that the first sign of one of these towns — Wuhu, Anking, Kiukiang — was usually its pagoda, a white crumbling tower on the riverside. Next followed the silvered tanks and naked bungalows in the compounds of the foreign oil companies. Beyond them the mission buildings loomed, sanitary and enclosed. Farther back from the river sprawled the ruinous walls of the Chinese city and along the water-side before it stretched its small Bund — a brick embank-ment lined with foreign and semi-foreign houses perching beside the big river like toys. On the towering shores ex-posed by the low winter water they were toys on a shelf.

During that winter of 1936–37 the water in the Yangtze dropped below the lowest levels previously recorded, and in December, usually only the beginning of the low season, it was already flowing fifty feet below its summer level, turn-ing its channel into a great steep-sided trough. As the deepest water flowed near the shore, our course generally lay within a few yards of one of the towering banks and for more than a week these long winding walls of crumbling earth were almost the only things visible from the small ship. Though they could hardly qualify as 'scenery,' they sometimes provided striking and unexpected vistas.

Their strangest effect was a negation of the sense of scale. The sixty-foot banks beside the mile-wide river had been cut by the rain and the current into forms which were more familiar to me in a sixty-inch size; they were eroded into the same rough gullies and escarpments which appear on a freshly plowed field or beside a hilly road after a freshet. Growing on the banks were clumps of reeds which increased the illusion, for though at a distance they looked like tufts of ordinary field grass, they were really ten or fifteen feet high. Whenever a man appeared on this huge scene, it was a shock to see him, as he was invariably less than knee-high to the size predetermined for him.

But in great quantities such midgets infested the brown shores. They fished, hauled boats, carried water, washed vegetables, spanked clothes, or simply sat observing the river. Most of all, they farmed. Armies of them busily pitted, scratched, and curried the soil. Viewed from the

steamer's deck far below, they demanded the cliché 'ant-like,' for their activities on the surface of the great layer of earth were heroicly tiny. Their stolid labor was particularly touching where the river had sucked whole fields down in dissolving steps toward the water, or where undercut patches of earth, neatly lined with vegetables, had cracked loose and were tipping out over the avid current.

Four days out of Shanghai the boat passed the immense Wuhan cities, Hankow, Wuchang, and Hanyang, sprawled out on the flat plain and, except for a few factory chimneys, invisible from the low-lying ship. West of the cities the river became much narrower and shallower, and was striped with sandbars on which long-legged birds promenaded gravely. In the low water it became necessary for the boat to anchor every night at dusk and to proceed very slowly, with frequent soundings, during the day. Farther west appeared distant mountains of shapes as strangely Asiatic as the humps of a camel. At first they were to be seen singly, some distance from the river, sitting like old men in solitary dignity. Then more of them appeared, approaching in lines and clusters. The sluggish river began quickening; its current increased, boiling up in hummocks over

hidden rocks and weaving itself into intricate patterns over
the shallows. Its brown surface was crisped in places with
foam, and in other spots convolved in heavy, sliding disks
of water. At length on an afternoon a week west of Hankow,
a high solid line of blue mountains rose up over the western
horizon. Straight into it the river incredibly led, through
an amphitheater of rocky, cone-shaped hills. On its north
bank, just short of the mountain wall, appeared the huddled
gray roofs of Ichang.

Beyond this point were the Gorges of the Yangtze and it
would be necessary to change to a smaller boat to go farther.
I was ferried ashore that evening in a creaking sampan as
the yellow light faded over the mountains. When I had
walked over the sloping foreshore covered with beggars'
huts and up the steep slippery stairs to the town, I found
that the city was engaging in an air-raid drill. All lights had
been turned off and in the close, odorous black streets, there
were no sounds but the scuffling steps and whispers of invisible multitudes. These preparations were later to be tried
only too thoroughly, for this city became the scene of one
of the most barbarous air raids of the whole war, when on
a sunny afternoon twenty planes arrived and plummeted

hundreds of bombs on it, burning two thirds of the city and destroying between two and three thousand of its people.

For several days I was delayed at Ichang by unusually low water; indeed, the official watermark, based on a record low in 1915, indicated that there was a foot and a half less than no water in the river. The foreign lines had already declared the rapids unsafe and discontinued their service for the winter, but the officials of the Chinese line on which I was traveling judged that there was still enough water in the Gorges to lubricate a small boat's passage over the rocks and within the week such a boat was dispatched.

It was scheduled to sail at dawn. I did not know that Chinese bedtime here was normally about nine and when I did come aboard at eleven on the night before, I found that the steward had installed a friend of his, a deck passenger, in my cabin for the voyage. When I appeared, a loss of face for someone was imminent. At first there was a feeble attempt made to prevent my coming aboard at all, but in the end I was accommodated in the quarters of the first officer.

The brightly lit cabin of this sailor was decorated with fir branches and glasses full of odd or pretty pebbles he had found along the river during his boat's nightly stops. There were two pictures on the wall over his desk; one, mildly scandalous, of a Buddhist monk making advances on a Buddhist nun, and another, printed in China's national colors — red, yellow, blue, black, and white — of a pretty girl and a monster. This was later explained to me as a demonstration of the moral that China's elements could with equal facility form either an attractive or a disagreeable picture. The only other personal belongings in the cabin were a huge assortment of Shanghai commodities, cheap imitations of foreign articles complete with English titles: 'My Dear Cigarettes,' 'Fairy Isle Cigarettes,' 'The Baby Cigarettes,' 'Modernistic Soap,' 'Butterfly Talc,'

'The Girl in Moon Dental Powder,' several rolls of an article called 'Red Ball Toilet-Paper Crêpe.'

Pleased with the novelty of a foreign roommate First Officer Liu, square-faced and smiling, made himself very agreeable. He helped me unpack, indeed insisting that he take everything out of my bag, perhaps to satisfy his curiosity as to the contents of a foreigner's luggage. As he experimentally knotted bows in my four-in-hand ties and squeezed color samples from my tubes of oils with Simian intentness, I became acquainted with his most distinguishing characteristic. He was a fountain of curiously wrought English. He proudly explained that he had learned some of it from books and some of it from passing travelers. Two of the books lay on his desk and they explained a good deal. One was called 'The Classified List of Miscellaneous Important Items' and aimed to provide the student with a suitable English remark for every possible conversational contingency. Some idea of its scope can be gleaned from the following extracts, taken at random:

> *Why does your father change his clothes?*
> *Did this man cut your finger?*
> *Go on: you walk too slowly.*
> *How many umbrellas have you?*
> *He is always getting drunk.*
> *He is in Hartford, Connecticut, America.*
> *He sprinkled my clothes all over with water and then run away.*
> *Don't soil my book or keep my book clean.*

The other was called 'Correctly English in Hundred Days' and its aims were set forth in the following preface:

> *This book is prepared for the Chinese young man who wishes to served for the foreign firms.*
> *It divided nearly hundred and ninety pages.*
> *It contains full of ordinary speak and write language.*
> *This book is clearly, easily, to the Chinese young man or scholar. If it is quite understood, that will be satisfaction.*

To me this book was extraordinary, incredibly. In its oblique chapters a whole fantastic world was unfolded. The section devoted to the farmyard referred to 'chickens and duckens,' while the chapter on animals described the 'tigar' as having 'two bright eyes and vary sharp legs.' Probably I can best suggest its unhinged universe and the dreamy style in which it was delineated by quoting in its entirety an essay on a familiar subject:

WATER

Water is the most useful thing. If we want to cook something we must use the water. We wash face and body must use the water. Everything must have water to living in anytime in anywhere except the dead things. Young man should do something. Young man should obey his parent. Young man should not gumbling. Young man should be diligent. Young man should be fairthfil. Young man should on guarrel. Post no bill. Spitting prohibited. No smoking. No admittance. Stop talking. Public Telephone. Please shut the door.

I wondered about the travelers, though; for when Mr. Liu's conversation was not quaintly irrelevant it was hair-raisingly obscene. When we finished unpacking, he knit his brows and, with the air of a man who knows what is expected of him, recited in painful sing-song several very sultry, foreign-style dirty jokes. 'Very interest' he called them, laughing and slapping his knees, but I don't think he understood them.

'The mariner's life is so dry,' he complained wistfully as he switched out the light and rolled into his bunk.

VIII. THE HIDDEN PROVINCE

Weighing anchor next day in a frosty blue-and-orange dawn, the ship sailed between two folds in the curtain of rock west of Ichang and entered an immense corridor formed by sheer yellow precipices piling one upon another to a height of more than two thousand feet. At that hour it was still dark on the river, with shreds of fog coiling over the roaring brown water, but far overhead the sky was faultlessly blue, and down the snow-capped mountains in the west a narrow area of ruddy winter sunlight was descending. More than a hundred feet above the boat the flanks of the mountains were veined with the marks of the summer floods; the long sloping beaches below were piled with rocks among which lay the bleached and sundered remnants of many junks and sampans and, in two spots at least, the wreckage of foreign steamships.

Deeper in the gorge the mountains approached till the floor of the canyon could hold nothing but the river flowing its twisted course between gigantic boulders. Unlike the peaks east of Ichang, which had been seated apart on the plain like dignified patriarchs, these monsters hulked together like a mob of old men, crowding to torment the river, leaning precipitously over it as they thrust great knees and elbows of rock before it. The closer they pressed the greater the river's frenzy became; it raced and dodged through the narrow gaps and churned desperately back on itself in the few wide passages. Sometimes it was inescapably trapped, caught between ledges of rock or masses of boulders fallen from the cliffs above. Leaping through such places, the water churned, shuddered, shattered, scattered, and fell.

At the first of the rapids the small ship advanced briskly into the heart of the huge millrace, its engines stoked to a pitch which made its whole fabric tremble. When it reached white water, its speed fell to an almost imperceptible crawl, but its engines beat faster and faster till its decks began to shake with the effort. Riding the surface of the huge current, it seemed to lose all its weight and raced along in one place, shifting skittishly at the suggestion of every wave. Only after minutes did the engines roar more deeply and the boat begin to edge up into clear water again. Never before had I thought of a ship as being capable of sailing uphill.

The steepest rapid, the Hsin Tan, was formed by a ledge over which the river poured, dropping eight feet in less than twenty-five. Hurrying halfway up this roaring incline, the ship slowed and then hung motionless, weaving perilously from side to side.

After five or six furiously stationary minutes, a line was thrown to a crowd of coolies who had collected on shore to profit by the emergency; this was used to draw a stout rope ashore and the rope in turn hauled over a thick cable of woven bamboo, reeled out through a pulley fastened just forward of the ship's waist. After considerable maneuvering by the gang on shore, one end of the cable was secured to a rock above the rapids while the other end was put in a windlass on deck. All of this was accomplished while the ship steamed feverishly full speed ahead in order to keep from slipping back, with its bow slanting uncomfortably up several feet above its stern.

When both ends of the line were fast, the ship was steered toward the far side of the river. Straining at the end of the cable, it curved out and slightly upstream. Then the wheel was thrown sharply toward the shore just departed from. The current carried the boat obliquely in that direction. The cable sagged and its slack was promptly taken up on the windlass. The ship returned to its course slightly above its point of departure and immediately swung out again on the shortened tether. Four or five such operations brought it to a place where the engines could resume their task.

At dusk we anchored for the night before the first sizable settlement since Ichang, the walled village of Wu-Shan —

Witch Mountain — set on a rocky shelf overshadowed by a dark triangular peak. Mooring near a pink sandbar on which a troop of ragged soldiers were scrambling about in a shrill game of handball, the boat was immediately surrounded by an untidy flotilla of sampans full of raucous vendors of oranges, cigarettes, wine, and peanuts. Several of the ship's officers and some passengers debarked to join the soldiers' game, and I went to walk up into the town with a fellow passenger, a young and very merry Jesuit from Java who spoke fluent French, English, Flemish, German, and Javanese and was then in the process of mastering his sixth tongue, Chinese. We climbed a slope dotted with fleshy green cacti, passed a crumbling pink temple, crossed a stone bridge over a deep ravine, and entered the horned gates of the town.

Along the narrow streets paved with huge flat stones stood half-timbered, thatch-roofed, houses, their roofs overhung by the spreading branches of banyans. The enclosing mountains loomed above the trees and over the peaks the sky was full of baroque gray clouds. This complicated scene was in as complete a contrast as possible to the bare, windswept, clay towns of the North, but in the dissimilar setting the same swarming people were busy, and though they spoke a different dialect, they wore the same blue clothes and pursued the same occupations with the same faultless humor.

At Wu-Shan I found that I had again reached country where a foreigner was a sight to be stared at and remarked upon. The towns in the Gorges were inhabited mostly by settlers from Szechuan and, as I was to learn, the Szechuanese were China's insolent champions in the art of baiting foreigners. While in the North only ill-mannered children had shouted 'Yang kwei-tzu' (ocean devil) when I passed, here grown men and women cried it after me, while the children ran off screaming with laughter at the foreigner's outsize features, or remarking on his terrible pale eyes which, as they said, could see three feet underground, though they couldn't penetrate clear water.

While we walked back to the ship, my companion told me a tale concerning a very tall missionary, six feet two or three, who one day shortly after his arrival in China was pedaling down the main street of the town in which he had been posted when an infant girl ran into the street and hailed him.

'Yang hsien-sheng' (ocean teacher or master) was the deferential term she used, so the missionary stopped to see what she wanted. Unwinding his legs from his bicycle he stooped down with his best 'What-is-it-my-little-one?' manner and laid his hand on the small girl's head. As soon as the child found the missionary's long visage on a level with her own, though, she dropped her respectful manner.

'Yang wa-wa' (ocean baby), she screamed, and ran off crowing in triumph. Of course an audience had collected and the missionary pedaled home with a good part of his face irrevocably lost.

On the second day the boat steamed through more forbidding gorges spectacularly striped with sunlight and shadow, past brown, yellow, and purple cliffs in whose crevices coffins were mysteriously wedged hundreds of feet aloft. In the afternoon it crawled between two precipices forming a natural portal which was, perhaps by the connivance of ancient geographers, exactly on the Szechuan-Hupeh border. The mountains receded slightly and under a misty blue sky the huge river curved among them, dividing to flow around glistening sandbars and romantic-looking little islands of dark tilted rock. The current which twisted about these boulders showed them to be as dangerous as they were attractive and as we passed them I could not but speculate as to the kind of Lorelei who ought to sun themselves here — almond-eyed Chinese charmers with gongs, drums, and huchins, who should pop their eyes as they chanted shrill

songs and eat melon seeds as they played. The only visible
occupants of the well-proportioned riverside, all of them
dwarfed to the size of monkeys by the immensity of the
valley, were gangs of boatmen laboriously marching up the
beaches dragging their junks against the current, miners
squatting in groups by the water's edge as they panned for
gold, and fishermen whose sampans dotted the river like
water-spiders.

Farther west the mountains receded still more, or, to return to the previous simile, the old men sat back and left the
river alone. Their character continued to soften until
finally they lay down, subsiding into a collection of rounded
hills, and presumably went to sleep, since they were covered
with a comfortable blanket of vegetation.

After the flat plains along the lower Yangtze, yellow with
withered winter foliage, this country beyond the Gorges
was fascinating in shape and enhearteningly green even in
January. Along the white beaches were fields striped with a
bright emerald fuzz of winter wheat; between them sprouted
plumelike clumps of bronzed bamboo. On the slopes above
were dark pines and yellow cacti, while on nearly all hilltops
spread squat, umbrella-shaped banyans, especially planted
in such locations, so I understood, partly for their holiness
and partly for their shade. Under the green the earth of the
hillsides showed a bright brick-red. The country was so
moist that even at sunny noon a faint mist hung over it,
silhouetting the irregular, leaf-embroidered shapes of its
hills, and giving it an extraordinarily rich and fecund appearance.

On the third afternoon from Ichang the boat moored at
Wanhsien, a smoky antheap of gray houses sprawled in the
lap of the hills at the top of a riverside cliff. From the beach
a wide staircase of hundreds of worn stone steps led straight
up into the city. Again I went ashore with the Jesuit, to
walk in the city and in a public park beyond it called 'The
Garden of the Four Seasons.' This enclosure contained,

among other things, a campanile, a basketball court, a Buddhist shrine, a tall tin bomb inscribed with anti-Japanese slogans, and an orchard full of fruit trees just then bursting into pink and scarlet bloom. As we strolled, my companion explained about General Yang, the recent war-lord Governor of Wanhsien, who had had the unusual park laid out. Though he was then in exile in the far southwest, banished by Chiang Kai-Shek, for years he had been an absolute monarch in the city. In some ways he had been a progressive ruler — he caused a fine network of motor-roads to be built around the city — but he was impatient in his methods. Once after a trip to Shanghai he decreed that all the townspeople should cut off their queues and discard their old-fashioned long gowns. When the populace refused to do so he posted soldiers armed with shears at the gates and had them snip all pigtails and cut all longer gowns to waist length.

On the sixth morning out of Ichang, the boat crawled around a bend in the river and came in sight of Chungking, piled tier on tier on a gigantic boulder between the Yangtze and the tributary Kialing, its bizarre appearance accentuated by great veils of mist seething before it — First Officer Liu had told me that the neighborhood of Chungking was so foggy that the local dogs barked at the sun whenever it did appear. The walls of the city were on the very edge of the precipices and from the gates long flights of crooked steps spilled to the river. Behind the walls the myriad roofs of the city were stacked in crowded heaps, and even before them there were clusters of wretched houses clinging to the cliffs and to the rocks below. Wedged into crannies and propped with tangled structures of bamboo, these hovels resembled so many birds' nests. The whole scene was stained with age; the cliffs particularly were veined with the garbage and sewage of centuries.

When the boat docked, the passengers were put through

a customs examination as stringent as if we had passed from
one country to another. I was surprised to see that the
swollen Szechuanese officials presiding were quite as
haughty with the down-river Chinese as they were with me,

and indeed referred to all of us inclusively as 'foreigners.'
In retaliation some of the travelers whispered sarcastically
among themselves of 'the rats of Szechuan,' as these proud
and fantastically insular westerners were commonly nick-
named in other parts of China.

When I disembarked, I seated myself in one of a line of
ramshackle sedan-chairs waiting on the foreshore and
was carried up one of the cliff-like staircases through a cas-
cade of descending pedestrians. After the city's piled,
medieval exterior and the slippery vertical alleys along its
water-front, it was surprising to find in the center of Chungking avenues capable of automobiles, full of a traffic that
was almost Occidental in quantity and speed, though still
thoroughly Oriental in quality. Jamming together to their
mutual peril in the rackety fog-shrouded boulevards were
carts, busses, sedan-chairs, trucks, litters, bicycles, rickshaws, donkeys, limousines, wheelbarrows, water-buffalo,
and motor-cycles.

The tide surged between rows of tall narrow shops so
flimsily built of plaster and lath that they seemed cut from
cardboard. The simplest were square, flat-fronted boxes
with glassless holes for windows, but many, even though already eaten away by the moist climate, gave evidence that
when freshly built they had been gloriously unique. They
were plastered, painted, and decorated with a giddy taste
which had known no limits except the size of their proprietor's purse. Across their façades stretched ornate cornices
and up and down ran clusters of columns — Baroque,
Gothic, Moderne, Hindu, Tudor, any or all. Between the
bands of ornament were phoenixes, flowers, shells, gourds,
dragons, fans, lions or clocks, rendered in plaster. Though
usually dedicated only to the gaiety of the beholder, sometimes these decorations were functional in that they symbol-
ized the nature of the building they covered. One drugstore
I passed had on its face a more than life-size man in colored
bas-relief, naked, with his stomach neatly open and all his

inner organs spread out in a pattern on the wall beside him.

Multitudinous banners and signs covered the façades, some printed in bastard English like these:

FALSE EYES AND DENTAL PLUMBING
INSERTED BY THE LATEST METHODISTS

or

LADIES TAILOR
CLIENTS MAY HAVE FITS UP-STAIRS.

Others were trimmed with unintelligible bands of Romanic letters, used for the elegance:

HZGRAMISTERLXHOTELSANGYHITAIFUMX

Many were magnificent black, red, or green lacquered boards on which golden Chinese ideographs had been inscribed in the old style, but even here the Western virus had entered and other signs bore ideographs distorted to snatch at the eye of the passer-by; ideographs whose lower strokes were fantastically elongated, giving them the appearance of mincing octopi; modernistic ideographs made of triangles; even ideographs which, to advertise more tellingly, were fabricated of the wares they praised — ideographs of socks and stockings before dry-goods stores, ideographs of macaroni before restaurants, and so on.

Behind some of the false fronts were roomy paneled shops where porcelain, spices, brassware, or pewter were displayed and sold in the traditional way. Some even were small factories where the wares to be sold were being made under the public eye. There were shops full of clacking wooden looms on which wide strips of luxuriant yellow and white silk slowly lengthened, shops where busy carpenters in leather aprons whittled and glued, clean-smelling shops where bleached strips of bamboo and rattan were woven into baskets or wicker furniture. I remember best a drum store in which an apprentice was beating on an unfinished tambour to test the tightness of the skin before driving in the nails to fasten it — as I passed, the rapid tattoo climbed and fell most engagingly in pitch, sounding over all the other noises in the street

For the most part, however, these stores were garish bazaars packed with sleazy imitations of Western goods made in Shanghai or Japan — tin thermos bottles and fountain pens, flimsy alarm clocks and phonographs, shoddy machine-made clothing, glass and celluloid jewelry, dubious patent medicines, poisonously perfumed toiletries of every sort. These goods were displayed in heaps and sold in as loud a blare of clanging Chinese jazz as a massed choir of cut-rate radios could achieve.

Though there was an electric light plant, a public bus system, and a telephone exchange in the city, the main advance of Western civilization as it then affected the mass of Chungking's populace was represented by these stores full of cheap machine-made folderols. It was to be the same in all the territory I visited of the same inaccessibility to the coast; I had entered the Gadget Belt.

Just as the modern West has so far taken from China only puzzles, lanterns, and similar bric-à-brac, quite ignoring those methods in the common arts of life — cooking, architecture, dress, recreation — which could be transplanted to good effect, so most of pre-war China had taken from the technical civilization of the West chiefly novelties of a varying degree of uselessness. The most widely known Western article in the interior, justifiably so in this one case, was the cigarette, which could be found in the remotest districts, but next to it ranked the tortoise-rimmed spectacles worn simply for adornment, either with no glass or with ordinary window glass in them. Following in popularity were such fripperies as painted celluloid combs and vases, tin thermos bottles ornamented with decalcomania roses, lead paperweights in the form of skyscrapers or mermaids, hand-mirrors decorated with photographs of movie actresses, and so on. These gew-gaws were bought and treasured in China in just the same way as flashy dragon-embroideries, soapstone incense-burners, and similar gift-shop junk from China are cherished in the Occident. To a Westerner it was startling enough to run across tawdry fragments of his own civilization isolated in a Chinese environment, but when the familiar objects were used as exotic details in a setting that was to the Westerner richly exotic, they gained a strikingly surrealist aspect.

As an example, I remember visiting a small provincial town where of an evening the local prostitutes were accustomed to ride down the main street in ox-carts, looking fabulously Oriental and picturesque in bright tunics and trousers, their hair adorned with silk birds and flowers. The girls from the wealthiest house, however, deemed this style of display old-fashioned, and in an effort to be attractively modern they rode on bicycles, not in carts, and dressed themselves in bloomers, middy-blouses, and tortoise-rimmed spectacles. So attired, they pedaled furiously up and down, certain of having attained the same temptingly exotic effect that the Occidental woman hopes to achieve when she dons a silk kimono and dabs Oriental perfume behind her ears.

In Chungking I stayed first in Chinese lodgings, actually in the Chinese Y.M.C.A., a bleak gray dormitory perched on the highest hill in the city, built around an asphalt tennis court and a playground containing another false bomb covered with anti-Japanese inscriptions. Here I went for the first time to a Chinese bath-house. Greeted by a brawny attendant in wooden clogs, I was ushered into a steamy common room to undress and drink tea, then into a tiled cubicle containing a foreign tub brimful of very hot water. After bathing I went for a haircut in the barber shop attached to the baths and, when I found that a shave was included, I let the barber have a free hand. I was content as he shaved my chin and neck, but then he went on to shave my cheeks, my forehead, my ears inside and out, the space between my eyes and eyebrows, and the inside of my nose. When he produced an ivory blade and offered to shave my tongue, I declined and left.

While traveling, I seldom had had the opportunity of such a thorough going over, and it had been humiliating to be forced to recognize that in this country of which I had been conditioned to believe the worst in matters of cleanliness, I was more offending than offended. Whether the yellow race is a more finished product physically, or whether it is because of its lighter diet, more moderate ways and sensible garments, the fact remains that the Chinese are naturally less gross than we Occidentals — they sweat very little and when they do, they sweat quite odorlessly. Testimony to this is borne by the dogs and water-buffalo of China, who fiercely dislike the smell of paler folk and either attack them or run away from them, according to their natures.

The smells of China are proverbial, but they should never be exaggerated into providing a smell for its people. The country does have an odor, a rich farmyard smell of natural decay. During my first days in China, I seemed to smell it everywhere, even to eat it and drink it at my meals, but it was no more disagreeable than the faint smell of burnt gasoline which oppressed me during the first days after my return to America, and as soon as I became accustomed to it, it disappeared. In the cities of China the smells can be unpleasant to the traveler, since the refuse from the walled houses is habitually thrown into the streets. But the courtyards of these houses, which the traveler does not usually have opportunity to whiff, are kept in unexceptionable state and the actual interiors of the houses are as clean as Occidental homes were before their occupants became germ-conscious. This is probably due to the individualistic convictions of the Chinese, which prevent him from taking an interest in keeping clean any places not directly involved in his own comfort, and generally speaking, the more public a place is, the dirtier it is.

But this same factor serves to keep the standard of personal cleanliness at a very high level. When confronted with a Chinese of position, immaculate in neat silk robes, with well-kept hands and shining face, I think almost any Occidental must feel himself a bit of an ape. Perhaps a good deal of this effect comes from the more stringent rules of Chinese etiquette, as cleanliness is indeed closely linked to propriety and few Occidentals can approach the personal control of a well-bred Chinese, who in social intercourse would never allow himself to slouch, grimace, blink, scratch himself, cross his legs, or exhibit restlessness in any other form.

Besides having a composure which gives him the appearance of possessing a very neat mind and body, the Chinese has other advantages. His simple silk robes are infinitely more manageable and easier to keep clean than complicated Occidental garments. The steaming hot towels with which he is greeted everywhere — in homes, restaurants, railways — enable him to keep his face and hands glisteningly dustless.

Also in the actual mechanics of personal hygiene he is allowed a freer hand by the attitude of his older and franker civilization. On hot days when perspiration is inevitable, it is quite proper for him to lift his arms and fan his armpits until they are dry again. Furthermore, toothpicks may be wielded without secrecy, and ears cleaned and tongues scraped without inhibition — special celluloid or ivory spoons and knives are sold for these purposes in toilet-goods stores. Noses are emptied frankly and directly onto the ground or into cuspidors, a practice which may be more decent than our own furtive habit of folding up the discharge in a cloth and carrying it around in our clothes.

Finally both sexes are free to clear their throats and spit whenever necessary, which is quite often in that dusty country. So often, indeed, that sensitive visitors to China — particularly upset, I think, by the spectacle of lily-like Chinese maidens hawking horrendously — have listed the spitting and the dust as the two most disagreeable aspects of the country, though it has been pointed out that at least the spitting helps lay the dust.

In general I should say that the Chinese have at least as lively a sense of cleanliness as we, though their concept of it differs in lacking the idea of cleanliness as a state of being sanitary. Also, to the matter-of-fact Oriental temperament, cleanliness never becomes a fetish, an end in itself, but remains a means toward the more obvious advantages of comfort and propriety. In the Chinese definition a clean house is an orderly house, where what should be dusted is dusted, what should be polished is polished, but only the few essentials — the table-tops, the beds — are immaculate in the Western sense; to the Chinese mind to describe a floor as being so clean you could eat off it would not be to compliment the housekeeper who had made it so, but would indicate that she lacked proportion. And so in personal hygiene, in the Chinese conception a clean person is a neat and well-behaved one whose clothes are pressed, whose face is hairless and polished with hot water, whose ears are waxless and whose nose is comfortably clear — not necessarily a person anointed with nationally advertised solutions, ready to be taken to a hospital without a change of underwear.

I stayed in Chungking for a week that first time, sometimes titillated, sometimes horrified, but always astonished by this metropolis of the West, the commercial capital of a rich but isolated and uniquely backward province the size of France. Walled off by mountains through which the Yangtze Gorges were still the only entrance, Szechuan in 1937 was a backwater where the old unregenerate ways of

China's civil war period survived. In 1934 Chiang Kai-Shek had entered the province in pursuit of the Communists, and then spent much of 1935 there in an attempt to reform it and turn it into a possible refuge in case of war. But Japanese pressure in the North had called him back to Nanking in November 1935, and he left with his work incomplete. As the wealthiest province in China, Szechuan was still the most corrupt. Its proletariat was impoverished by its officials and war-lord generals — in some sections, the farmers were still being forced to pay their taxes for as many as fifty years ahead. Those at the top of this system came to Chungking to enjoy their wealth, while its victims came to the city to beg and to die.

Through Chungking's semi-foreign avenues frequently roared limousines full of well-upholstered officials and their families. On the edge of town stood the imposing villas of the war-lords, built in the foreign style with many unexpected luxuries. One which belonged to a certain General Fan even had a glassed-in tennis court attached, probably the only one of its kind in Asia. In this connection I was told that Fan was so devoted to the game, as a spectator, not a participant, that he had had all his eight wives tutored in it so they could play for him at any time of the day or night. Indeed, his sixth wife was lady tennis champion of the province, though whether wife because champion or *vice versa* I could not learn. When Tilden and Vines had come to Shanghai a year or two back, Fan invited them to journey the thousand-odd miles to Chungking to play for him and was mortally affronted when they refused.

Similar evidence of the character of these leaders is supplied by the tale of one of Fan's colleagues who decided to enter the theater business. A touring company of Shanghai actors had spent a recent season in Chungking, and reaped a large financial harvest as their performances were a welcome improvement over the usual run of crude provincial talent. The General concluded that if the Chungkingese would pay so much to see Shanghai actors, the Shanghai-landers would be equally eager to watch performers from Chungking. He bought up a cut-rate troupe of backwoods actors and shipped them off to Shanghai to make his fortune. Naturally, they could not even make expenses.

In Chungking's pullulating streets, however, it seemed that those who were not noticeably well dressed were very shabbily dressed, while a great majority were in filthy rags. Crowds of unfortunates shivered along the streets, ate in the gutters, and slept in doorways. Their desperate need and great number were demonstrated by the way ragged little groups would swiftly congregate to whisk away anything dropped or spilled. When a house burned on the street where I was lodging, even before the flames were out police had to be posted to prevent the mobs of vagrants from making off with the charred and still smoking wreckage.

Many of the paupers could not wait until things had been dropped or spoiled before snatching them; the streets swarmed with pickpockets and others, less professional, who simply grabbed and ran. Favorite victims were old Chinese women who because of their bound feet could not give pursuit, and it was not uncommon to see such old grand-dams yowling and tearing their hair as nimble beggar boys ran off with their market baskets. The active were victimized too, and I was told by a foreign lady that once, while she was riding down the main street in a rickshaw, a man stepped up to her, lifted the hat off her head, and disappeared with it.

There were also quantities of professional beggars, so miserably diseased and deformed that it was almost impossible to believe their ills self-inflicted. In deserted alleys, however, I sometimes came across them busily scraping their sores open again, like tidy shopkeepers who dust and rearrange their goods between customers.

It was pathetic that, in the face of the ravenous need of these multitudes who must employ every scrap of material for continued existence, some things should be exempted from use by superstition. The Szechuanese believed that when the straw sandals (tsou-hai) they wore were discarded, they must not be destroyed or the feet that had worn them would feel pains. Consequently those who were discarding shoes liked to throw them up over telephone lines to decay unmolested; dangling so on the crazily looped wires were enough tsou-hai to make fuel for many a pauper's fire. The Szechuanese also preserved the old Chinese belief that papers on which ideographs had been written were sacred and must be burnt lest they meet with uses which might defile them; there were public receptacles along the streets from which written matter was regularly collected and burnt, and these were sacred even to penniless scavengers.

Against a background of medieval squalor, the various idiocies of the Gadget Belt which I observed in the foggy streets stood out with a strange effect. I remember a small shop window on a steep dark alley where a Chinese dentist advertised his office with some life-sized colored photographs of American movie actresses. Though the ladies all wore the customary expression of refined invitation, the dentist had taken steps to make their charms still more pertinent, and stuck into those famous smiles was an arresting display of real gold and silver teeth.

In a wider street, beside a food-store adorned with dried snakes and the varnished carcasses of chickens, stood a shoe-shop specializing in boots for the Tibetan trade. Before it hung a magnificent pair made of white felt and embroidered purple silk. Eventually they would tread the rocky surface of the earth's most mysterious land, probably on the feet of a feudal prince or grand lama. Until then, they were wrapped in cellophane.

In Chungking I went to one of the missions to ask advice about travel farther west and, hospitably passed along from hand to hand, came to meet a few of the non-missionary foreigners in the city. Not long after arriving, I was invited to stay with a group of these people, and during the few days before my departure had my first and only taste of the lunatic boredom of life in a small treaty port. Perhaps those I stayed with were in an uncommonly bad position; they lived on the city side of the Yangtze, separated by a tedious journey in litters and sampan from the settlement on the south bank where almost all the other foreigners lived clustered around the Chungking Club with its tennis court, pool tables, library, and bar.

The house where I stayed was set behind a bamboo palisade on an isolated hillside otherwise covered with the tiny fields and tumbledown straw huts of truck-gardeners. It had been built by a wealthy Chinese banker and its big square bare rooms were in such completely foreign style that inside them one could easily imagine oneself in the suburbs of Pittsburgh, Milwaukee, or Oakland. I understood that the house was one of the very few in Chungking with running water, and the oddly assorted people who shared it had nothing in common except their mutual love of self-effacing plumbing. The evenings I spent in this pocket had a dreamlike vacancy; the valuable running water came from a tank on the roof which could be filled only by hand, and when the householders sat in the living-room after dinner, toying with old newspapers, listlessly reading books, or angrily writing letters, there was a heavy hostile silence broken only by the creaking and stamping of a line of coolies walking up and down a ladder outside the window, balancing buckets of water for the tank on the roof.

IX. OVER THE HILLS

From Chungking I planned to travel to Chengtu, the Szechuanese capital, two hundred and fifty miles farther west. The safest and most comfortable way was by plane, but that was naturally expensive. There was also a five-year-old motor highway, the first real automobile road ever built west of Hankow, and already an important link in the network of strategic roads which the Nanking Government was pushing to completion in the west; at Chengtu it joined the recently opened road to Sian and at Chungking it connected with the highway lengthening southward to the French railway in Yunnan.

On a misty January dawn I walked to the bus station in Chungking's western limits and in company with two dozen assorted Chinese climbed into a ramshackle carryall about the size of a station wagon. When we had assumed our positions on the narrow seats, attendants and friends of the passengers began thrusting through the windows quantities of luggage: suitcases, baskets, bedding, babies, fiddles, fireworks, thermos bottles, melons, rugs, parasols, cooking utensils, clocks, chickens, and other portables. The engine started, the car began to tremble, and gradually the paraphernalia shook down into a compact mass little more than waist-high.

In the wet gray light the bus jounced rapidly out of the city, through a jumbled neighborhood where stood the homes of the province's successful merchants and retired generals. The bleak, garish villas were scattered over a group of small bald hills, surrounded by mangy bamboos and banana trees. The spaces between the houses were crowded with conical grass-covered mounds and it was a shock when I realized that the section had been a cemetery before it became a suburb.

Beyond this grisly development the road climbed the side of the foggy Yantze valley, tunneled through a ridge, and emerged on a damply sunlit region of rolling red-clay hills. Szechuan's literary name is 'The Garden of the Flowery Kingdom,' and as I had visited other places in China with equally charming names, I was surprised to find that this country was very much like a garden. The resemblance was not caused by flowers, of which there were few in January, but by trees and shrubs; the hills were naturally grown with a variety of decorative plants usually found in the same locality only by artificial means. There were clumps of palms and pines, cacti and willows, cedar and bamboo. Separated by clear green streams and neat fields these tangled groves gave the country a lush, parklike appearance, suggesting one of those eighteenth-century engravings of the tropics as imagined by an artist who had never visited them.

Set among the small hills and valleys were capacious farmhouses with light plaster walls criss-crossed by weathered half-timbering which gave them somewhat the appearance of Tudor cottages. At intervals there were shrines and temples covered with crumbling orange-pink stucco. Through this placid scene the bus caromed at a hair-raising speed, leaving behind it a trail of dust, frightened animals, and laughing or cursing farmers. At half-hour intervals it stopped in attractive country villages of whitewashed, blue-trimmed houses and all the passengers got out to drink tea, stretch their limbs, and haggle amiably with the crowding vendors of oranges, cigarettes, and seed-cakes. The pattern of the journey was becoming monotonous when, late in the morning, the bus overtook an army on the march.

The troops I'd observed in the more accessible parts of

China had been mostly of a type which showed the influence
of Chiang Kai-Shek's foreign military advisers and his
'New-Life' movement; dressed in neat uniforms they were
to be seen drilling with discipline or marching off armed
with spades and patriotic songs to attack a municipal ditch.
These troops we passed in a cloud of red Szechuan dust
sang no songs nor did they march. They swarmed along
the road and through the adjoining country without any
sort of order. Some wore uniform coats or hats, but the
remainder of their costumes was dictated by individual
tastes and means. All were armed with the traditional
umbrellas and carried as well numerous washbowls, tea-
kettles, flashlights, towels, uncooked vegetables, and extra

sandals — these were slung over their shoulders or tied to their clothes with twine. Many who had guns swung their smaller effects in cloths tied to the gun-barrels in Dick Whittington style. Those who could afford to rode in sedan-chairs or rickshaws, and those who had pets — dogs, birds, monkeys — carried them or led them on strings.

I understand that by now such musical-comedy Chinese troops belong entirely to legend, and to dally for a moment with the impossible it seems a pity that, instead of their being replaced by organized and mechanized warfare, their way of fighting could not have been declared by international agreement to be the standard style. While it might not lead directly to victories, both sides lose in a modern

war, and at least the individual combatants were more
comfortable waging one in which trickery was more important than bloodshed, and battles could be postponed
because of rain.

In the late afternoon the bus crossed a narrow green river
on a barge and ascended through a white country town on
the opposite shore. On the crowded main street it swerved
through an arched gateway and stopped in what had once
been the porticoed court of a theater, more recently used as
a garage. Beside it was a one-time temple converted into a
hotel. With comic complaints and much laughter the passengers untangled their numb limbs and trooped in a body
into the stone-paved court of the inn; after the crowded
hours on the bus, it was pleasant to be shown into a small
square room where one could expand to the proportions of
a small square bed.

In the many whitewashed cubicles on the hotel's second
floor, the guests sat beyond open doors, refreshing themselves after the day's drive with tea, food, and cheerful
torrents of that intense but aimless conversation which the
Chinese so enjoy. Through the rooms the hotel attendants
bustled, shouting good-natured sarcasms to each other as
they carried towels and bowls of clear steaming water, arranged piles of bedding, or emptied spittoons. In the corridors vendors of cigarettes and sweetmeats wandered, and
one peddler of pills who as he shuffled back and forth
chanted a melodious but melancholy description of the
car-sickness his wares would remedy.

At nine o'clock all the lights in the hotel were arbitrarily
turned out and, as the human noises subsided, another
clamor waxed. The very planks of the building began to
shake, but not until one of them ran across my hand did I
realize that this new uproar was caused by rats. In face of
the invisible horde one could think that the Pied Piper himself had come in on the bus. Stamping, scratching, and
screeching, they held carnival until dawn.

On the second day's journey toward Chengtu some diversion was provided by three professional mourners who boarded the bus at one of its stops. They were making a business trip, for they were swathed in funeral white, and as they got on they moaned and beat their breasts in simulated woe. As soon as the car started, however, they neglected their duties and began to take a cheerful interest in the scenery. Then the mourner in the middle was spectacularly car-sick over the other two and for the rest of the trip the trio attended strictly to their business.

Late that afternoon the road arrived on a crest from which a wide tree-filled plain was visible. There were glimpses of quiet water under the trees and above the thick green foliage curled smoke from the chimneys of many farmhouses. The bus clattered down the slope, out onto the plain, and shortly arrived in a scattered suburb dominated by the tall East Gate of Chengtu.

For more than a month I had been proceeding westward across China, and though I did not yet want to abandon the direction, Chengtu was the last city of any size short of the frontier and I planned to stay in it long enough to draw from the new setting I had reached. Just before leaving Shanghai I'd bought my first box of pastels and on the trip west experimented with the medium. Finding that it adapted itself to my limitations better than any other I'd tried, I decided to make a sustained effort to investigate its possibilities. Also, since an attempt to make a complete record of this country seemed impossible, I decided to limit myself to portrait-making. I was particularly interested in doing pictures of the tribes people of Szechuan as a comple- ment to my pictures of Mongols, and already had in mind a rather vague plan of making a collection of pictures of as many as possible of the non-Chinese peoples of China.

There were no foreign hotels in Chengtu in those days, for indeed there were less than half a dozen non-missionary foreigners in that city of almost a million people. As I did not want to live in a Chinese hotel for a long period and still did not want to go to the trouble and expense of setting up housekeeping for myself, I settled down to boarding with a family of American missionaries on the campus of the West China Union University. The college buildings occupied an area nearly a mile square just beyond the south wall of the city and were handsomely set among wide lawns and gar- dens in astonishing contrast to the crowded Chinese farm lands and graveyards surrounding them; with its straight, tree-shaded avenues and rows of perfectly Occidental buildings, the compound was without parallel in all the territory west of Hankow, possibly west of Shanghai, and it is only natural that it should have become the refuge to which so many of China's universities have since retreated.

After having gone fifteen hundred miles into China, it was slightly unsatisfactory for me to end up in an enclosure where everything was as nearly like America as circum- stances would allow, but settling in with the missionaries provided no more difficulties than a stranger settling into any unfamiliar domestic establishment would encounter and after having accommodated myself to Mongol life these small adjustments were easy. As a matter of fact if I had not done so I should never have got along so well with my drawing. In the family were two boys, fifteen and eighteen years of age, without whose help I could never have done what I did. Both spoke fluent Chinese and being entirely indifferent to the ridicule such undignified behavior provoked were always willing to go with me into the streets, where they would not only attempt to persuade any passers-by I selected to come and sit for me, but could usually get them to do it for twenty or thirty cents.

I found that I could complete between two and four pictures a day, so at least twenty times a week we set out into the ramshackle streets by the South Gate to seize models. We brought back peddlers, soldiers, beggars, students, coolies, a Buddhist priest, a Taoist sorcerer, a midwife, a tinsmith, a ragpicker, a carpenter, a cook, and so on. As a general rule we could only persuade members of a class low enough to feel they could not ignore what money I had to offer. The plump merchants in black silk robes would listen to the proposition with amusement, then snort and move away remarking loudly that it was foolish to think they would take so little money to sit for a picture for someone else when they could afford to have real photographs taken for themselves. There were some exceptions; one very handsomely dressed old man in a silk bonnet like a crusader's hood, and on another occasion, a bright-eyed Mohammedan teacher with a glistening bald head and a long curly black beard, were not only delighted to sit, but refused to be paid for it. On the other hand, a roadside beggar we approached haughtily rebuffed us, saying he could not afford to leave his business for my price. Next day the rascal sidled up and said he could sit now. It developed that he had got his son to take over his position in the gutter; I passed the place later and saw the child sitting with his legs rather amateurishly cramped into the attitude

of deformation which was his father's stock in trade, weaving his head in the same startling fashion and slyly reciting the same story of woe.

Another beggar I drew had no simulated troubles. I found him lying on the marble bridge over the river which bounds the south wall of Chengtu and was instantly struck by his piercing expression of despair. He was an emaciated young fellow in scanty rags, barefoot, with a sort of makeshift splint on his right leg. As he sat for me I learned that he was a native of Chungking and had there been impressed as a baggage coolie for the army of one of the provincial generals who was making an expedition against a rebel tribe on the Tibetan border. He was taken with the army almost to Batang, five hundred miles west of Chungking and about two hundred and fifty west of Chengtu, but in the mountains he had the misfortune to fall and break his leg. As he was no longer of use, he was turned out of his job. He had somehow dragged himself through the mountains to Chengtu and was then begging to get money for food and perhaps shoes for the rest of the trip. I was glad that a favorable exchange rate made this charity one I could afford.

Once we had persuaded the models to sit, they generally went through the rest of the process without further demurring. In doing these pictures, I aimed to achieve a rapid, rather broad, impression of the type represented rather than an individual portrait; in some cases the likeness came

first, but with others, as soon as I found I had completed a sketch which pleased me, I made no further attempt to put the specific face on paper. The attitude of my sitters depended very directly on the extent to which I produced a likeness. Some who had been reluctant to come were interested when they saw their own or their friend's faces appear and subsequently became helpful in securing more models. Others who were not content with their images went away grumbling, embarrassed or resentful, feeling they had been made fools of even though they had earned wages for sitting in a chair.

One very old peasant woman whom we found collecting twigs in a thicket near the college was almost panicked by the suggestion that her picture be done, but at the mention of money she wordlessly trotted after us to the compound. When she saw the paper and crayons, her uneasiness returned and it was rather difficult to get her placed. At intervals throughout the sitting she would silently get up and begin to steal down the steps of the veranda where I worked. At a cry or a move from me, she would return and shyly seat herself again without a word or change of expression. Her wrinkled old face made her a simple subject and as it happened her picture developed into a good likeness. When it was nearly finished, I invited her to look at it. She said nothing, but thereafter she no longer tried to escape. Even when the portrait was done she did not care to go, and until I packed my things and took them into the house she remained by the easel, occasionally fingering the edges of the picture and smiling secretly.

When I had been working for a week or two, some of the missionaries interested themselves and helped me procure models of a sort I could not pick up on the streets. A doctor who ran a clinic in the city invited me to come and pick sitters from among his patients and here I was able to do men of a more prosperous kind; when I had selected one, he would be railroaded in to me by the internes and told that if he didn't sit there would be no treatment today. Three ladies who ran a girls' school, which was considered the most stylish academy in West China and was attended by the daughters of many wealthy officials and several minor war-lords, suggested that, as I had not yet drawn any young women of a proper sort, I should choose a few models from among their pupils. There were numerous other kindnesses; indeed the nicest compliment on my painting I ever received came from a missionary lady encountered here. She was a fat and jolly spinster from the heart of the Bible Belt.

'Oh, boy!' she gurgled. 'Some of these pictures just hit me all over.'

I was strongly advised to stay in Chengtu through February to avoid traveling during the celebration of the New Year. In the old Chinese calendar there were no holidays during the bulk of the year; the nation simply worked for eleven months and then went on vacation together for the twelfth. So far in the interior the old way prevailed. February remained a month during which little was done and for the two middle weeks all business was suspended. Besides being a time of celebration, this was a period of financial reckoning, and all through the festival the country was considered unsafe, as many whose debts exceeded their assets customarily tried raising the money by amateur brigandage.

The previous winter in Peking I had celebrated the Chinese New Year quite thoroughly, for in the house where I was living, the servants had been given permission to observe the occasion as they pleased, and five dollars with which to do so. They garlanded the house with sprigs of pine and bamboo, pasted red papers printed with good wishes on all the gates and cupboards, and erected in the dining-room a small altar on which they placed pictures of the household gods, incense, and offerings of fruit. On New Year's Eve they stayed up gambling and shooting off fireworks and at midnight invited us into the courtyard to kow-tow while a picture of the kitchen-god was burnt with a salvo of five crackers, sending the deity off to make his report on the year's events in the household. Only at three in the morning were the celebrations concluded when we were wakened again to eat bowls of soup, full of meat cakes to bring luck.

Needless to say, no such heathenish goings-on took place in the compound where I spent my second Chinese New Year. Still it was pleasant to walk through the dark and empty streets of Chengtu on New Year's Eve, noting the singular hush and seeing the cozy, private-looking glow of lights which glimmered through the shutters behind which each family sat eating and celebrating by itself. On New Year's Day, too, the streets were attractive, bright with scarlet New Year's placards and full of holiday loiterers in vivid new blue clothes; it was customary for the coolies to wear their annual change of clothes for the first time on this day.

Every afternoon of my time in the city, when I had finished drawing I walked into Chengtu to be refreshed by the tumultuous life of the streets and by the cigarettes which were unwelcome in the compound where I lived.

Between the college and the South Gate stretched crowded graveyards and rich fields of reddish earth, lined

with green rows of winter crops. Along the river by the city wall were lumberyards and lines of wattled shops and inns; in the riverside groves between them old men wandered with their caged birds or sat in the sunlight rolling polished walnuts about their palms to keep their fingers supple. On the riverbanks beggars fished, soldiers washed their horses, and housewives their vegetables.

Beyond an arching stone bridge rose the tall city gate, guarded by spruce Central Government soldiers and adorned with posters from Nanking advising the citizenry to brush their teeth and drink boiled water, as well as local proclamations ordering them to pay their taxes and hate the Japanese. Inside the walls were meandering residential alleys lined with high gray-and-white stucco walls, quiet except for the noise of children and the cries of wandering peddlers, but between them a turbulent street of wooden shops led to the center of town.

Side by side here were raucous tea-shops full of loungers sprawling in bamboo easy-chairs and listening to the chant of professional story-tellers; spice-shops lined with rows of fat blue-and-white crockery jars; wholesale rice-shops with waist-high piles of the pale grain lying on straw mats or heaped in baskets; sweet-shops where half-naked coolies pulled huge masses of yellow taffy on hooks driven into the walls; shoe-shops where child apprentices glued together scraps of many-colored rags, layer upon layer, to make soles for slippers; wet food-shops where heaps of green vegetables lay glistening on the damp pavement; dry shops with trays of seeds and nuts, dried ginger, dried peppers, dried figs, and dried octopi, and sometimes straw sandals, firecrackers, candles, toilet-paper, and kindling-wood as well. This street of stores was always noisy with cries, laughter, the shuffle of feet, the screech of the oilless wooden axles of water-carts, the jingle of the small bells on coal-carts, or the vibrating clang with which itinerant street barbers advertised their approach — this was an oddly penetrating noise made by drawing a rod rapidly up through a long pair of metal tweezers. Farther in toward the center of the city the crowding sounds were augmented by the clack and clatter of wooden silk looms, the tapping and filing of metal-workers, the spasmodic gargling of engines in hidden garages, and the distinct ting-ting-ting-tsing made by the plucking of the odd wood and wire tools, like long violin bows, used to fluff out cotton for the stuffing of pillows and quilts.

About a mile and a half in from the gate, the street widened and the traffic quickened with shoals of rickshaws, weaving bicycles, and a considerable number of new foreign automobiles. The buildings here were of three or more stories, with fanciful plaster façades partially covered by blue awnings hung from their eaves. In their open ground floors were big bazaars full of fine silk or china; also clothing-stores with complete stocks of foreign apparel; bookstores hung with patriotic, educational, and seductive posters; drugstores selling such Western products as Baby's Own Tablets, Odorono, contraceptives, Pinkettes, and gas-masks, and more conservative pharmacies which offered wapiti-horns, mandrakes, dried toadskins, and mummified vipers coiled up in little silk-lined glass boxes. In this cen-

tral section were the big restaurants and theaters, and here
at all hours of the day and much of the night walked swarming multitudes in blue robes, arguing, bargaining, eating,
idling, in the stridently exuberant clamor of Chinese music
spewed from hundreds of radios in the open stores.

My favorite walk, however, was to the public park west
of the main street, a pleasaunce which was once a garden
in the traditional Chinese style, with rockeries and camel-
back bridges, but which had more recently been altered into
a triumphant apotheosis of the culture of the Gadget Belt.
Crowded together here in an area about the size of a city
block, crawling always with holiday-makers, were gaudy
bandstands, tea-houses, toilets, grottoes, bowling-alleys,
pleasure-domes, and pool-parlors. There was a Gothic
arbor which contained a zoo, and a rococo pavilion housing
a museum of military objects ranging from quilted Ming
armor to hand grenades. There was a garish movie house,
directly behind which were lodgings for Living Buddhas
visiting from Tibet. There was a small formal garden in the
Versailles manner, and a bicycle rink where the up-to-date
youths of Chengtu rode hired wheels round and round until
they were dizzy, and jubilantly sounded their klaxons until
passers-by were deaf.

Towering fittingly over this hurlyburly was a monument
celebrating the completion of a railway which had never
been built, a spike of an architecture as arresting as its
history. Its plaster heights rose nearly a hundred feet to
an undersized cupola of purple tiles and were decorated
with big bas-reliefs of railway equipment — a switch, a
section of track, and so on — which with a modicum of dis-
tortion had been made to form Chinese characters of auspicious meaning. At the base of the column was a larger
bas-relief of a train, with a stone locomotive which suggested a baby carriage containing a barrel and a telephone
booth, and a coal car which was Noah's Ark on wheels.
Blatantly unstreamlined, the train was striped with bands

of acanthus leaf and egg-and-dart moulding; its smoke-stack had a floral border. The miraculous wagon was equipped with golden wheels and bells and, as I remember, emitted a chaste puff of gilded smoke.

This memorial was an interesting by-product of the affair which overturned the Manchu dynasty. Ever since the time when the first railway was built in China there had been plans for the opening of the immensely rich province of Szechuan by a line from Hankow to Chengtu, and in 1910-11 the necessary money was raised by subscription in Szechuan and Hupeh. A course was plotted through the Gorges along the north bank of the Yangtze, an elegant station was built in Ichang, a commodious station hotel was constructed in Chungking, and this shaft was thrown up in Chengtu. Before more than a few miles of track had been laid, however, the Government in Peking awoke to the potentialities of the project and declared that when finished the railway would be Imperial property. At this the Szechuanese rebelled and, as the time was ripe, their action led to a nation-wide revolt.

The Chengtu revolutionaries were fantastically colorful in the Szechuanese manner — they costumed themselves as heroes of the stage and their energies were chiefly occupied in tying ropes across the main streets so that when Imperial officials rode by in their litters they would have to get down and crawl under, losing face. Though the revolution as it spread became serious enough, its effect on the project which had begun it was also in the legendary celestial style; in the uproar the man in charge of the railway funds absconded with them to the International Settlement in Shanghai, where, as I understand, he is still living in a lavish manner. No more work was done on the railway.

During those winter weeks I came to know Chengtu quite well and should judge that it will eventually be chosen the capital of New China. Its inaccessibility is now an advantage and the nature of its plan and location make it a more suitable city than overcrowded Chungking, or Kweiyang or Yunnan Fu, both of which are in territory too unproductive to support a metropolis. If the Government does establish itself in Chengtu, it will not be a new thing for the city. It was a capital during the period of the Three Kingdoms and its plan retains an Imperial scale. In its center there are still the walls of a former Forbidden City which, when I was there, enclosed a provincial university. In this connection I understood even then that the college was to be ousted and a large civic center would be built in its place. As funds for the construction were to come from Nanking, it was presumable that even before the war the Government had its eye on Chengtu as its seat if it should be forced to move west.

While I was in Chengtu, however, the city hardly seemed an ideal place of national refuge. The trouble had begun when Chiang Kai-Shek was imprisoned at Sian. General Liu Hsiang, the number one war-lord of Szechuan until 1935 when Chiang marched in, had decided that this was a Heaven-sent opportunity for throwing off Central Government control and reasserting his old power. General Liu was a typical old-style war-lord; though he was progressive enough to like ice-cream and drive a Packard, he nevertheless relied in all decisions on the advice of a soothsayer known as Fairy Liu, who read the future in the entrails of animals. The chief obstacle to his revolt was a detachment of loyal Central Government troops which Chiang had left in Chengtu against just such an emergency. They were quartered in a military school in the north city and on Christmas Day itself, General Liu, on the advice of Fairy Liu, had the school surrounded by his provincial troops. The attack was scheduled for nine in the evening, but at five in the afternoon word came through that Chiang Kai-Shek had been released. Declaring that he had a head-ache, General Liu postponed the war and went to the country for a rest.

After this fiasco which had deplorably revealed so much that should have been kept secret, several of the minor provincial generals formed a clique to get rid of Liu Hsiang and to drive out the Central Government, too, if the opportunity should offer; all these factions had troops in the city and while they invited each other to start something, Chengtu passed a jumpy winter. At New Year's time the customary fireworks were strictly forbidden, lest the noise of firecrackers be used as a cloak for a surprise revolt. Several times during February the number of troops policing the streets was increased and sometimes the gates were arbitrarily shut in the daytime as the rumors began to fly. One afternoon when I walked into the city I found barbed-wire barricades piled in readiness by the city wall and soldiers posted twenty or thirty feet apart all down the center of the big streets. On a morning later in the month, when some guns were fired in test at the arsenal, the city was convinced for hours that civil war had actually begun and uneasy groups congregated in the streets to listen for more explosions.

Toward the end of my stay in Chengtu, I was pleased to find that I could get a few tribes people to sit for me. There were a number of aborigines from the mountains to the west who lived in the city, making their living as masons. The Chinese of Szechuan traditionally built their houses of wood, wicker, and stucco, and consequently there were few good Chinese masons; when stone work was needed for modern buildings or the linings of wells, these mountain-dwelling aborigines, who always built their own houses of stone and were hence expert masons, were employed. When I first arrived in Chengtu, I thought such tribal workmen were rare, and, contracting with a sharp curio-dealer of tribal blood to supply me with models, I fell into an unsatisfactory situation. He would not bring models for less than two dollars apiece and even so brought very few —

only those who would agree to give him a sizable cut, I concluded. One day in the market, however, I found myself followed by an inquisitive tribesman. Turning the tables, I followed him. When I discovered where he lodged, I returned to visit him with one of the boys from the mission and asked him to come and sit. He was not only delighted to come, but also brought a number of his friends and later passed the word along to such an extent that before long groups would come to the mission almost every day, eager to try this strange but easy way of earning money.

Most of them were of the Heh-Sui, or Black-Water, tribe from the mountains in the extreme northwestern corner of the province. Though I understood there were always a certain number on the plain, that year there were more than usual since the Chinese Communists and the Government troops who were pursuing them had recently been through their country and many of their villages had been burnt, and their lands ruined, by one side or another.

There were also members of the Chiang and Hsifan tribes, as well as a few pure Tibetans; they were all monkey-like little people in bulky burlap garments, both men and women decked in crudely handsome coral and silver rings and necklaces, with their long hair dressed in braids. When they came to be drawn, they would chatter incessantly in their birdlike tongue and show much delighted curiosity about the foreign fittings of the mission compound. For speed and simple effect I did their portraits without back-

grounds and in a way that was a loss, as the incongruity of their barbarous appearance on the prim porches of the mission was striking.

Against such a background their behavior seemed equally strange. One old Tibetan lama had apparently forced himself to come only to still the urgings of avarice; he seemed in mortal terror all through the sitting and crouched away from me between two wicker porch chairs, chanting protective prayers which he read from a curious board-bound book. Another lama, of tribal extraction, was of exactly the opposite disposition. He could hardly be forced to stand in front of me, so anxious was he to look over my shoulder. He chatted gaily to himself all through the sitting and when it was over gave me two presents — a piece of hard brown gum stamped with an image of Buddha and a handful of shriveled black pellets, which he presented as if they were of great value, though they seemed to me to be only dried rabbit droppings. Later I learned from a Tibetan scholar that they were made of dust and the feces of the great Living Buddha at Lhassa.

Most engaging of all was a wizened old tribeswoman who through her streams of unintelligible chatter displayed such a cheerful personality that when her picture was finished, the lady of the mission came to the veranda and presented her with an orange. The old woman ate the fruit with appreciative dispatch, then took the peels and wove them ornamentally into her hair and set off down the road, whistling.

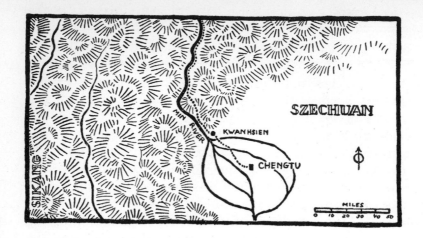

X. THE FRONTIER OF THE
FLYING HORSE

THE aborigines I drew in Chengtu had aroused my
curiosity about their country, and on a morning in early
March I left the city in the company of one Chinese
servant to travel into the mountains which separate the
basin of Szechuan from the Tibetan plateau.

Beyond the West Gate we walked for nearly a mile through
suburbs, first past urban lines of wooden shops and inns,
then past thatched huts, finally past tall whitewashed
watchtowers and out into the wide country. Over the long
red road a blue sky arched hot and cloudless. Beating on
the earth beside it, the sun stirred up summery odors.
Through the dust trudged a scattered multitude of blue-
coated farmers, and a line of half-naked coolies wheeling
toward the city wooden barrows on which huge squealing
porkers were strapped stomach-uppermost, their oily black

bellies shining iridescent in the sunlight. The clustered trees along the road were growing new leaves at the ends of their branches and these bursts of fresh emerald growth spotted against the blackish older leaves seemed like masses of vivid green flowers. Under the branches the thatched farmhouses stood almost hidden behind towering hedges woven of growing bamboo. Between the dark, luxuriant groves the entire countryside was planted with a magnificent crop, then in full blossom. This was the yellow rape or sesame plant, cultivated for the oil its seeds yield; it was a bush growing three or four feet high and flowering in a mass of canary-colored blooms. Mile after mile the brilliant fields spread away from the road, of a yellow so intense that the brassy humming of the million bees among the blossoms seemed almost the sound of the color. Between such blazing acres and an indigo sky, the green trees and grass looked black and the rich red earth seemed purple.

Though it was possible to do this first leg of the trip either by bus or rickshaw, I wanted to walk to get in condition for the mountains. Such an attitude was incomprehensible to my servant, a thin, rather shifty, chronically embarrassed-looking young fellow named Li. Before we had gone two miles he asked for an advance of his wages — they roughly equaled four American dollars a month — and with the money he hired a ride in a wheelbarrow. At the next village the idlers in the tea-house were much amused.

'The servant rides, but the master cannot,' they called after us.

I was considered to have lost so much face that Li, merely by his connection with me, lost some too. Thereafter he would only ride his wheelbarrow in the country where the road was empty; at the entrance of every village he dismounted sheepishly and walked.

By nightfall we had covered twenty of the thirty-five miles to the mountains, and I was exhausted when we stopped at a roadside inn for the night. Passing through a ramshackle tea-shop open to the road on two sides, we were shown down a passage hung with strings of drying peppers, into a court lined about with one-story buildings of wicker-work and wattle. Through the broken window-lattices on which chickens had roosted for the night, groups of dark figures could be seen sitting in the wretched light of vege-table-oil lamps. In the court two donkeys and a horse made soft noises over their evening food and a scabrous beggar grunted comfortably as he washed his feet in a wooden trough.

Li managed to secure place in a small room with a door still on its hinges and a window which was not only intact, but had been freshly papered and promised some privacy from the crowd which I knew would collect as soon as word spread that a foreigner was inside. When he had arranged my blankets on the straw of one wooden bed and lit one of my candles beside it, part of this scene at least took on an aspect of familiar comfort. Immediately, too, the landlord appeared with a great iron kettle and poured a steaming jet of hot water into a wooden footbath, a tin washbasin, and a blue-and-white china cup containing tea leaves.

As I dawdled with my washing and my tea, the inevitable crowd collected and the open door was soon packed with a phalanx of wide-mouthed, wide-eyed country faces. When I decided to change out of my sweat-stained clothes, I shut the door, but when I had finished dressing I heard a rustle by the window and, turning, saw the white paper pane dotted with dozens of black holes, behind each of which a dark, unwinking eye sparkled. As I watched, there was another scratching sound; a damp finger plunged slowly through the paper and was withdrawn, and another eye appeared.

In half an hour Li arrived with a tray bearing a heap of rice, a bowl of cucumber soup, and two freshly fried plat-ters of stew — peppers, mushrooms, and beef, and cabbage and pork. When this had been eaten, the last grains of rice washed down with the last gulp of soup, my surroundings inevitably took on a more attractive appearance. After dinner there was nothing to do except lie in bed and smoke and watch the other travelers gossiping or gambling, but physical fatigue and the sedative effects of Chinese food made any alternative undesirable. The easy decline of the senses into a comfortable stupor, the slow quieting of the inn, and the gradual extinguishing of its lights   all these made the squalid scene grow slowly pleasant. The only check to this comfortable collapse into sleep was a visit to the latrine in the back court; it consisted of a precarious scaffolding of flimsy boards built over a pit in which lived two huge black swine, peculiarly formidable when obscured by the leaping shadows of candlelight. But once securely established in bed again, the inn seemed cozy, and when the world had narrowed down to the few square inches of familiar blanket immediately under my nose, I felt completely at home, if not specifically home.

I had decided it would be easier to travel according to Chinese routine, so I had myself waked with the others next day before daybreak and set out immediately, having taken nothing but a dark cup of tea — these country Chinese ate only twice a day, at ten in the morning and five in the afternoon.

The morning was foggy and veiled under coiling gray clouds of mist, the fields of intensely yellow rape had an evil, sulphurous appearance. Though occasionally after heavy rains the mountains of the Tibetan border were supposed to be visible from Chengtu, I had not had the luck to see them, and as the sun began clearing the air and we progressed over plains which tipped more sharply uphill, I kept my eye fixed above the trees ahead. Even so, when the first line of a summit floated out of the mist, it was breath-taking because it appeared more than twice as high in the sky as I had expected. In the next ten minutes range after range appeared, piling up in the west and north like a gigantic blue staircase, suddenly changing the scale of the houses and trees along the road, converting the open plain into a valley. It was hard to believe that these were only the foothills, that the twenty-thousand-foot monsters which dot the Chinese Himalayas could not yet be seen.

Late in the morning a pagoda appeared above the trees and beyond it rose the hooked roofs of a town, enclosed by a crenellated wall following the ridge of the lowest foothill. We ascended a twisting street between tumbledown inns, crossed a rushing green canal on a covered bridge lined with tiny shops, skirted the mossy walls of the city, and at last entered them through a dank stone passageway. This town, Kwanhsien, was the last settlement on the Chinese plain, the terminus of the mountain trail to Tibet, and appropriately its walls enclosed an area of which half was level and half was steep as a roof. All its houses were built on the flat land about the south gate, as tightly packed as if they had been shaken down from the slopes above. This provided a dramatic beginning for the mountain trail, for in the very center of Kwanhsien the road to Tibet branched off uphill from the main street, mounted steeply over the housetops, and wound toward a gate in the ridge above. At the foot of the ascent, I bought food in a crowded restaurant, and while I ate, Li, on his own initiative, hired a coolie to carry his luggage, and the coolie, after inspecting the load, impressed his ten-year-old nephew to carry his own effects. In the early afternoon we four set off up the mountain road.

From the gate in the back wall a huge panorama opened. Below to the rear were the gray roofs of the town and beyond them the green plain sloped down into the misty distance. On either side, as far as the eye could see, a massive blue wall of mountains rose straight from the level farmlands. Before the gate ahead a rocky green river —

the Min — roared out onto the plain and farther to the west its valley could be seen emerging from the mountain mass, flanked by ascending chains of peaks.

Just to the west of the gate, the ridge backing Kwanhsien was cut by a straight-sided ravine through which ran a canal leading to the river about a quarter of a mile upstream. At the place of juncture the canal widened into an area of sand about two hundred and fifty feet across; it was separated from the river by a long dam, its sides made of wicker cylinders full of boulders, its central part of timber and brushwood. Through this barrier only a trickle of water seeped to flow down the sun-bleached canal-bed.

The Chengtu plain, at the northern apex of which Kwanhsien stands, is in effect an inland delta of the Min, built of alluvium brought down the mountains and deposited where the current slackens among the gentler hills of the Szechuan basin. This plain, which embraces about three thousand square miles, was originally dry, useless country,

but, with the painstaking ingenuity which characterizes
all their practice of agriculture, the Chinese have fertilized
and irrigated every square foot of it and turned it into one
of the most productive areas in the world, capable of five
crops a year. All the canals built on the plain are constructed to lead into this main canal at Kwanhsien and by
demolishing the dam at its head enough water can be deflected to irrigate the whole plain. The wisdom with which
this system is arranged and the workmanlike way in which
it has been carried out — the ravine through which the
canal leads is an artificial one — are impressive enough
alone, but I think the project is made unique by the circumstance that it was conceived and executed more than
two thousand years ago and has been in continuous operation ever since. The canals are contemporary to the Great
Wall and have surpassed that barrier in usefulness if not in
size, for there has never been a serious famine on the
Chengtu plain.

Later in the spring I was to return to Kwanhsien on the
occasion of the 'Opening of the Waters,' as the festival
celebrating the breaking of the dam and the deflection of
the river into the canals was called. It was an impressive
event, given real drama by the fact that the year was de-
veloping into an abnormally dry one and a rather serious
famine threatened in sections of the province less fortunately irrigated.

In the brilliant April sunlight thousands of blue-coated
spectators from all over the plain had assembled for the
ceremony, standing among the glistening white boulders
on the noble riverbanks, and on the graceful bamboo bridge
which was looped across the river and canal just below the
dam. First a sacrifice under the direction of old General
Liu Hsiang was made in the shrine guarding the dam; a pig
and a chicken were slaughtered and samples of the various
grains raised on the plain were burnt. Next a patriotic
speech was made by a uniformed representative of the

Nanking Government, who orated on a flag-hung stand, his skull flashing with sweat as he gesticulated in the sunlight. Then toward noon, after several salutes had been fired, five or six workmen picked their way carefully out onto the center of the dam and began chopping at its supports.

The barrier had been constructed so that its whole center section depended on one great prop. After several minutes' work the subsidiary supports were all removed; water began seeping through the dam at several points below and all the workmen but one retreated to the shore. As the remaining coolie began to hack at the crucial support, the whole huge audience fell silent, concentrating on this single tiny figure in the center of the sunny valley and the widely echoing chock-chock-chock of his blows.

Finally the great timber began bending and splitting with reports like pistol shots. The workman ran nimbly back across the top of the dam. For a moment the beam still held, then it toppled, as if in slow motion, and as it fell the first thick creamy wave of water curled over the dam, throwing high in the air several huge cross-timbers. Suddenly the whole central bulwark collapsed and a tumbling body of water burst down over the bone-dry sands of the canal bottom.

After the drawn-out suspense, the release of this flood was a dramatic catharsis; my impulse was to yell, and I think that in a crowd of Occidentals witnessing such a scene, pandemonium would have broken loose, with hats and pop-bottles thrown into the air, screams and cheers. From the close-packed multitude of Chinese farmers, though, to every man of whom this water was life's blood, there came only a long sigh or gasp, of wonder or satisfaction — almost the same sound the waters made.

When I returned to Chengtu by bus that afternoon, the car overtook the vanguard of the water about fifteen miles out on the sloping plain. Down the narrow, sun-baked ditches the sparkling tide was speeding, its first pushing waves dotted with dry leaves and twigs, filmed over with patches of dust. Out into the waiting fields it spread, in darting rivulets which lengthened down the plowed furrows like parallel squadrons of racing snakes.

Late that evening the water reached Chengtu, and walking in the country outside the city it was inexpressibly satisfying to find the formerly empty ditches brimful of water which liquidly reflected the light of the moon.

Descending to the riverbank above Kwanhsien, we followed the Min up its shapely valley, between slopes on whose lower flanks rape-fields were terraced in curving yellow stairs and whose steeper sides were dotted with dark tea-bushes. We walked past clumps of lilac and forsythia, past scattered coal-mines and pink brick-kilns which had a familiar, industrial look, though they were being operated in a manner which had not changed in two or three thousand years. Over the smaller tributaries of the Min the trail passed on wooden bridges with crudely carved and painted arcades. Over the larger streams it crossed on swaying catwalks woven of bamboo cables.

We stayed the night in the main valley, in a wooden inn which curiously resembled a Swiss châlet, but next day struck off up the wild little valley of a turbulent brook, through a chasm whose sides were hung with vines and tufted with long grass in which bloomed fiery blue violets; we were to cut across through the mountains and rejoin the Min farther up its winding course.

All morning we climbed a stone-paved trail, switching back and forth across sparsely farmed slopes on which timber and shrubbery grew in a wild and luxuriant fashion I had not seen before in the used Chinese countryside. The higher we went, the cooler it became, and when we reached the pass in the early afternoon we were assailed by an Arctic western wind in sharp contrast to the muggy mildness of the valley. Though the sun above was brightly visible, the country from which this wind blew was unfortunately veiled in mist; the snow-covered peaks which had chilled it were invisible, and before the pass stretched only a great gray void in which the shapes of the nearer mountains loomed faintly. From the depths of the chasm ahead, at least five thousand feet below the top of the pass, there came the faint, steady roar of churning water.

Though on maps the border of China is represented considerably farther west, China can really be said to end at this first range of mountains. The territory to the west is Chinese only in the sense that North and Central China are now Japanese; the Chinese do control the cities and the communications, but the back country is tribal and entirely independent. All this territory between China and the more populated and accessible sections of Tibet is little known, some of it entirely unexplored. All of it is very high, crossed by immense mountain ranges, one of which, the Amne Machin, contains peaks which are still so little known that they may prove as high as Everest. It is furrowed into precipitous valleys by a series of great rivers; one of its wonders is a territory where within fifty miles of each other spring the headwaters of five of Asia's mightiest rivers — the Yellow and the Yangtze of China, the Mekong which divides Siam and Indo-China, the Salween and Irrawaddy of Burma. Another of its wonders is the Likiang Gorge, two miles deep, where the Yangtze flows from an elevation of eight thousand feet to five thousand, between one mountain approximately eighteen thousand feet high and another of twenty-two or twenty-three thousand.

Botanically and zoologically the region is even more a backwater than the mountain-ringed Szechuan basin. Several of the world's rarest animals — the takin, the golden-haired monkey — are found only behind its mountains, and it is, of course, the center from which pandas can be exported with such fanfare. The Chinese have stories of still stranger animals, and until the country is more thoroughly explored, perhaps such tales should not be too emphatically rejected. Indeed, in Chengtu I was shown a pelt alleged to be that of a flying horse which had been found in one of the more inaccessible valleys. The skin was of an animal about the size of a fox; it had four legs and two wings and was covered all over with white down. When I saw it, it had been mounted by a Chinese taxidermist who had embroidered a red-silk smile on it and trimmed its feet with red-flannel ruffles, but I was told that foreigners who had seen the skin before these additions were made reported that the animal from which it came must have been a genuinely freakish specimen, if not a freak species. The Chinese called the beast the 'tien ma,' or heavenly horse, and explained that its normal habitat was the Western Heavens. It was rare elsewhere because the only specimens caught farther east were those that had wandered out and got lost.

The human inhabitants of this western region are as queer in fact and rumor as the animals. The Chinese have stories of dwarfs, giants, and men with tails. The existence of the dwarfs has really been verified by missionaries; though as far as I know no one has been into their country, small specimens have been seen elsewhere — they are in demand as domestic slaves among the larger tribes. It is possible that they have lost stature because of some dietary deficiency in their isolated valley.

The only evidence of the existence of giants is unfortunately negative; in one district the natives of normal size do build houses with very small doors, to keep them out. I was told that in former times when the monsters were more numerous, the smaller people used to wear loose metal tubes over their wrists so, if they should be seized, they could slip their hands out and run away. The number of big fellows was later reduced when it was discovered that if liquor was left out on the hillsides they would drink, brawl, and kill each other.

The existence of men with tails is still more hypothetical, but at regular intervals rumors which spread as far as the Shanghai papers have been circulated of corpses with tails being found in the rivers washing down into China from the inaccessible heights of this region.

Whatever the substance behind such stories, the people who are known to live here are strange enough. Cut up as it is by mountains which isolate all its valleys, the region is inhabited by an assortment of tribes   the Chiang, the Jairong, the Hsi-Fan, the Heh-Sui, the Nosus or Lolos — about whom the only facts known are negative. As their language, their customs, and their appearance indicate, they are not of Chinese or Mongol derivation. They cannot readily be identified as Tibetan, nor from what I subsequently saw of both would I judge that they were related to the Miaos, the aboriginal inhabitants of South China. As nothing is definitely known about them, the usual speculations have been made. They can as well be linked to the American Indians or the Lost Atlantis as to the Chinese, and at least one missionary working among them has become convinced that a certain group, the Chiangs, descend from the ten lost tribes of Israel. In support of his contention the Chiangs are monotheistic, live in flat-roofed houses of a strongly near-Eastern appearance, and are the only people of farther Asia who carry burdens balanced on their heads.

Below the pass our path wound down in handsome loops through dense thickets of scrub bamboo three or four feet high. The plant was the food of the panda and one of the reasons why that beast was so hard to capture; the thickets were so dense that it was impossible for a man to walk through them without a trail. This shrubbery shone a fresh spring green in the sun, and although no flowers were visible under it, the path passed at intervals through areas of delicious floral scent.

By late afternoon we reached the Min again. Here there were no more sloping farmlands nor wooden villages; indeed, no houses except a few miserable inns, for even Chinese farmers could hardly make a living in this perpendicular gorge and the tribes people preferred to build their villages in less accessible valleys. The mountains rose straight and rugged from the river to the sky, making a gigantic rocky corridor whose walls were dark with thickets of pine and rhododendron and whose floor was white with bleached rocks and sand.

As the roaring which floated to the summits had indicated, the river itself was drastically altered. Here it was a mountain stream of clear green glacier water, spurting and whirling as it cascaded down its rocky course. It was a mountain stream enlarged to incredible proportions, though, tossing its tons of shattering water among boulders the size of houses. Its tremendous noise filled the valley with a booming that was so persistent and so capable of swallowing other sounds that it soon made of itself a sort of silence. The ear became accustomed to it and no longer noticed it; it was audible only when the path had passed through a thicket or behind a heap of boulders and came out over the river again — then the noise would strike the ear afresh and fill the air with thunder.

Through this roaring sunshine the road to Tibet twisted up the valley, skirting sometimes over high ledges cut into the mountain-side and winding sometimes among the boulders of the river-bed. Along it plodded a steady stream of laden carriers. Tea was the chief article of commerce being carried west, though I did pass consignments of tobacco, porcelain, wine, and similar amenities. The returning traffic was in skins, feathers (golden pheasant feathers from this region are used in headdresses for the Chinese theater), salt, and herbs — bundles of this last commodity were pleasant to encounter, as sweet or pungent odors hung about them and lingered after the carriers had passed.

Of course there could be no wheeled vehicles on such a mountain trail; I passed several caravans of small, quick-stepping horses harnessed with bells and red tassels, but the bulk of the traffic journeyed on the backs of men, women, and children. These carriers were chiefly members of the aboriginal tribes, stocky and immensely vigorous little people who like bugs could march along under burdens of approximately twice their own size and weight. The normal load ranged from two hundred and fifty to three hundred pounds; tea could be conveniently bundled down into a parcel about six feet by three, but when the cargo was of straw sandals or some other commodity whose bulk was great in proportion to its weight, the man beneath it did indeed resemble an ant making off with a bun. Naturally the carriers could endure such burdens only with frequent rests. They carried T-shaped sticks on which to balance their loads while stopping for breath, which they did about every two hundred feet. When they rested they would purse their lips and whistle with that same slight, piercing sound which rubber dolls produce through their stomachs.

I spent a week walking in this valley, progressing up from one grand mountain amphitheater to another. Each morning we roused ourselves in some frowsy inn — the deeper in the gorge, the more like a hencoop it would be — and soon after dawn set off up the steeply winding trail. Each day the hot sun moved overhead from the eastern mountains to the west and the bright area it lit slid from the western mountains down to the river, up again, and out the valley's eastern rim. In the canyon, the steep, shaggy mountain-sides, faced with cliffs and boulders, and the flashing thundering river combined in a wild free landscape as much in contrast to settled China as the bare table-lands of Mongolia had been.

And like the Mongols, the cheerful, ruddy, wild-haired tribes people who trudged along the trail were as different

as possible from the Chinese of composed appearance and behavior. As in Mongolia, I again suspected that the Chinese were right in classifying Occidentals as outer barbarians, for, as with the Mongols, I immediately felt an affinity to these savages. After the Chinese who had so

much more control than I could manage, it was a pleasure
to encounter people who must also be visibly moved.
Many of the aborigines had never before seen a white
person, and when I passed some would wave and shout with
pleasure at the strange sight, while others were frightened

and ran off the path praying aloud. In particular it was agreeable to get away from the impersonal but merciless curiosity of crowded China, where privacy was unknown and politeness a complicated formula, and enter this wilderness whose dwellers accustomed to solitude would be embarrassed to stare for more than a moment at another person, no matter how unusual.

At intervals along the Min single cables of woven bamboo were strung over the river between the cliffs, but I did not understand that they were bridges until I saw a stocky old tribesman use one as such. Fastening himself to a crude wooden pulley looped over the cable, he spat on his hands, shouted, and leapt backward from the precipice, plunging head foremost and upside-down toward the center of the river. When the bottom of the arc in the cable had been reached, he began to pull himself slowly up, hand over hand. When the opposite cliff was reached, he unhooked himself and proceeded nonchalantly along the shore, whistling.

Far up the valley I reached a rapids where lumber which was being floated down to Kwanhsien from the virgin forests of Songpan had jammed in a narrow gorge. Hundreds of naked pink logs were wedged among the rocks, grinding and rending as the force of the water hurled them into dams and then snapped them apart again. Let down into this confusion by ropes from above were dozens of aboriginal lumbermen. The path passed along the top of a precipice at this point and at the far bottom of the abyss beside it these men looked no larger than the black birds which circled excitedly in the air above them. Nimbly they ran about on the slippery rocks in the river, prying and poking at the timber with slender bamboo poles, dodging the flying logs and dashing waters. They worked with fury, and whenever a knot of lumber finally dissolved and thundered downstream, they would yell so triumphantly that they could be heard even above the tumult of the river.

This valley of the Min had but recently been the scene

of another heroic conflict, for it was one of the river valleys up which, two years before, the Chinese Communists had been pursued in the course of their long trek from Kiangsi to Shensi. There were still the remains of fortifications on both sides of the river. On the far bank were the Communist lines, makeshift trenches dug in behind boulders high in the mountains. Dotted on the near bank were the strongholds of Capital, round mud forts with straw roofs on stilts which gave them rather too much the appearance of garden-houses.

I tried several quick landscapes in this valley; for my last I seated myself on a rock jutting off from the path at one of its highest and narrowest points. Below my dangling legs a cliff dropped sheer to the river at least two hundred feet below. Absorbed in the drawing, I did not notice a caravan approaching from behind and I was horrified when the first horse passed. There was not more than three feet between me and the vertical mountain wall on the inside of the trail; startled by the unaccustomed object in its path, the lead horse snorted and tried to stop. Then, pressed on by the animals behind, it began nervously edging past, its burden catching on the rocks on the far side and making it still more skittish. When it was halfway past it whinnied and with a flourish of hoofs which missed my face by inches plunged off down the path at a gallop.

Each one of the forty-three following horses passed in the same way. I sat petrified, and seeing the animals trotting wildly down the valley ahead, their loads joggling askew, felt certain that if I wasn't struck by a horse, I should be pushed into the river by the drivers. When the last horse had been panicked and the caravan-men did come up, however, my discomfiture must have been greater than theirs. They examined me and my drawing attentively, made a few cryptic remarks in the aboriginal tongue, and then ran down the path after the horses, laughing heartily.

My main point in making this trip into the mountains had been to get drawings of the tribes people, and I was disappointed to find that all the aborigines on the road were either too shy or too busy to be drawn. Li was unable to prevail upon any to sit and his efforts only resulted in making them angry or painfully embarrassed.

One morning, having just been politely but conclusively rebuffed by a tittering family of fur-hatted Jiarongs, I was feeling particularly discouraged when I encountered a magnificent-looking mendicant lama dressed in a yellow tunic and red jester's hat. He was chanting and shaking a rattle made of a human skull as he walked beside the river and seeing him approach I felt as a stamp collector must on finding some rare piece of triangular postage. By the gift of several packages of cigarettes I managed to get him seated on a rock, bewildered but timidly grinning. I got out my drawing-board with excitement and it was the last straw to have the fellow leap to his feet and run up the hillside as soon as he realized that the foreigner was to stare at

him with his terrible pale eyes. I began to think that I should do better to return to Kwanhsien and try to find subjects among the numerous aborigines who came there to trade, as I had found that, by settling in one place and accustoming people to the idea, it was never too hard to get models.

When I left Chengtu I had intended going into the mountains for about a hundred and fifty miles, to the monastery of Tsakaloe, but when I got beyond Kwanhsien I heard a report that the monastery had recently been burnt to the ground, either by raiding Communists or bandits. Also Li's diffident manner had proved a front, and at the rate at which he was spending my money, squeezing at least half for himself, the sum with which I had left Chengtu would hardly last all the way to the monastery anyway. I heard also a fairly reliable rumor of bandits on the pass before Tsakaloe.

The factor which finally led me to turn back was perhaps foolish, but to me it was the strongest of reasons. Just

before I left Peking, a friend of mine had had so acute an attack of appendicitis that he had to be operated on less than four hours after the first symptom appeared. Try as I would to fight it off, the knowledge that I was to travel in country where such a mishap would not be an inconvenience but a disaster had convinced me that I, too, carried a time-bomb planted in my middle. At first, when I thought that the appendix was on the left side, I felt I had twinges on my left side. Later, when I learned that the appendix was on the right side, I was sure I had pains there. On that walking trip, as soon as I realized that I was completely out of the reach of any hospital, I became convinced that my appendix was simmering. (When I did return to Chengtu, I had myself fluoroscoped and, being assured that my appendix was normal, was able to forget its existence again.) It was a minor dilemma, as my curiosity about the country

ahead and my pleasure in what I'd already seen of it urged me on just as strongly as those factors held me back. On the day I changed my plans, I walked all morning, torn between the two impulses, but finally I did turn back, having gone only about halfway to Tsakaloe. The achievement involved in such a trip was negative. I hadn't gone anywhere, but I had at least left China. That broad land through which I had been moving westward all winter lay entirely to the east; to the west were only the fabulous vacuums of Tartary and Tibet.

On the noon when I turned back, I reached a place where the trail zigzagged up the face of a precipice. From its highest point a jagged snow-mountain was visible, floating like a feather above the head of the valley, and toward it the river I had followed up from the sea wound through a deeper, steeper trough. Just at the right time a herd of yak, the first I'd seen outside a zoo, came lurching down the path, their massive bodies covered with tattered whitish hair, their long horns cruelly curved. Their Tibetan herders were handsome brown people, dressed in furs and hung with slabs of ornate silver jewelry; they were startled at sight of me, and I could hear them muttering protective prayers as they passed. The sun was out, the river sparkled, and the dark mountains beside it were dotted with the pink blossoms of wild-cherry trees. It seemed that all these things combined in the perfect antithesis to that drizzly dawn in Shanghai when I had started west.

After returning out of the mountains, I stayed in Kwan-hsien for a week in order to do some of the pictures I had been unable to make on the trail. As I had anticipated, I had no trouble procuring models in the city; the tribesmen living in Chinese territory were less shy than those in the mountains and when word spread that the foreigner would pay thirty cents to anyone agreeing to sit still for an hour, they came flocking.

Also on my return I was fortunate in falling in with just the person who I think was best able to help me. This was a young tribesman, a Jairong, whom I encountered outside the walls of Kwanhsien. From the first he showed himself an unusual fellow. On seeing me, he approached without timidity and in excellent Chinese asked Li who I was and what I was doing. He came with me to my lodgings and was intensely interested when I showed him my drawings. I did one of him which pleased him and every day for the rest of my stay in the city he brought me other tribesmen to draw. His assistance was invaluable, as besides Chinese he spoke at least three tribal dialects, and whenever I saw any aborigines on the street whom I particularly wished to have sit, he did his best to persuade them. I was never able to establish his identity entirely to my satisfaction; he seemed to occupy a peculiar place in the life of the town. He had no visible occupation, but his clothes were the best I'd seen any aborigine wearing and on his thumb was an exceptionally fine coral and silver ring. He was as well known and popular among the Chinese as the aborigines of Kwanhsien, and he could not walk down the street without being hailed numberless times and stopped for consultations by a wide variety of people. He was, I know, a person of importance in his own tribe, perhaps the son of a chief or minor princeling. I finally decided he was living in Kwanhsien for his own amusement and had gained such local celebrity simply by reason of his intelligence and attractive personality. His name was Sana and his place of origin, as near as I could make it, was Suichen.

Most of the tribesmen in Kwanhsien were from the nearer valleys and their native appearance and behavior were considerably diluted by Chinese influences. Shortly after I returned to the city, though, a caravan came in from the extreme northwestern corner of the province, the Amne Machin area which is one of the last unexplored sections of the world.

The first I knew of its arrival was when I encountered one of the drivers on the crowded main street of Kwanhsien. That was a mildly ridiculous event. He saw me just as I saw him and both of us stopped stock-still in amazement. For both of us the other was an unprecedented novelty; I had certainly never seen anything like this huge, copper-faced youth dressed in skin boots, leopard-trimmed fur coat, and immense sheepskin hat. We approached and stood staring at each other, making a conspicuous pair as both of us stood more than a head taller than the rather squat Szechuanese in the street. A large audience collected and began to make sarcastic remarks about the two kinds of outer barbarians. The tribesman prowled warily around me, looking at my clothes and then began examining my pockets with an air of deep mystification. Finding a package of cigarettes, he gestured that he would like to smoke,

so I offered him one and lit it for him. It was apparently his first cigarette, but he drew the first draught deep into his lungs. Immediately he was doubled up with a fit of coughing, and the Chinese crowd, by that time so large that it blocked traffic, burst into roars of laughter. His face crimson with congestion and embarrassment, the tribesman pushed his way through the jeering spectators and hurried away.

Later that day I saw the other drivers in a store where they were bartering rock salt for Chinese whiskey, and all of them looked as Attila's warriors must have. Their bulky fur togas were pushed down to their waists in the warmth of the shop, exposing huge bronze chests and arms. In the shadows their eyes and teeth glinted as bright as the ornate silver fetish-boxes they wore on chains around their necks and the huge silver hoops they wore in their left ears. When I passed, they waved their arms and seemed pleased at the unusual sight, but later, when I asked Sana to invite them to sit for me, he was oddly reluctant, intimating that these were bad people to deal with. After repeated urgings, however, he agreed to go with me, and next morning we went outside the north wall of Kwanhsien to the valley which was by tradition set aside as a camp-site for Tibetan and tribal caravans. At the foot of the valley, on the banks of the glistening Min, the drivers were seated around a smoldering fire. Sana went to speak with them, approaching within fifty feet of the fire and then waiting silently until asked to come closer, a mountain custom, I understood, and one which in the wilderness could mean death if broken. When he returned, he said they had agreed to come, so I went back to my lodgings and waited; I was staying in the gate-house on the compound of Kwanhsien's only missionary, a Canadian lady absent at the time. All that day they did not appear and I began to worry, as I had heard that the caravan was to leave on the day after. Sana would offer no assistance, however. His previous attitude toward the tribesmen was accentuated and he flatly refused to go look for them.

Finally, just at dusk, there was a noise of howling outside the mission and in burst my prospective models, all of them dead drunk. Li and the mission Chinese ran out into the street and the tribesmen were thrown into such glee by this effect of their appearance that a table was overturned and two dishes broken. After some maneuvering, I managed to get the leader seated by my drawing-board and very conveniently he passed out. Though the light was failing and the model awoke twice to vomit onto the floor, I was able to complete a sketch of sorts.

When the drawing was done, the fellow roused himself and, apparently feeling good as new, called his drivers into the front court of the mission. Joining hands they formed a circle and began a slow, solemn, skipping dance. As they danced, the leader sang in a high, slightly nasal tenor. His song was monotonous but melodic, full of sliding notes and minor tones, with the same queer faraway quality I had admired in Mongol music. After they had danced awhile, two of the tribesmen took my arms and insisted I join the skipping circle. If this had not happened — I felt a fool since all the Chinese had seeped back into the court when they heard the singing and were making cutting remarks about the behavior of savages, brown or white — I should

have been more impressed by the strangeness of these goings-on. Even as it was, the odd measures of the song
seemed to speak of distant, infinitely desirable valleys full
of clear rushing streams and ringed about by wonderfully
tall mountains. That evening I should have liked nothing
better than to go back with these fierce but agreeable savages into whatever unlikely country they inhabited. But
as I've explained, my journey toward such territory had
been a fiasco, and it was typical enough of this leg of my
trip that I should have watched the odd dance, which was
my nearest approach to the land I should have liked to
enter, inside the prosy precincts of a mission compound.

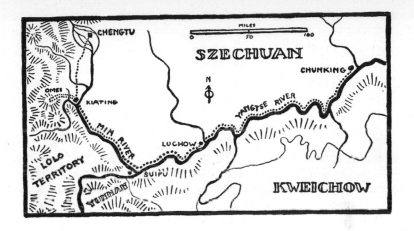

XI. A FOGGY MOUNTAIN
A SUNLIT RIVER

Returning to Chengtu, I stayed on in the city through April, boarding as before at the mission while I did more drawings and made another try at writing. Soon the full heat of the Szechuanese spring reached the city and around the dark mission buildings suddenly bloomed gardens of subtropical luxuriance where the warming air was full of voluptuous odors and quivered with yellow, cream, scarlet, black, and lavender butterflies.

By the end of this tantalizing period I was avid to be on the move again; my first step was a day-long bus trip southward to Kiating, a town from which I intended to climb near-by Mount Omei, highest and most beautiful of China's nine sacred mountains. This was a pleasant drive over lush, river-veined plains and through nicely wooded red-clay hills, given a slight edge of suspense, however, by the fact that a bus on this run had shortly before been way-laid by bandits. Fortunately they had been very amateur marauders and instead of aiming at the tires had fired wildly into the car. Although two passengers were wounded and one was killed, the bus had escaped.

Late in the afternoon my car arrived uneventfully at Kiating, a close-packed city whose crenellated red walls rose at the confluence of the Min and Tung Rivers. Eighty miles south of Chengtu, its vegetable setting was almost tropical, with palms and large-leafed vines making a jungle of the groves outside its walls. On the banks of the Min across from the city a row of small, hump-shaped hills pro-jected abruptly from the plain and in a red cliff on the side of one, a hundred-foot Buddha was carved, overlooking the river and the town with an ancient stone smile.

Although a day's walk west of the city, Mount Omei was nevertheless in the prefecture of Kiating and I found that the local magistrate embodied the first difficulty of the climb. In Chengtu I had been advised that, as there were perhaps bandits operating on the mountain that spring, it would be sensible to take a guard with me. Two soldiers were deemed sufficient. I made the mistake of applying for two and was consequently ordered to take four. As I later learned, to get two I should have asked for one — the num-ber was automatically doubled, as the larger the guard, the larger the fee.

On the morning of departure four soldiers appeared. Selecting the two more timid-looking ones — all four were boys of eighteen or nineteen — I sent them away and set out; the rejected pair followed along the street a hundred feet behind until I could think of no more ways of saying 'no,' then they caught up with the rest of us, grinning.

With my army then I left Kiating through the morning mists, passing out of the city under a ruinous red sandstone gate and down a red paved road on which hundreds of tiny frogs were leaping like grasshoppers. Our path led along the banks of the Tung, a swift-flowing, dark-green stream, growling with the reverberation of the thousands of rounded boulders it carried in its current. A few miles out of the city we crossed in a flatbottomed ferry expertly manned by two garrulous old ladies and struck off cross-country, through yellow fields of winter wheat, past gigantic thickets of bamboo, and bleak mulberry groves denuded of leaves to feed the famous silkworms of Kiating. The early mist gave way to a fine rain and, as the day wore on, this increased to a downpour. We sloshed over muddy country roads, along endless ramps winding between water-filled paddy-fields. Even the farmers had gone indoors and the country was almost silent. Only by the streams the huge current-driven bamboo water-wheels creaked protestingly as they revolved and lifted endless cans of water up the banks. On the flooded rice, the falling rain sizzled and hissed maliciously, and from our feet came the peculiarly sordid, squelching sound of water-filled shoes.

Late in the afternoon the steady rain gave way to a series of brief violent showers and the low-hanging clouds began whisking off toward the north. As they moved apart, there were hints of a sun above and fleeting glimpses of wooded slopes ascending from the plain ahead. Our road trended upward, passed through the small town of Omei-hsien, and wound into the cloud-covered foothills of the still invisible mountain. We followed a fern-banked stream up an increasing slope until dark, then stopped for the night in a draughty, time-blackened wooden temple.

It rained all night, and next day the world was still sealed under a sky of lead-colored clouds which truncated the green mountain ahead at a point only slightly higher than the temple where we had slept. Our trail led over a flank of the main mountain to the banks of a rocky river and thence up its valley, between mountain walls which narrowed and steepened. There were some farms and villages along the lower, flatter reaches of the stream, but they rapidly decreased, and at the last settlement the road pre-empted the only flat ground, so the village was built on the road and the public path wandered engagingly through the corridors and kitchens of most of the houses.

Soon the valley was a real ravine with sheer limestone walls. In the cliffs beside the path, polychromed images of Buddha had been carved. Out of the mountain walls rushed the waters of underground streams, many jets with such force that they spurted clear of the rocks and fell straight into the river below. In a ditch beside our path a dwarf woman was washing clothes and later there scuttled ahead of us a great green crab with orange legs — exceptional sights, suitable to see on the approach to a holy mountain.

In this valley my guard made me stop while one of their number ceremoniously fired two shots into the air. Up to this point the four adolescent warriors had been delightful company, for they took the trip as a holiday and commented favorably and at great length on everything we passed. From here on, though perhaps they laughed more than ever, they kept their rifles always cocked and walked two ahead of me and two behind, so that as we slipped and stumbled up the wet path it seemed there was no direction in which I could look without staring down the barrel of a loaded gun.

Farther on the ravine widened into a noble mountain arena clothed with stands of dark timber and dominated by the fog-shrouded peak which towered ahead in a staggeringly vertical wall. The path crossed the river on a granite bridge, climbed out of the valley on the opposite side, and began ascending the crest of a spur of the main mountain mass. This spur was in effect a range of small mountains itself and the comb along which the path led was as twisted and serrated as the spine of a dragon. Each peak in the line jutted far above the preceding one and climbing the ridge was like ascending the back of a dragon bent on flying to heaven.

We had by this time reached the sacred precincts and the

slopes were clothed with forests. Under the tangled trees by the path bloomed scarlet azaleas, pink roses, small green orchids, and blue and yellow violets; there were multitudes of Jack-in-the-pulpits, apparently identical with the American variety, though here they must have been preaching Buddhist scriptures. The air grew cooler and beyond the trees ahead the clouds sometimes shifted to reveal stunning glimpses of the wall of Omei's peak, the Ch'in T'in or Golden Summit, which on this eastern side rose sheer for nearly a mile.

At intervals I stopped to make quick sketches, stenographic jottings of the mountain forms untidily erased and written over with the names of colors. My soldiers were immensely interested the first time, but when no recognizable pictures emerged they became worried and upset. Whenever I sat down to draw thereafter, they stood about me and prevented any curious pilgrims from approaching near enough to see my work — this could have been out of consideration for my comfort, but from their attitude I judged it was out of embarrassment and a fear of the effect on their face any public knowledge of their employer's vagaries might have.

In the afternoon we stopped at a small shedlike temple for food. The strictest Buddhist principles are observed on Omei; no living thing may be killed and consequently meat is not available. Nevertheless, the monks have devoted much time and energy to devising ways of varying their diet and easing their carnal tastes, and they can cook combinations of seaweed, mushrooms, and vegetables so that, in appearance, in texture, and sometimes in flavor, they resemble meat. They counterfeit chicken best, but the pseudo-pork and pseudo-beef are tasty in their own ways. After hours of climbing, these masquerading vegetables seemed extremely appetizing, particularly since they were served on a table under which a glowing charcoal brazier counteracted the clammy mountain airs outside.

My pleasure in the meal was marred only by the presence of a monk who thought he could speak English. Apparently he had learned it from a Chinese-English grammar which eschewed the Romanic alphabet and expressed English words with a string of Chinese characters whose sounds approximated the necessary English syllables. Through much of my meal he hung over my chair mumbling, 'Hua teu dei shih,' and other incantations. Not until I had gone several miles farther up the mountain did I realize that this initial sentence was, 'What do you desire?' and I should then have regretted my cool reception of such politeness if it hadn't been for something which occurred when I was finishing my meal. It was plain that the monk had boasted to his friends of his ability to speak the alien tongue and when the foreigner was unable to understand his efforts he was naturally on the brink of a loss of face. Just as I left he redeemed himself by pointing scornfully at me and declaring to the company at large, 'Ta bu-tung Ying-kuo-wha. Ta shih Mei-kuo-ren!' (He understands no English. He's an American!)

Late in the day our path began its vertiginous zigzag up the bald flanks of the Ch'in T'in. The fog here clung close around the rocks and the altitude — this point was at least a mile high — was indicated only by the cold winds blowing out of the void, and by the increasing stubbiness of the vegetation which grew as rankly as below only in the most sheltered crevices. When darkness fell, we stopped in a moss-covered red temple in a grove of pines among whose branches a few disconsolate monkeys were roosting. Though I esteemed this temple chiefly for the vegetable stews which came piping hot from its kitchen, its monks considered its most exceptional feature to be a small deep pool sunk in the rocks beside its terrace, fenced about by a marble balustrade. This well was called the 'Elephant's Bath' and was one of the mountain's major shrines.

The holiness of Omei dates from the semi-legendary day when Pu Hsien, a disciple of Buddha, rode a white elephant loaded with Buddhist scriptures from India into China and so began the conversion of the Chinese to Buddhism. He is supposed to have come as the crow flies, through the clouds, but his way was long, and apparently when he reached Omei his elephant needed cleaning; the legend explicitly mentions that he bathed his mount in the little crevasse. The legend does not say, but it also seems likely that the elephant's journey ended here, for while one can see how such a sizable beast might be fitted into this well-like pool, it is hard to imagine how it could possibly be got out again.

On the third day, another foggy one, we climbed the last rounded slopes of the Ch'in T'in through thickets of thorn, bamboo, and huge dark-leaved rhododendron trees covered with white, scarlet, and lavender blossoms. In the protected valleys grew tangled little forests made odd and somewhat unwholesome-looking by the rains, which were almost constant at this altitude. Most of the trees had been killed by the damp and on their bare decaying limbs grew many vivid lichens, fungus, and parasitic vines. On the ground beneath them lay a deeply matted carpet of gray moss, and it was uncanny to walk in dead silence among these sick, fog-shrouded trees, through blood-red pools of petals fallen from the parasitic flowers growing on the limbs above.

After some hours of stiff climbing on wet flights of crude stone steps, we reached the lowest point of the actual summit. For another mile the path lay along the comb of the invisible precipice of the Ch'in T'in, through brown thickets and under windswept black pines. Here the fog was still thicker and now that there were no more slopes to be seen above, however dimly, the rocks and trees by the path seemed afloat in the void. The two-mile abyss stretching below the cottony-white walls was evidenced only by the voracious silence which lived behind them, swallowing all sounds without trace of an echo.

The actual summit was a bleak beak of a crag projecting out into vacant whiteness. On the very highest rock, literally hanging over the abyss, was a squat little stone shrine. This was the ultimate goal of pilgrimage and its sides were covered with names and prayers in Chinese and Tibetan, some written on papers pasted to the rocks, some scratched into the walls themselves. Though on the plain at Kiating the subtropical spring was already in progress, here it was nearly freezing, and immediately upon arrival I went into one of the wooden temples near the summit for hot tea and a turn at a charcoal brazier. It was as well that my thoughts

were on my feet and in my stomach instead of contriving some significance for the time and the place. As soon as I entered the temple, a beaming monk came to me and carefully unfolded a paper he took from his robe. It was the sports page of a Shanghai paper, six months old, and from its greasy appearance had reached the top of Omei wrapped around someone's food. He politely intimated that I should read from it so that all might hear how the outlandish inscriptions were spoken. As soon as I began, a crowd of gray-robed monks collected, standing in appreciative silence and enjoying to the full the rich uncouthness of the foreign tongue. I'm certain, though, that the sounds of the language could not have been half so strange to them as they were to me, hearing my own voice reverberating last year's racing results through the prayer-halls of Buddha's Golden Summit.

When I was done, one of the monks hustled off to his living quarters, and soon returned with a small object clutched in both hands. He pushed through the circle and proudly displayed a half-used bottle of medicine made in Shanghai, with a title in English, also made in Shanghai:

THE CONSCIENTIOUS GINSENG EXTRACT
Good for the Brains and Marrow
and Recommended to Men Lacking Blood.

That night I was accommodated in a corner cubicle in the largest temple dormitory. It was a clean room with fresh straw on the bed and walls of a cheerful scarlet, but one glimpse out its window or through the wide cracks in its rickety floor offset all these advantages. The dormitory was built on the very brink of the precipice and this particular corner projected out like a balcony over a vast amount of nothing. Only fog could be seen below, but it was explained to me as one of the attractions of my room that the vertical drop below was almost three quarters of a mile.

I had planned to remain on the summit three or four days, at least until clear weather, but I'd counted on providing for only two soldiers. All four had taken it for granted that I was to support them in the style to which they were unaccustomed — that evening I could hear them enjoying a jugful of Chinese whiskey in the next room. Since with my limited Chinese I could not shout them into more frugal ways, and since in any case their amusement at my irritation could always cut me short, after a short reckoning I realized that I should have to leave the summit early next day — fog, rain, or shine — if I was to return to Kiating solvent.

Next morning the fog was thicker and I spent some time at the summit, glumly enumerating the marvels I should have been able to see. On any clear day the western horizon would have been ringed with the snow-mountains of the Tibetan border, while to the east should spread the verdant hills and valleys of Szechuan. On rarer days, when the sun and the clouds were properly disposed, below the Ch'in T'in should have bloomed Buddha's Glory, an illusion of concentric rainbow circles similar to the Brocken Specter and so striking that devout Buddhists have thrown themselves through it to destruction on the cliffs below. On still less frequent occasions one should have been able to see the ghost of Pu Hsien trotting down the sky on the ghost of an amiable white elephant. Of course the finest sight could hardly be expected, since it has never been seen except on the advent of an entirely virtuous ruler. Then two phoenixes soar up out of the void before the summit, rolling their bronze eyeballs and twirling their twelve-feathered, five-colored tails. 'Buddha comes! Buddha comes!' they squall, and come he does, floating plump and serene in the heart of a lotus.

For me nothing stirred in the mist; only a fine rain began to fall as we left. As we climbed down the side of the summit, though, a breeze blew from below and suddenly the whole upper half of the Ch'in T'in swam out of the white sea of mist. It was an immense and rugged apparition, a wall of cliffs capped by a forest of pines. For nearly five minutes it was visible. Breakers of fog billowed in slow motion against it, slipping up its face and seeping off through the trees on the top. Too soon a tidal wave of white rolled up from below and obliterated it.

It was a tantalizing clue to the hidden panoramas which surrounded me. The arrangement of pines and rocks against the blank background of fog had been in the best style of Chinese painting and I suppose I should have been satisfied. But as an Occidental with an incurable tendency to literalism in my own painting, I preferred to see it all and I stamped downhill through the fog, steaming with frustration. As I attributed my premature return to the costly tastes of my army, it satisfied me to run downhill until out of breath, then sit on a rock and watch the antics of the soldiers as they scrambled to catch up with me, at the same time trying to prevent their guns from tripping them or banging their shins hard enough to bruise them. This went along very well until I inadvertently sat on an anthill instead of a rock. After that all jokes were at my expense for the rest of the trip.

We reached the town of Omei-hsien at the foot of the mountain in one day; that afternoon the fog thinned and before sundown the summit of Mount Omei, impossibly high, peered down at us. Next day its blue bulk stuck up into a cloudless sky, and even from Kiating its scornful presence was visible.

After two days in Kiating I hired a sampan and sailed for Chungking, about two hundred and fifty miles downriver. As an example of the cost of travel in inner China, it took the equivalent of nine American dollars to hire the craft and its crew of three — the price included rice for myself and servant for the duration of the nine-day trip. It was even more of a bargain than it may seem at first statement, for those days were probably the most enjoyable of all my time in China.

The sampan was a flatbottomed craft twenty-five feet long and perhaps five feet wide at the widest. It was very shallow, drawing less than six inches, and its sloping sides

curved gracefully up to a square bow and stern. In its waist was a cabin of straw matting; ahead of this were benches for the oarsmen and behind was a raised deck for the pilot. This meager craft was also a floating house of the sort in which millions of Chinese spend their entire lives; in its bow was an iron bowl for fires — this was the kitchen — and under the matting, mattresses were piled — this was the common bedroom. The whole wide river was the domestic reservoir and cistern.

The age of the vessel was undecipherable, its appearance ramshackle in the extreme. As I discovered during the voyage, its side planks had in many spots decayed to the consistency of cheese and with little effort a finger could be worked clear through them. The wet planks of its bottom were infested with the pupae of some insect and every day one or two of them would crawl up through the floorboards into the sun, crack their shells and fly away, leaving empty pink carapaces like the ghosts of small winged lobsters.

The owner-pilot of the boat was a jolly, huge-faced oaf

from the country behind Kiating, who spoke his Chinese
with a backwoods burr so thick that even the servant I had
brought with me from Chengtu could hardly understand
him. He never entirely got over the novelty of being at
close quarters with a foreigner, and when not steering,
eating, or sleeping, would sit regarding me like some large
dog, his wide mouth gaping and his tiny eyes glittering with
idiotically pleased astonishment. His oarsmen were his
small son, a thirteen-year-old who did most of the heavy
work aboard, and a rickety and garrulous old man who was
perhaps his grandfather. When I stepped into the sampan
at Kiating and saw this crew, I had doubts of our ever
reaching Chungking, but I was reckoning then without
our strongest force of locomotion, the swift currents of the
river.

We left on a misty but already hot spring morning; it
was about the tenth of May. Once untied from the landing
by the water-gate of Kiating, the boat slid out into the
current and sped rapidly down past the red walls of the
city, past the giant Buddha gazing from the hillside with
his wig of vines and his lap full of trees. Down the green
river it glided, into a full nine days of delight.

The weather, which had been so unaccommodating on
Omei, showed a change of intention for this trip and each
day was finer than the last. All nine had the same pattern,
almost monotonous in their consistent perfection. I now
remember them all as one, particularly since the circum-
scriptions of life on a small boat allowed no variations of
my own routine.

Each morning we poled away from shore about an hour
before dawn and moved slowly down the river, the oars
creaking and the oarsmen grunting as the sky turned from
black to bronze to stone-color. All the mornings were foggy;
sky and water were uniformly gray and the fresh green
shores showed only in streaks between layers of rising mist.
Very gradually did the sun appear, first a white china disk

in the fog, then a silver one, finally an unbearable presence in the sky.

Always sparkling in the sun, the stream wound among rounded lines of hills and mountains, over a shallow bed nearly half a mile wide. It had not yet begun to rise from the melting of the Tibetan snows and on either side of it stretched shingles of glistening boulders. Every four or five miles there were shoals bared by the low water; over these the current ran swiftly, foaming and leaping, but between them it slowed into long lakelike stretches of placid water. Traveling so close to the river we were very conscious of its changes. Through the rapids the sampan shot with breath-taking speed, but propelled by narrow oars it progressed almost imperceptibly across the burnished surfaces of quiet water. Every fifteen or twenty minutes the pilot and the rowers left their work and as the sampan slipped backward or sideways downstream, they squatted under the matting, eating melon seeds and taking alternate puffs on a tiny long-stemmed pipe.

By noon we floated through a blazing world, over molten waters and by shores where the glaring sunlight robbed even the vivid red earth and green trees of color. At its zenith the sky became so dark a blue it seemed black and under the trees and awnings on the beaches lay inky shadows into which all living things retreated to doze.

On the sampan these hot hours were devoted to eating and sleeping. The pilot and his old assistant retired to their beds spread under the matting and the young oarsman busied himself with the preparation of our midday dinner. In the white glare of sunlight the flames from the fire he built in the prow were invisible, and in the general warmth its heat was almost imperceptible; its streams of pungent blue smoke seemed to materialize from thin air. Swiftly and expertly the boy would go through the ritual of rice-making; first cleaning his utensils with a bamboo whisk-broom, then boiling some river water in the great flat iron pan, placing over it a wooden drum with a slatted bottom, pouring in rice and more water, fanning the fire for endless minutes, finally scooping out a bucketful of tasty but gritty food. When he had emptied the water and fried a handful of greens and pork scraps in the iron pan, the meal was ready.

After eating there was a siesta for all, during which the boat was allowed to drift as it willed. It was very pleasant then to lie in the shade in the center of the sampan, lulled rather than disturbed by the distant cries over the water and the faint swishing and clicking of pebbles and sand which could be clearly heard through the thin planks of the bottom.

In the middle of the afternoon when the heat had somewhat lessened, the boatmen went back to work and I generally spent the next few hours swimming or sunning myself. The country Chinese, even these boatmen who spent the better parts of their lives afloat, never went into the water. Though I did sometimes see small children sporting in the shallows, judging from the amazement the plain fact of my swimming provoked I should say that none of the river-men knew how to swim or knew that it could be done. The first time I undressed and prepared to dive, there was consternation aboard; the pilot grabbed at me while the others shouted and emphasized in pantomime that the water was over my head and I should be unable to wade. When I insisted on going in and then swam back to the boat, I was confronted by a string of ludicrously gaping faces. Later, when word of the foreigner's freakish talent had spread from boat to boat, other craft often came close to ours while their crews invited me in dumb-show to jump into the water and perform for them.

Still my audiences could not enjoy the swims as much as I did myself. The river was warm, clean enough, full of currents in which it was possible to float motionlessly downstream, brushed and gently pummeled from head to heels by the interweaving water. By instinct I avoided all but the shallowest dives in this reputedly treacherous river, and it was as well, for when I reached Chungking I heard it was a tradition that whoever dived below the surface of the Yangtze never came up again.

In the late afternoon, as the sun descended and the atmosphere yellowed with dust, the colors of the landscape grew in richness and intensity; the river and sky turned a burning blue to which the reds and yellowish-browns of the shore made sumptuous contrast. The new green of the leafy trees on the banks turned to emerald, the clusters of pines seemed black, and the ripe fields of early wheat were dusky gold. In this vibrant, darkly sunburnt picture, the ivory walls of the whitewashed farm villages and the lighter patches of the cream and purple thunderheads which sometimes moved across the far horizon stood out with telling effect.

At sunset we always anchored for the night by some river town or village. The settlements were unpleasantly dirty in contrast to the noble stretches of empty beach, but like the river itself this valley hid a certain amount of menace under its agreeable surface and bands of marauders sometimes raided its shores. Though bandits had been known to shoot at boats in the river in daylight, their more common practice was to wait until their victims had come to shore; consequently it was imperative to anchor within reach of a sizable town by nightfall. Some stretches were considered particularly treacherous and I'd been warned in Kiating that unless we entered on them before noon, allowing plenty of time to get through by dusk, we should anchor and not proceed until next day. Fortunately all these danger zones fitted into our normal schedule and we were not delayed.

I always slept in the boat and, bandits aside, the nights on the river were almost as idyllic as the days. The sky was tropically speckled with huge stars and flickering swarms of fireflies. As an only flaw there were also swarms of ravenous mosquitoes, seemingly the size of flying mice and almost visibly dripping malaria germs, which bred on the river-front and at the departure of the sun rose humming to the attack.

For two days from Kiating we floated southward down the Min, the same stream I had followed into the mountains above Chengtu. Though it was here a smoother, larger river with only a few mild rapids, it still retained its clear green color. At Suifu, however, some fifty or seventy miles from Kiating, it was joined by a turbulent brown river flowing out of the mountains to the west, and their combined waters, dramatically mingling below a pagoda-topped red hill, turned and rolled eastward toward the distant Pacific. The river flowing from the mountains is the one marked on Occidental maps as the upper Yangtze; it is indisputably larger and longer than the Min, but as its course lies entirely among the inaccessible mountains of Tibet, the Chinese characteristically ignore it. They have always considered the Min to be the main stream, since it flows farther through strictly Chinese territory and is thus more useful to them. In any case, the waters of the two streams flowing eastward from Suifu were indisputably the Yangtze and even here, more than a thousand miles from the ocean, unquestionably a great river.

Gliding on its sunlit surface were crafts of all descriptions, of types which had not changed for centuries. The largest were rafts of lumber being floated down from the mountains to the cities in the east; some were hundreds of feet long and on them were built whole villages of straw matting.

By far the most numerous were the junks, chunky brown craft varying from thirty to eighty feet in length. Though all of these were equipped with masts and were of the same appearance as seagoing junks, the nature of the river made sailing almost impossible. Going upstream they were towed by crews of naked coolies on shore who labored at the end of long ropes fastened to the tops of the masts. Along slow stretches of the river the coolies could walk erect, chanting as they pulled, but in the rapids heart-breaking effort was necessary; then they had to use not only their legs but their arms for leverage — they crawled painfully through the boulders and sand, and from a distance they resembled herds of monkeys.

Going downstream the junks were a noble sight. Their masts were removed and with their upcurving lines they resembled archaic Egyptian or Phoenician galleys, to which indeed the first Chinese craft of this design must have been contemporary. On their forward decks stood twenty or thirty oarsmen wielding long sweeps, and to keep in time they sang and stamped as they rowed. Their chant was usually a simple one of two or three notes; they would repeat it again and again, faster and faster, as they rowed and stamped with increasing speed and vigor. When, in perhaps ten minutes, the limit of endurance had been reached, they would hold the straining tempo for a minute or two, then with a long exultant shout drop their oars and sit down to rest while the galley continued to glide on its momentum. It was always exciting to see one of these oddly shaped craft speed past, its long oars flashing and splashing in unison as over the waters floated the strange rhythmic cries of its crew.

There were also swarms of smaller boats such as the one I traveled in. Besides the traffic bound up or down river there were local boats; loaded cross-river ferries skulled with long poles; sampans full of peddlers rowing out to passing ships to offer vegetables, kindling, whiskey, or cookies; even the miserable crafts of water-going beggars. I remember best a ferry which crossed before us one morning bearing a bride on the way to her wedding. Far ahead on the north shore we could see the blue sedan-chair of the go-between and the bright red one of the bride being carried down to the river; they were loaded into a boat which began to cross slowly and passed within a few feet of us in midstream. The go-between, a neat old lady with white hair, was sitting in the sunlight, but the bride had to remain shut in her win-dowless box of embroidered red silk which had been sealed in her own home and was not to be opened until it had been set down in the house of her as-yet-unknown husband. We floated on down the river, but far behind I could see the red and blue sedan-chairs being unloaded on the south shore and carried up the sloping bank. It was a lovely scene — the day was spaciously blue and the distant scarlet chair made an apt fleck of color in it. It seemed a pity that the bride could not have known something of the appearance of her progress, instead of having to crouch terrified, as she must have been, in her dark and airless box.

Pictorially, all these river landscapes were built up from a horizontal, from the rippling surface of the river itself. Almost as flat as the water were the pebbly shingles and sandbars emerging from it, but above them curved the steep fifty- or sixty-foot banks which would contain the river during the summer floods. Behind the banks stretched gently sloping plains and on them the striped red and green hills were piled, most of them rounded but some squarish, some conical, and some even of the eccentric hand-made shapes to be seen in Chinese landscape paintings. Above the hills, far in the distance, stretched ranges of dark blue mountains.

Particularly by the rapids, many hills stood close to the river, faced with precipices in which square-doored caves had been cut. Whatever prehistoric race carved these cliff-dwellings has vanished without a trace — the Chinese have no record of them — but presumably they were the an-cestors of the mountain aborigines. When I passed down the river their caves were being used as homes by beggars, lepers, and other outcasts. Sometimes the hills pushed their presence on the traveler in more emphatic ways. In one curving narrows lay an extraordinary little island-hill, its stone sides as square and tall as if they were built of masonry. Around it the greenish current ripped and whirled hideously and on its vine-covered top was a pink shrine to counteract the influence of the malignant spirit which had managed to capsize so many boats here, drowning so many boatmen.

In another narrows a line of cliffs plunged directly into the water and before them the river gurgled ominously even in this low season. I was told that at flood-time the current here formed a maelstrom capable of swallowing whole ships; even large junks which had strayed into it sank slowly and vertically out of sight, and when the tops of their masts had disappeared they were never seen again except as scattered clots of timber and battered bodies floating far downstream.

Along both the Min and the Yangtze the country was thickly populated and the shores were always dotted with blue-coated people, some working on the river, some on its banks, some in the fields beside it. All level ground was under intensive cultivation and many of the hills were terraced. Spaced only a few hundred feet from each other, white and gray farmhouses dotted the fertile country, standing among the green feathers of giant bamboo. Every three or four miles there were mud-walled farming and fishing villages high on the riverbanks, and perhaps every twenty a gray town of five or ten thousand. Besides these there were some real cities — Suifu, Luchow — which might for their size alone have been well known if they had been anywhere but in the crowded interior of China.

When we anchored before a settlement for the night, I went up into town for my evening meal, a habit I had formed on the first evening of the voyage when I chanced to notice my pilot lading water from the river into our rice, just as the fat owner of the next sampan upstream was urinating majestically overboard.

It was always extraordinary to walk up into these obscure and crowded little settlements as the yellow and purple evening light faded from the sky, through steep narrow alleys lit only by torches and crude oil lamps. More than any other towns I visited they were of ancient China, and in their streets and squares, full of turbaned crowds moving through the ruddy light and flaring shadows, nothing had really been changed since the days when the whole world was torchlit or dark.

And they were medieval in more than appearance. Returning to the river-front through the black streets of one, I was brushed against by a begging monster with a head slightly larger than normal, but a body no bigger than a

starch box. The bones of his arms and legs were of normal
length, but they were covered with nothing but pallid skin;
flesh and muscles seemed to be entirely lacking. Strapped
to the back of a man who seemed to be his brother, he moved
down the alley with his dead limbs dangling horribly, looking like a great white spider.

In another such town I encountered a woman who was
carrying two children, one in each of two baskets slung
from a pole over her shoulder. The older child was unre-
markable, but the other seemed to have met a violent death.
He was sprawled stiffly in the basket, his clothes clotted with
dried blood and his face covered by a flat masklike scab
through which no features could be seen. The woman was

moaning and screaming as she walked and I should never
have suspected her of being a professional beggar if I had
not heard subsequently that she had been frequenting the
neighborhood for at least three weeks, during which time
the bloody child had not been observed to decompose in the
slightest.

Some evenings we reached our anchorage before dark and
twice I tried sketches, though I should have realized that
as an Occidental in these seldom visited towns I was too
conspicuous to begin with. On one occasion I sat in a side
street to make a pen drawing of a shop-front; within three
minutes I was surrounded by a mob of more than seventy-
five gapers. I knew that I had made a mistake, but the
mood of the crowd was jocular, and though they continually
jammed in between me and my subject, a polite smile and a
swimming motion with the arms could always move them
back again.

Several children edged through the crowd and stood behind me, breathing down my neck and pinching inquisi-
tively at the fabric of my shirt. Soon one in particular, a
swollen little boy about ten years old, began to make himself annoying. My ink-bottle stood on the pavement beside
me and the child insisted on edging his feet too close to it
for safety. For five or ten minutes, during which the sketch
progressed hardly at all, he kept inching up and each time I
pushed him back. Finally he jogged my elbow and I pushed
him with it, perhaps too strongly, in the stomach. Without
a word he disappeared through the crowd and, thinking I
was done with him, I went on drawing.

Suddenly a handful of pebbles, dust, and dried dung was
thrown at me from behind. It cascaded over my head and
shoulders and piled up on my drawing. Turning I saw the
same child staring at me with a parody expression of surprise
on his round face. No one in the crowd laughed, however.
There was an ominous silence and, realizing that I had committed what for a foreigner could be the dangerous offense of
appearing ridiculous, I got up quickly and left.

A few nights later I had the sampan anchored a little
offshore, in water two or three feet deep, and, thinking
myself safe from curiosity, began a chalk portrait of the old
oarsman. Before long two coolies waded out and stood attentively by the boat to watch me work. In twenty minutes
there was a crowd large enough to surround the boat, all of
them standing in water halfway up their thighs. It was plain
that all would have liked to sit in the boat to watch more
comfortably, but my pilot lay in the stern, mumbling bellig-
erently, and no one wanted to be the first to take the step.
Finally a husky soldier with a salmon-colored face
splashed out and joined the audience. I had learned that
among Chinese a face of that boiled pink shade could only
come from much yellow wine, and I was not surprised when
he pushed through the crowd, seized the gunwales, and
vaulted into the boat. Immediately a half-dozen others
began climbing in. All of us in the boat jumped up. The
boat lurched. The soldier, still weaving to regain his balance, fell backward into the water. As the surprised crowd
began to mumble resentfully, my boatmen hurriedly cast
off, swept their oars along the gunwales to free them of
knuckles, and rowed to the other side of the river to moor
for the night.

The settlement on the opposite bank was only a collection
of temporary mat-sheds built on the sands and the banks
behind. I had known that in the late summer the Yangtze
was capable of rises so rapid that they were sometimes fatal
to the beach-dwellers, and here I heard an odd incident of
the floods of the previous year. It seemed that an old
woman living in a hut on the beach had decided her death
was near and invested her life's savings in a magnificent
coffin. Shortly after the coffin was delivered, the river rose
unexpectedly, surrounding the sandbar on which she lived.
It continued to rise and, deciding that she might as well die
in her expensive coffin, the old lady stepped into it. Soon

the river swallowed her house and all those around it, drowning many, but the coffin floated off on the current. Next day it was found on the shore about fifteen miles downstream and in it the old lady was still snugly ensconced, alive and perfectly dry.

On the eighth day out of Kiating we anchored at a larger town — Changchung, I believe its name was — and going ashore I found that I had re-entered the Gadget Belt. The two main streets of the city were lined with pseudo-foreign, white-and-pink plaster houses, and were wide enough and flat enough for rickshaws. Probably in compliance with the whim of some official, all the rickshaw coolies carried dinner-bells which they tinkled as they moved, making a pleasant addition to the usual clamor of Chinese street-life. In Changchung I saw again for the first time in weeks advertisements in near-English, two of them worthy of record. One proclaimed the 'Hsin Lee General Store' and bore the cryptic motto, 'I'm on the Globe.' I thought at first this might represent a garbled memory of Shanghai-American slang — 'I'm on the ball' perhaps — but in the corner of the sign there was a picture of a geographical globe. The other adorned a store which had long since closed down and I regret that I was never able to examine its wares. The sign proclaimed, 'The Blue Sky and Art Company.'

On the ninth morning a strange rattle broke the calm of the river; I was astonished when I identified it as a pneumatic drill and saw tiny figures preparing to blast high on a cliff on the north shore. As I subsequently learned, they were preparing for the long-awaited Chungking-Chengtu railway. Toward noon a smoky factory swung unexpectedly into view on the riverbank and on the hills behind it appeared villas of an unmistakably European appearance. Rounding the next bend, the sampan slid down into the welter of boats clustered below the busy antheap of Chungking.

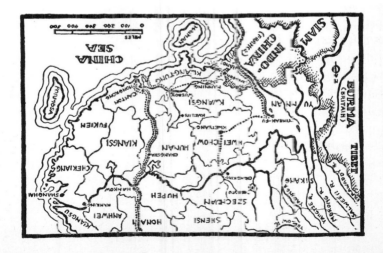

XII. DRAGON COUNTRY

As we prepared to moor by the wide shelf of pebbly beach, there was a droning in the air and a fat tri-motored passenger plane soared down over the roofs of the city. Its silver wings flashing, it swerved and sank gracefully past the huddled gray walls, past the tall veined cliffs, past the narrow slatted sails of the junks, landing finally on a sand-bar two hundred feet away. It was the semi-weekly plane from Shanghai and had left the coast a thousand miles to the east at just about the same time of morning that we had started down-river from a point perhaps ten miles to the west.

When I came to Chungking from Shanghai, the city had seemed remote and intriguingly Oriental. Approaching it from the other direction, it was an urbane metropolis. When I paid off my servant and the boatmen and ascended through the bustling streets to the same lodgings I had thought so bleak in January, I found myself in the lap of civilization. I got into a bathtub for the first time in three weeks and, much more luxurious, had my first glass of beer in four months. I was delighted to find that I could examine Shanghai papers less than two weeks old, and could even go to the movies again — which soon I did, but on the screen was Shirley Temple and in the rickety theater were not only too many enthusiastic people, but also several large and fearless rats.

Of course Chungking was changed by more than my attitude; in January it had been muffled in winter fog, but in May it was frying under the full heat of summer. For at least eight months of every year the city's climate was tropical, and somehow its flimsy streets seemed more suitable under the glaring light, certainly more picturesque. Over the crowded houses were great p'ungs — shields of matting on bamboo frames — and in the streets were awnings, lattices, and umbrellas which cast dark shadows of intricate shape. The passers-by all wore wide straw hats and almost all carried fans. Sitting at leisure in their small-clothes, in shops or tea-houses or on balconies, drinking tea, smoking, toying with their pet birds or monkeys, the gentlemen of Chungking were agreeable to watch. Walking by in their silk robes slit to the knee, their faces attractively moist with sweat, the young girls of Chungking were disruptingly lovely.

The downtown streets were unusually crowded during those last days of May; through them long lines of coolies supervised by soldiers and police were carting heavy wooden cases down to the river. I heard that the threat of a provincial revolt under Liu Hsiang and others had again become acute; these cases contained silver bullion being shipped down-river to safety from the banks of Chungking.

Though in Shanghai in December there had been rumors of a road under construction between the provinces of

Szechuan and Yunnan, I had been unable to learn how nearly finished it was and what traffic was allowed on it. In Chungking in May I found that the road south had been completed during the winter and a public bus-line was already operating over it. From Chungking this road ran south for about three hundred miles to Kweiyang, capital of Kweichow, there joined a road from Changsha, capital of Hunan, and led west about five hundred miles to Kunming, or Yunnan-Fu, capital of Yunnan. Of course it is now an invaluable link in China's network of strategic highways, but when I set out on it just five weeks before the outbreak of war, its existence was hardly known outside western China; it was one of the most extraordinary aspects of those feverish preparations which finally rendered the country capable of real resistance at almost the moment war broke.

I left Chungking early on a hot summer's morning — very early too, for though these busses did not start the day's runs until eight or later, tickets went on sale at six, and so great was the crush that it was advisable to reach the station soon after five. I was ferried across the Yangtze as the rising sun turned sky and water to molten brass and cast yellow light on the topmost houses of the tall dark city. On the brown shores the growing light revealed multitudes already astir — figures in summery white who fanned themselves as they wandered along the beaches. Half a mile up from the shore, the Chungking terminus of the bus-line was a blue shed jammed with a jabbering mob and incredible assortments of baggage. In the yard before the station stood the three busses into which all the people and material were to be packed. It was almost nine when the caravan finally ground off and the busses began whining in low gear along a well-graded road up the slopes bounding the Yangtze to the south.

Ascending these hills on my way out of the province, I finally saw evidence of something about which I had heard reports ever since arriving in Szechuan. The low water which had made my trip up the Yangtze Gorges difficult was an early result of a severe drought which gripped the province in the fall of 1936, making the winter crops almost entirely a failure. In Chungking in January I'd been told that the number of local beggars was already swelling with famine refugees. When I was in Chengtu in February, the situation became serious enough for the municipal government to declare a period during which it would be illegal to slaughter animals — a Buddhist remedy for drought. In March and April the need for rain became more acute, and even though the Chengtu plain was fully irrigated, various other means of attaining it were tried. The Rain-Gods were taken out of their temples and placed in the sun in the hope that this would make them so uncomfortable that they would summon rain. A great image of the Rain-Dragon was constructed of bamboo and pine branches and carried through the streets by young men naked except for loin cloths; crowds followed them, throwing buckets of water on the dragon.

At the same time harrowing reports came in from the northern part of the province where the situation was already acute. Many farm families were reduced to eating mud; it was alleged that a certain kind of white clay was even quite palatable when fried with vegetables. There were rumors of cannibalism, and desperate farmers were said to be exchanging children with their neighbors so as not to be forced to kill and eat their own young.

When I began traveling in the country I heard of misery which seemed blacker because of the ignorance which accompanied it. In Kiating just before I arrived, a pig with a malformed snout had been discovered and in the belief that its freakishness was the cause of the famine, it was placed in a flower-decked litter, conducted by a rejoicing crowd to the execution ground, and formally shot.

From the back country came the story of a mob of frantic farmers who had rushed into the magistrate's compound in the local market-town, chopped down the official flagpole, and burned it. The explanation was that the Chinese characters meaning flagpole (ch'i kan) also meant 'all drought.'

By the time I returned to Chungking, the grain from the fall harvest had been consumed throughout the countryside and the deadly business of mass starvation was well under way. Refugees were flocking to the city. Some committed small crimes in order to be thrown into prison where they would eat regularly, and hundreds pilfered among the food stalls on the streets, thinking the flogging they received as punishment a cheap price for a handful of food. During April and May the police removed from the streets of Chungking an average of one hundred corpses a day.

It may seem odd that I could have lived four months in the province without detecting signs of this catastrophe, but in the crowded cities it was hard to distinguish famine victims from the many wretches suffering from more usual causes, and when I did go into the country I traveled almost entirely along rivers where the effects of drought were naturally small. Going away from the Yangtze on that last day in Szechuan, however, the extent of the disaster was only too apparent. The earth was baked like a brick and on it all vegetation was brittle and brown, filmed over with dust. The paddy-fields by the road, which at that time of year should have been full of water dotted with green shoots of rice, contained nothing but cracked, dry mud. In the barren, sunstruck fields whole farm families sat drearily hacking and hammering at the clay, pulverizing it so that if some rain should fall these shards might soften more quickly into useful earth again.

I think it was fortunate that I had served an apprenticeship in the mountains and on the river before I undertook the journey through the giddy hills of South China in the heat of early summer.

The bus in which I left Chungking had only a few benches around the walls and we passengers sat sprawled inextricably together on the floor and on boxes, our legs and luggage woven into a fantastic web. The company included a Buddhist priest, a fat official and his wife, three soldiers, two students, several merchants, and a farm family consisting of man, wife, grandmother, two children, and four chickens. Though pinned motionless from the waist down, my fellow passengers were naturally not cramped, physically or mentally. As the speeding bus jolted the bodies and bundles into new patterns, all sat talking together, gesticulating at each other or at the flying scenery and laughing with high and ceaseless good humor. In the sunny weather the crowded car soon became a traveling oven, for most of the windows were kept shut against the dust. Before long the mingled travelers began taking off their clothes and by midday I sat bathed in sweat, my own and others', surrounded by a merry crowd of half-naked folk, while the air in the bus was not only full of flailing arms and fans, but also of clothes being patiently waved to create a breeze.

At the frequent stops, everyone disembarked to stretch and eat and drink. Tea, fruit, seed-cakes, sugar-water, spiced spaghetti, and corn on the cob were popular solaces after the discomforts of travel. Oranges and long sticks of sugar-cane were purchased in quantity and taken along to be consumed on the bus. For half an hour after every stop, the space in the bus which was not already occupied by the active limbs of chattering people was full of flying orange seeds and peels aimed from mouths turned in the general direction of the windows, of long sugar-canes flailing wildly as their owners gnawed on them, and of expectorated wads of fiber from these canes, chewed dry of their goodness, and also aimed generally at the windows.

The nerves of a Westerner are no match for those of an Asiatic; I was less able than the other passengers to sustain good humor under the routine discomforts and I began to be impatient with this flamboyant and persistent eating, for whenever the bus negotiated any steep hills or a series of sharp curves, a good many passengers succumbed to car-sickness. All through the first day I had to sit next to the small son of the farm family. At every stop he was plied with food of all sorts by his doting parents; he always gobbled it down, and shortly after the bus had started would vomit with equal facility until he had got rid of that batch and was ready for more at the next stop. Although not many of the adults were quite so regularly affected, every sharp descent took its toll. The women in particular were susceptible and just the sight of a hill ahead would set them to moaning and clasping their throats in anticipation.

Most passengers carried two patent remedies for the failing; Tiger Crackers and Tiger Balm, the first to be taken internally, the second externally. I was politely invited by my seat-mates to partake of both medicines whenever we went through hilly country. I managed to avoid eating any Tiger Crackers, but once after continued urgings rubbed some Tiger Balm on my cheeks and forehead as directed — it was a purplish alcoholic ointment cooling to the skin. When it was seen that indeed I did not sicken, everyone was pleased and public faith in the medicine was bolstered; it had just failed notably in two instances.

The farm people preferred to have themselves pinched by their neighbors at the approach of nausea. The pinching was done with the knuckles and the favorite points of application were tender spots such as the nape of the neck, the Adam's apple, or the inside of the elbow. It was a cruel-looking business, raising dark-red welts on the patient, but as far as I could see had no preventive effect.

The oldest farm woman was never sick and was consequently contemptuous of the pinching. I particularly remember this wrinkled old beldame, though, because she was riding with her small naked grandson in her lap and frequently when the bus slowed or stopped she would hold the infant's little behind out the window beside her, hissing through her teeth to give him the idea.

On the first scorching day the bus wound through typically Szechuanese red hills, into a region of limestone mountains thickly timbered with pine and bamboo. In the late afternoon it zigzagged up over a handsome ridge marking the Kweichow border and descended to a narrow town, Song-k'an, strung along a river in the ravine below. The hotel here was built under a colossal banyan on the outskirts of town by the river's sandy pink shore. In the upper gallery of the inn, we guests sat as the light failed, eating melons, drinking tea, and admiring the antics of a cageful of monkeys, the prized property of the landlord. On the beach below, a dozen tanned and naked soldiers were washing some black horses and from beyond the town floated the marching songs of other soldiers at their evening drill. After dark we were summoned down the ladder-like stairs into a stone-paved court and at trestle tables lit by torches ate the colossal meal for which, with a night's lodging thrown in, we were paying fifty cents apiece (fifteen in American money.)

The border mountains were apparently an important factor in Szechuan's drought, for next day, on the other side, the weather was rainy. Starting at seven the bus skittered up and down more tree-covered slopes, lurching perilously around fog-shrouded curves. In the afternoon it threaded through a series of attractive mountain valleys, intensively farmed, where black cypresses stood between blond fields of wheat and mauve expanses of opium poppies. It stopped for the night in Tsun-Yi, a whitewashed town sprawling over the gray rocks of a shallow mountain pass. Here the hotel was inside the walls, and when I'd been guided through a courtyard full of potted flowers, I was ushered into a room with a balcony overlooking the bustling main street, a thoroughfare which became alive with great globular yellow lanterns as the evening turned blue.

On the next day, a fresh and delightfully cool one of swiftly moving clouds and spotty sunlight, the bus climbed through a succession of wider valleys, among green mountains which grew smaller and sharper with each mile. There was ample evidence that this highway was a very new one, built through territory which never before had sounded to the peals of a klaxon. The animals by the road were still dumbfounded at sight of an automobile and surprised water-buffalo would frequently run amok and gallop down the road ahead of us for hundreds of yards. The country people had not become entirely accustomed to motor traffic either and at the approach of a car would scurry back and forth across the road like their own chickens. Entering a village, the driver, the mechanic, and many of the passengers would lean out the windows shouting warnings to all to get out of the road and sending imprecations after those who failed to do so.

On one occasion a small naked boy ran so close in front of us that in a swerve to avoid him the driver nearly plunged the car into a ditch. The child fell down beside the road and lay there quaking with terror at his narrow escape, whereupon the driver stopped, jumped from his seat and kicked him twice in the stomach. It was a brutal business but must have lessened the chance of that particular child's killing himself under the next bus.

In the larger towns the crowds in the streets were often so thick that the bus had to slow to a crawl, and once its speed was no longer lethal, no amount of honking or abuse could move strollers out of its path. Then the mechanic had to crawl out on a mud-guard, grip the radiator-cap with one hand, and with the other reach out to slap the scalps of the most obstinate and deliberate.

Still the most striking evidence of the highway's recent construction was the driving technique of the chauffeurs

who conducted the bus over it. With foreign-style motoring caps worn rakishly backward as they had seen them worn in the movies, they spurred the rickety vehicle as fast as possible over every inch of the way, charging with glib recklessness around the blindest corners. Though the road had only been in use for a few months, in several places beside it already lay the gutted and crumpled carcasses of earlier busses. Fortunately there was practically no other automobile traffic, no private cars whatsoever and usually only three or four busses to be passed each day. There was much non-motorized traffic, though, for the highway roughly followed the course of one of the old mandarin roads; we passed and panicked a number of horse caravans, many of them loaded with choice Yunnan opium. The periodic stops in villages and towns provided a respite from the continued suspense, except on occasions when one of the drivers opened a fresh can of gasoline and started sloshing it into the tank, a lighted cigarette dangling sophisticatedly from the corner of his mouth.

Four or five hours from Tsun-Yi, the bus emerged on a strange plain scattered with hundreds of sharp little mountains from seventy-five to five hundred feet high, shaped like teeth, like bottles, like beasts, like boxes, like knives, like dragons, like anything but mountains. Between the knots of abrupt hills the land was quite flat or at the most slightly rolling. It was in some places so rocky and in others so highly cultivated as to be treeless, but the sugar-loaf pinnacles strewn about on it were clothed with luxuriant bushes and vines. The effect was extraordinarily artificial, more like the landscapes of Chinese Art than I would have believed possible. As I later learned, all the central part of Kweichow was of soft limestone and not only contained such abnormal hills, but was irrigated by rivers which were inclined to disappear underground, sometimes flowing invisibly for miles before returning to the surface.

When the afternoon light was turning cool and yellow for a quick mountain sunset, the bus banged across a rich stretch of irrigated fields to Kweiyang, the compact capital city of Kweichow, lying in a saucer-shaped valley ringed about by the grotesquely spiky hills.

Once Kweiyang had evidently been a crowded, walled town, but recently wide highways had been cut through it and lined with semi-foreign stores of a uniform and extremely attractive type. The façades of all buildings on the main streets stood flush with the curbs and all had colonnades through the face of their ground floors, forming continuous arcades on which the shops opened. All of them were freshly whitewashed and all had blinds and trimmings of solid black. The city was built on slightly rolling land,

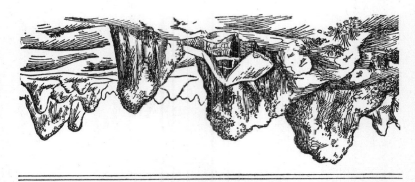

and between the rows of severe zebra buildings the spacious, rather empty streets sloped gently up and down, covered from curb to curb with clean pink sand. Above the ends of these odd avenues, full of the clear liquid light of the plateau, the strange little mountains poked their lopsided summits, emerald green in the last rays of the sun.

In the hotel at Kweiyang I stayed the first night in a room next to one occupied by a military tai-tai — officer's

wife — who gave a shrill mah jong party lasting well into the small hours. Toward midnight, when I'd retired and was trying to sleep despite the racket, a small furry creature hustled through the curtains of my door and scuttled under my bed. In a minute the entire mah jong party was in my room, laughing and holding lamps aloft. Several fell on their knees and after poking under the bed brought out the creature. It was a small black bear. The tai-tai seized it, slapped it, and kissed it, and then with a hoot or two at me the party went back to their mah jong.

In a few days I started westward by bus toward Yunnan, planning to stop off at Nganshun, the largest town in western Kweichow, to do drawings of the aborigines who were numerous in that part of the province. It was a half-day's trip from Kweiyang to Nganshun, up a gently tipping plain dotted with thousands of green hills shaped like the fins and flippers of dragons. The town of Nganshun was still medieval in style, but as liberally whitewashed as Kweiyang — I understood that all these Kweichow towns had recently been cleaned and furbished for the benefit of a party of Nanking officials who had just made a tour of inspection down the new highway into Yunnan.

I soon regretted that I had not come into Kweichow until my money and my drawing materials were nearly gone; the tribes here were far more numerous and accessible than those farther north. Kweichow had been the last stronghold of the aborigines who originally inhabited all China south of the Yangtze, and though Chinese outposts were earlier maintained in it, it was not really brought into the Empire until the eighteenth century, practically yesterday in Chinese history. Even later, though Chinese colonists occupied its more fertile valleys, the province remained a self-governing state in all but name, and it was not until 1934, when Chiang Kai-Shek invaded it on the heels of the Chinese Communists, that Kweichow actually came under the control of the National Government. Though now completely under Chinese rule, the population is still at least half aboriginal. Some of the tribes are partly sinolized, some still in their native state — some 'raw,' some 'cooked,' as the Chinese say.

I believe that all of the aborigines of Kweichow are considered to belong to one group, the Miao nation, but the nation has at least seventy subdivisions — tribes whose dialects are mutually unintelligible and whose customs and

costumes vary sharply. Though in the past the tribes frequently fought with the Chinese or each other, and some
groups in the north still have a reputation for fierceness,
most of them are now peaceful, almost plethoric, farm
people living amicably mingled together.

Apart from their extraordinary picturesqueness of appearance which infected me with an itch for the paper and
crayons of which I no longer had a supply, the cheerful
natures of the tribes people attracted me and from what
I could learn of it from other sources, their civilization
fascinated me. A curious negative quality seemed to per-
meate all their ideas and beliefs. They had no gods in our
sense, but feared demons — by the roads there were sometimes painted stone images of these in a style rather similar
to the totem poles of the Pacific Indians or the wooden
fetishes of Korea. Many of the tribes practiced couvade,
that custom which prescribes that when a child is born the
mother must go off into the fields and drop it without fuss,
while the father takes to his bed for several days and becomes the object of all solicitude and sympathy. To celebrate holidays these odd people staged horse-races without
beginning or end, even without winners; the participants
simply rode round and round the track as they pleased,
starting whenever they wished and stopping as soon as they
became bored. Unfortunately the Miao had no written
language in which to record the growth of their attitudes,
but the lack is explained by a legend curious in itself:

It seemed that they once lived farther east, near the
purely Chinese territories, and there they had known and
used a few Chinese characters. But the Chinese were too
crafty for them, and at length the tribes decided to move
west. On their migration they came to a great body of
water, perhaps Tung Ting Lake. They were puzzled as to
how to cross until they saw water-spiders walking on the
surface of the water and decided to imitate. They swallowed so much water that they swallowed all their characters with it.

Through the missionaries at Nganshun I got in touch with a converted Miao tribesman and through him I was able to find several models, really as many as I still had paper for. Once I went with him to a market fair to sketch, walking eight or ten miles out into the country through a petrified forest of needle hills. The booths of the market were dotted over a rocky saddle between two hills and around them surged hundreds of blue-coated Chinese and tribes people in embroidered clothes. From a distance the fair appeared as a strange crawling mass of brown and yellow disks of various sizes, for in the intense white sunlight the stands were shaded by great umbrellas and the people who walked among them carried parasols or wore cartwheel hats of basketwork. This chattering throng wandered among piles of fruit, vegetables, shoes, china, cloth, ironware, baskets, displays of rainhats and raincoats skillfully woven of straw by tribeswomen, and heaps of bamboo imported from Szechuan and offered at great profit in this plateau country where the plant could not be grown. There were frivolities too: a trained monkey which wore a comic series of tiny hats, turning itself into a soldier, a merchant, an actor, a priest; a soft-drink stand which featured a jolly pottery Buddha spitting sugar-water; many counters where peppered noodles, the Chinese equivalent of the hot dog, were sold.

My drawing here was not successful because as soon as I began to work I attracted a crowd which exceeded even that around the performing monkey. In order not to be cut off from my models, I had to have them stand within a foot or two of me. I had nothing to sit on but a low rock, and as my face was thus on a level with the model's knees, I began to foreshorten in an exaggerated fashion, turning out monstrous sketches with pinheads and giant feet.

I was able to make more interesting pictures when I went with my guide to his home village about two miles from Nganshun and he had members of his family put on their

wonderfully embroidered ceremonial clothes. The village
was similar to a Chinese farm settlement, consisting of
a half-dozen rough, thatch-roofed stone houses clustered
inside a protecting wall. Here about fifty Miaos, a dozen
black swine, and two hundred chickens lived in an amiable
welter. I did my drawings in the home of the head man,
distinguished as the only structure of dressed stone and
finished woodwork in the village. In the next room was the
village school, very recently established as part of a program inaugurated by Chiang Kai-Shek to hasten the as-
similation of the tribes in the interests of national solidarity.

I was told that in this connection a bounty of thirty
dollars had been offered by the Government for every mar-
riage between a Chinese and a member of the tribes.
Smaller rewards were given to influential aborigines who
would cut their hair and dress in Chinese style. I understood, however, that the process of sinolization was proceeding very slowly, since the pride of the Chinese and their
contempt for the tribes was equaled only by the pride of
the tribes and their contempt for the Chinese. From what
I could see of the posters and lessons on the walls of the
schoolroom, the tribes children were being taught to read
and write the Chinese language and were also instructed in
the rudiments of modern hygiene. I must say, though, that
while I was there the only activity conducted by the two

bespectacled but roguish young Chinese schoolmarms was the singing of 'San Min Chu I' (the Chinese anthem) and the constant use of one thing which was plainly the most popular benefit of the alien culture. This was a ping-pong table.

After a week in Nganshun I set out westward again toward Yunnan-Fu. The road soon wound into irregular, broken country where the pinnacled Kweichow plateau gave way to ranges of real mountains running north and south. It was a handsome region, wild and sparsely inhabited, where comblike peaks covered with velvety grass separated valleys thickly grown with vines, shrubs, and occasional palms. In early June the slopes were blossoming with quantities of pink and yellow roses and a blue flower similar to the forget-me-not. It was a country of many water-falls; there were dozens of white threads of spray cascading down the tall sides of the valleys and at one point the road passed beside a monstrous cataract where a full-fledged river plunged over a ledge at least two hundred feet high. The tribes seemed to outnumber the Chinese here and by the road walked Miao women in embroidered and fringed costumes, their headdresses hung with silver coins.

This territory, which until a few months before had been completely inaccessible, could not long remain untouched, for in the cuttings beside the road the red earth was frequently veined with black deposits of coal lying on the surface, almost ready to be picked up without mining. Among the mountains the motor highway which had opened the district seemed the more remarkable; in one place it descended an almost vertical precipice on a dozen hairpin switchbacks. Unfortunately bridge-building had lagged behind the road-building, and the bus passed over most rivers on crude hand-propelled ferries. One narrow stream was even crossed on an ancient suspension bridge formed of boards laid across two chains, a wobbly structure dating

from the days when this route was an Imperial Mandarin trail.

Hour after hour, day after day, the bus wound over the sharp hills, through groves of dark pines dotted with scarlet azalea, over rushing mountain streams, down slopes terraced with emerald rice-fields, through villages of gray limestone houses, past whitewashed temples with ornate painted gateways. All this country was handsome and unexpected, and some of it was beautiful. To me the shifting landscapes were naturally exotic, but they were saved from the static and rather stultifying charms of the picturesque by their number and infinite variety. Like the countrysides of America and Russia — the two other great continental nations — this Chinese land had a pictorial quality best defined as an active one, since it opposed the static uniqueness of the picturesque with a condition in which individual places were only combinations of things which were the same over a huge territory. As the bus swooped down a slope toward a cluster of farmhouses around a green pool or ascended through a rhododendron-covered ravine, I was always conscious that behind these hills hundreds of similar hills stretched toward the horizon and these houses and towns were duplicated with small variations across a continent.

As a traveler it was useful to recognize that the picturesque was tiresome except as a novelty and if there were only one of a thing it was hardly worth bothering about. Even though I was not entirely aware of this at the time, I did immensely enjoy the unfolding panoramas of similar paddy-fields, hills, groves, and pagodas as the bus wound through the thousand wrinkles of the great surface of China. In retrospect the idea is still more satisfactory. The memory of the few unique places in China, the few sights — the Imperial quarters of Peking, the Gorges of the Yangtze — gives me less pleasure than the fact that I can now look at a map of China, select some anonymous place far in its heart and remember that there, for instance, between a rocky river and a blue mountain, a whitewashed inn stood in a rustling grove of bright green bamboo, facing down the valley to where the horned gate of some obscure country town was silhouetted against the sky.

PORTRAIT

DRAWINGS

A PROFESSIONAL BEGGAR OF PEKING
One of the most profitably pathetic men in the business.

**FARM-WOMAN FROM THE COUNTRY NORTH
OF PEKING**

*Drawn during the war when she had refugeed into the city
with nothing but her six-year-old granddaughter and a
flock of sheep.*

A PEKING CARPENTER

This man came to mend the gate of the house next to mine and was disgusted with the prospect of sitting for his picture, obliging only out of politeness to my servant. Several times he got up and walked away.

YOUNG TOBACCO MERCHANT, NORTH CHINA
*A more prosperous man than most of those who would sit
for me. He did because he himself painted.*

SUBURBAN HOUSEWIFE, CHENGTU, WEST
CHINA
*The wide black turban is a Szechuenese remedy
for headaches.*

A CHENGTU RAGPICKER

COOLIE FROM CHUNGKING
This man was the one with the broken leg.

SZECHUANESE FARMER

JAIRONG TRIBESMAN FROM THE SIKONG
TERRITORY BETWEEN SZECHUAN AND TIBET
Drawn at Kwanhsien, Western Szechuan, where he had
come to trade skins for tea.

HEH-SHUI TRIBESWOMAN FROM SIKONG

Drawn at Chengtu where her husband was an expert welldigger.

JAIRONG BOY

HEH-SHUI SHEPHERD

*In the interests of realism he blew a single piercing note
on his flute throughout the sitting.*

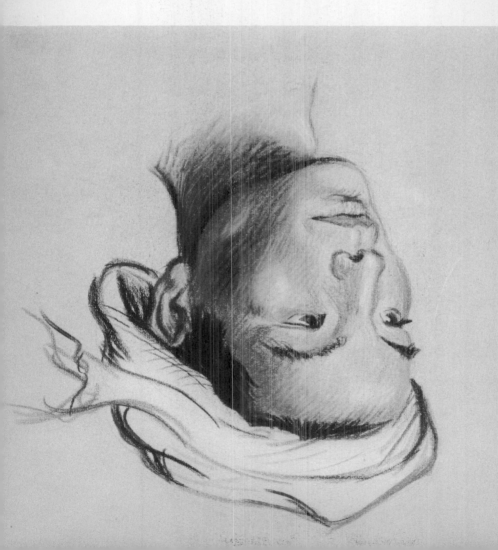

JAIRONG BOY

He attempted to tear up this portrait when it was finished.

FARMER OF THE MIAO NATIONALITY, B'A TRIBE,
FROM NGANSHUN, WESTERN KWEICHOW

XIII. WEST, SOUTH, EAST,
NORTH

ALL the way west the road trended up toward the eight-thousand-foot plateau of Yunnan. The air became thinner and even so late in the year the nights were really cool. Then on a showery afternoon the bus reached Pan-hsien, the last town in Kweichow, and all the other passengers debarked. At ease for the first and only time in a Chinese bus, I was driven up over a range of mountainous hills from whose summits a wide petrified sea of green, blue, and purple peaks was visible. Descending, the bus reached an arch of basketwork ornamented with fir branches and faded paper flowers, standing forlorn on the bare hillside. This was the actual gateway to Yunnan, erected for the benefit of the recent inspection party from Nanking, and beyond it the road became really excellent, smooth and cleverly graded and furthermore decorated at its borders with patterns laid out in white, mauve, and red sand.

The first settlement on the other side — Pengyi — was a slatternly little walled village set beside a marsh at the bottom of a red-clay valley. As the Kweichow and Yunnan provincial bus-lines did not connect on any regular schedule and even in Pengyi no one knew when the next bus was due, it was no pleasure to regard the prospect of an indefinite stay here — even now I particularly remember the inn at Pengyi, since it was there that I found a pile of excrement in the center of my bed, whether left by a child or a dog I could not determine. I thought it very fortunate when a decrepit carryall arrived late that first evening and after

some confusion in the matter of purchasing a ticket, occasioned by the fact that in Yunnan there were three distinct currencies in simultaneous use, I was able to leave next morning. Just how fortunate I was I did not realize until I had reached Yunnan-Fu and learned that the last traveler to come across the border had been forced to wait eight days in Pengyi to make his connection.

As the Yunnan bus sped west, the verdant mountains flattened out into wide, rather arid, yellow hills dotted with cactus. In the valleys and along water-courses, tangles of tropical foliage glistened. Here the farmhouses were fort-like buildings of yellow clay, with flattish tiled roofs and sloping walls reminiscent of Tibetan architecture. The people along the road were dressed in clothes of extravagant parrot colors, or garments on which wide bands of embroidery enlivened the conventional peasant blue. There were also many tribes people strolling in costumes checkered and tasseled with red, black, or yellow, their feet encased in thick-soled, hook-toed shoes, their necks hung with silver bangles.

The bus reached the capital on an afternoon when fat

purple-and-white clouds were moving across the sky trailing
gray curtains of rain. It descended toward a wide, hillgirt
plain on which a lake and citified lines of trees could be seen
between the showers, and rolled down a long straight avenue
flanked by real sidewalks. Even before I reached the center
of town, the urbane and Occidental air of this street made
me realize that I had crossed China and come out on the
other side. Soon there appeared severely rectangular houses
of white, yellow, and pink stucco, of exactly the narrow,
blank-faced sort to be seen in French provincial towns.
They were the first structures of a genuinely European appearance I had seen in months except for those fragments
preserved behind the walls of compounds like the oddities
they were. Through the streets of Yunnan-Fu came a
sound which made me realize still more vividly that I was
on the edge of the world of international, Occidentalized,
civilization again — this was the shrill tootling of the French
trains shuttling about in the yards outside town.

I found a friend from Peking stationed in Yunnan and
stayed in the city for a week. It was a pleasure to associate
with moderately profane foreigners again, to eat and drink

in the foreign style, to hear American jazz, even from records cracked and overused, to examine foreign newspapers and magazines only two to eight months old.

As the people and landscape of Yunnan had seemed less akin to those of China than of the hot countries of southern Asia, so the capital seemed quite apart from the cities north and east of the mountains. The Chinese crowds in the streets were still more gaudily dressed, and leavened with quantities of tribes folk and lolloping little Tonkinese in brown or white pajamas. The buildings between which they strolled were uniquely colored — apple-green, mauve, and scarlet — and covered with a tropic blossoming of ornament. Also the city's foreign trimmings were modeled on French rather than American or English patterns. Its main streets had no three- or four-story shacks in the sky-scraper style or brick structures of Victorian pseudo-Gothic as in the Yangtze ports; instead the tumultuous and vari-colored life of the Chinese markets was compressed into a long line of gray buildings with uniform façades, a faint, faraway echo of the Rue de Rivoli.

The life of the foreign colony was naturally dominated by the French, for of the several hundred foreign residents less than half a dozen of the non-missionaries were American or English. Instead of revolving around 'The Club,' as it would have in the anglicized society of a Yangtze treaty port, life centered on 'le Cercle Sportif de Yunnan-Fu.' Here the Yunnan gentlemen gathered in near-English tweeds to drink 'le wheesky,' but in the lounge, where at one of the clubs to the north a group of astringent English women would have been knitting or a team of American women would have been playing ruthless bridge, there were to be seen rather stocky *jeunes filles* and *chic* but mustach-ioed young matrons playing ping-pong in black satin after-noon dresses cut so low as to show the huge crucifixes bouncing between their powdered breasts.

I left Yunnan for Hanoi by train, in one of a line of stocky little red cars drawn by a Toonerville engine. Though the cities were less than three hundred and fifty miles apart, this was to be a three-day trip, as the line descended from mountains eight thousand feet high, shuttling back and forth over innumerable zigzags, through more than two hundred tunnels.

Through the first day the train wound over huge bare hills, across mottled yellow slopes gashed with patches of bare red day and spotted with cloud-shadows. In one of the valleys we skirted a bright cobalt lake. In others there were turbulent red streams on whose banks glistened stands of banana trees — untidy groves of greasy, bladelike leaves under which the unripe fruit was to be seen growing upside-down, as it seemed to me. All day the vegetation grew more luxuriant and by afternoon the cuttings beside the track were covered with long tangled grass in which grew quantities of white lilies and pink orchids. At dusk the train stopped for the night at a railway village and there I found that as an Occidental it was incumbent on me to stay at 'le Bungalow de Compagnie,' a small pink hotel with excellent French food and a small zoo of local birds and monkeys, but at a price which shocked me after Chinese inns.

On the second morning the train began winding down a narrow river valley at the bottom of which was a vivid tangle of bushes and vines. Soon the valley widened, then its whole bottom dropped surprisingly away. The river swept over a cliff, falling in delicate cascades to a jungle floor far below. Instead of twisting down the bottom of a small valley, the train was abruptly winding along the rim of a huge green canyon.

Laboriously it crawled around the edge of the abyss, threading in and out of the cliffs through dozens of tunnels, detouring up the narrow valleys of tributary rivers to lose altitude more gradually. In one spot it shot out of a tunnel directly onto a bridge; the walls of the stream cascading far below were both sheer precipices and at the other end of the bridge the train plunged into the face of another cliff.

Between the cluttered trees on the floor of the canyon there opened green caverns full of twisting vegetable stalagmites and stalactites. The air was hot and almost visibly humid; the big leaves shone as if freshly wet and over the cascading brown streams the spray-filled air itself seemed to glisten. Through a sweltering yellow afternoon the train curved out among smaller hills increasingly over-loaded with swollen foliage, and at dusk it reached the frontier. Crossing a steel bridge over a brown river over-hung with blossoming scarlet trees, it left China, entered Indo-China, and stopped for the night at the town of Lao-Kay, a cluster of whitewashed European and Asiatic build-ings set on the violently green riverbank.

Anxious to avoid the expense of another 'Bungalow de Compagnie,' I accompanied a jovial, gat-toothed porter to a Chinese hotel in the village — the Hotel Thinzel — where I found lodgings of satisfactory price. French influence was evident here in the wallpaper of my room, luridly trellised with pink and purple roses the size of cabbages. On the wall was a highly colored chromo of a nude Chinese girl smoking a cigarette on a foreign couch, beside a dragon table on which stood a parrot, a thermos bottle, a gong, and a telephone. She lay in a pavilion in a garden ringed about by skyscrapers and down the path toward her was cycling an enthusiastic executive in a blue serge suit and a sun-helmet. Behind this picture lived a pair of nervous lizards who darted up and down the walls barking intermittently like small fox terriers.

Next day the train sped southward over the plains of Tonkin, past rounded green and azure hillocks, past swamps of lotus and mauve water hyacinths, past straw villages and cream-colored French stations and barracks which

looked peculiarly raw and angular in the soft Asiatic landscape. In the evening it arrived in Hanoi, a pale, cluttered
city stretching out on the green plain beside a wide *café-au-
lait* river. In the pompous yellow station I was approached
by an affable old Cantonese who explained in French that
he was from the Hotel Thinzel in Hanoi and had been wired
of my arrival by his colleague in Lao-Kay. He led me off to
his hotel, directly across from the station, and installed me
in a whitewashed room furnished with a huge black-wood
bed and four brass cuspidors, one in each corner.

That evening, as the sky turned pink, green, scarlet, and
purple before the tropic night, the European appearance of
Hanoi's electric-lit streets seemed somehow extraordinarily
unconvincing to me. At the same time, though, it gave an
air of masquerade to the hordes of Asiatics who swarmed
out onto the cooling pavements. The giggling Tonkinese
and Annamites in flowing tunics and pajamas who packed
the trams and stood in queues outside the cinemas had a
very carnival appearance against the prosy Occidental
background; even those who affected European dress
favored only the more gala French fashions — the men
were boulevard dandies with bérets and light suits much
nipped in at the waist, while the women wore frocks which
in soberer climes would have been party dresses. After
China, these whispering, waltzing, little folk seemed a
typically tropical people, gay and improvident children of
nature, and the streets of their city were soft with a less
reasoned, more physical atmosphere. Under the street lights
the Tonkinese men in gauze turbans joked and scuffled
among themselves with a juvenile glee which I had never
seen among the cheerful but composed Chinese, while the
Tonkinese women lolled and chattered and flashed their
black-lacquered teeth with a freedom and a flirtatious
consciousness of their sex absolutely unknown among the
attractive but proper women of China.

In the center of Hanoi was a quarter purely French where

lived the officials and business men who ran the city and its
hinterland; with its white hotels, theaters, and restaurants,
and its leafy park laid out around a charming little lake, this
section made a stunning façade for the less shapely structure
of colonial imperialism. As I walked there the lake surrounded by dark tropical trees was reflecting the last peacock colors of the sunset. In one of the pale buildings
beside the park a long café glittered, and on the brilliantly
lit pavement before it native flower-vendors stood knee-deep
in barbaric heaps of yellow, purple, and blood-colored
blossoms. At the pink metal tables the French colonials
sat in white suits with their slim native mistresses or their
black-browed French wives. As I passed, the café band
was playing Ravel's 'Bolero,' with emphasis on the brasses,
and the rather phony excitement of this music floating out
into the Asiatic night made the whole scene almost too
luridly like one of those felicitous oleographs of 'Life in the
Colonies,' printed in full color in a Christmas number of
L'Illustration.

Next day I left Hanoi to the northeast, traveling to
Langson by train, across the humid delta lands and into hilly
country pierced by sharp black limestone peaks like those
of the Kweichow plateau. I shared a third-class seat with

a portly Annamite lawyer in white pajamas and black turban, who bulged his eyes with concentration and seized on the opportunity to corroborate his ideas about America.

'Tous les Américains sont millionaires.'

'Aux États-Unis, toutes les maisons sont cinq cent mètres d'altesse.'

Or really embarrassing under the circumstances, 'Les Américains n'aiment pas les nègres.'

At the Langson Station I was greeted by a round-faced young Chinese speaking excellent French and passable English who informed me that his uncle was the manager of the Thinzel at Hanoi. After apologizing that there was no Thinzel at Langson, he guided me to a comfortable and inexpensive Franco-Annamite hotel and after dinner insisted on taking me to tour the night clubs which the municipality of Langson had provided for its French garrison. I felt this last courtesy was not entirely disinterested, for with us went some of his friends, a party of dapper young Cantonese, and as soon as we arrived at the first cabaret they asked for a partner for me and demanded to be shown the new American dances. The girl they selected must have been a half-caste, as she had a jutting bosom which contrasted strikingly with the spindly shapes of her colleagues.

'Mae West, la voilà!' cried one of the Cantonese, immensely pleased with himself.

'All the foreigners like to dance with her,' explained another, beaming at me.

Later we went to a cabaret which had vermilion walls and ceiling, and was lit by lamps with scarlet shades. All the dancing-girls wore salmon-colored robes and the effect was very much that of a school of pink fish afloat in an aquarium full of ketchup. For music there was one of those glass-fronted contraptions which contain a mechanical marimba and a gloved hand playing a violin by machinery. Beside the robot sat a live Tonkinese musician jubilantly augmenting its jigging French jazz with a bass drum and a pair of cymbals.

Owing to a temporary disruption of the regular bus service, I left Langson to cross the border in a private car with four Cantonese traveling salesmen, a red-bearded French priest, and two pet monkeys. Through a steaming June morning we rolled rapidly westward over excellent graveled roads and after a two-hour drive reached the border station of Dong-Dang. When we had registered our departure at the little French customs-house, we turned off on a twisting, grass-grown trail and jolted down it until we were halted by a rusty chain hung across the way. The chauffeur honked his horn vehemently for some minutes, and finally a sheepish coolie came out of the bushes, grinning and wiping the sleep from his eyes. He removed the chain and we proceeded up the wretchedly rutted path toward a gap in the small range of mountains ahead. Cutting across the pass above was a great wall, black with moisture and fringed with weeds. At a crumbling gate in the belly of this winding snake of masonry we were stopped by a troop of soldiers armed with fans and conducted to the Chinese customs-station just inside. While we waited two hours until the official in charge should come back from his lunch, I realized that I had indeed returned into China.

And just as on the September evening when I descended into it from the desert tablelands to the north, but much more strongly, I realized that I was delighted to be back. On my first return I had been pleased chiefly as a traveler, delighted to be leaving the fantastic but empty plains of the Gobi for the most crowded, various, and spectacular country in the world. Coming back up from the cluttered jungles of Tonkin my attention was naturally not taken by China's visual complexities, and in any case I relished the second return as considerably more than an improvement in the quality of the sight-seeing. After a sojourn in a country which was not really a country but the colonial possession of a European power, it was a pleasure to return to

a land which was run, however haphazardly, by its own
people. China was still unique as the only great country on
the Asiatic mainland to have resisted the advance of Western imperialism; it was basking in a period which now seems

golden as it preluded the attack of imperialism at second hand, from the other direction.

But as I realized while we waited in the heat at the border, amused by the soldiers who detained us — in the shade of the gate an awkward private was practicing calisthenic exercises with a real beheading sword instead of the usual wooden one; cheers, warnings, jeers, and essays at mimicry from his audience attended his efforts but in no way influenced them — the essential reason why I was so pleased to be returning was that I had become fond of the Chinese and enjoyed being among them.

I suppose the civilization which produced those humorous outspoken soldiers and their four hundred million countrymen, and the one in which I had been reared — the oldest and the youngest, the farthest east and the farthest west — differ as much as is possible for two institutions built by the same human race.

Occidental nations, it seems to me, and America more drastically than any other, have built their civilization as a mechanical one, and not only in the plain sense of the word, though in that they have produced an unparalleled amount of paraphernalia; even in the abstract adjustments the Occidental method has been mechanical in that it aims primarily at shaping the environment to fit man. Chinese civilization has grown along a belief that it is more convenient and suitable to shape man to fit the environment; theirs is a mental rather than a physical civilization, to such an extent that it can really be defined as an attitude, not a structure. This divergence may be the natural result of the disparity between the ambitious Occidental temperament and the matter-of-fact Oriental one when confronted by the same problems of existence.

In the West the mechanical approach gives the appearance of having created a much larger and more complete civilization, since more of it is tangible. In the matter of religion, it has produced a huge bulk of recorded dogma insisting on a universe patterned around mankind and a deity who will furnish a comfortable home for it to retire into afterward. In the matter of man's relation to other men, it has evolved unprecedentedly complete forms of government, which prescribe exactly the individual's duties to society and assure him of what he is to get in return.

Its material equipment, the actual tools for the reshaping of the physical environment into a comfortable berth for man, has reached an unprecedented pitch of efficiency. Indeed, so great has the bulk and elaboration of this machinery become that in America, at least, the mechanical civilization already gives a picture of its ultimate future, or the future as it hopes to make it; an age in which all the difficulties of environment are eliminated — the moral, mental, and social difficulties, of course, but particularly the physical ores — an air-conditioned, sterilized, sound-proofed future in which all civilization becomes one great machine aiming to present to mankind at its kernel a surface as agreeably smooth and completely featureless as the inside of a cocoon.

Perhaps in its young days two or three thousand years ago Chinese civilization also aimed at subduing the physical world and shaping it around man's convenience. At some point in their development, however, the Chinese apparently came to believe that the more intricate mechanical adjustments were unnecessary, as man could attain the same harmony with his environment simply by accepting it as it was. A donkey or a litter was satisfactory transportation for a man who was not in a hurry; feather beds and upholstered furniture were unnecessary for those who had taught their bodies to sit or lie without restlessness on firm surfaces.

This may be the inevitable viewpoint of an old civilization, which like an old individual has lost its desire to change its surroundings and instead is content to fit itself into them. But in any case, in China the contraptions of mechanical

adjustment have been very satisfactorily replaced by an attitude which in itself forms a civilization as complete and practical as could be desired.

Of course a certain amount of mechanical civilization has always managed to survive through the centuries. There have been a good many enduring social and political usages, though these have not generally been efficient when applied to any but local problems. There has always been a great mass of homely well-tried methods which made the common acts of life — eating, drinking, and so on — as pleasant in China as they were anywhere. Otherwise, however, the country's great civilization has been stored entirely inside its people and has consisted of a marvelous spiritual resilience, a vital but controlled temper to be seen in all the behavior of the Chinese, in their calm content and their unflagging good humor.

By the time I entered Kwangsi, the summer heat was pressing with infernal weight over the southern provinces

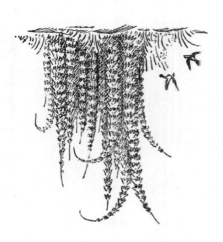

and it made me very aware of the discomfort of the unfamiliar and disorganized ways of life imposed by travel. I'd had my fill of bus travel or rapid travel of another sort, and as it was decidedly not the season for slower and more interesting journeys, I grew restless, anxious to press on as fast as possible. All through the rest of my progress through South China I hurried in anticipation of my return to Peking, where I planned to enjoy a settled life again for a month or two before leaving for America. This circumstance was fortunate, for while it spurred me on too rapidly to learn anything sensible of the country through which I passed, it got me to Peking on one of the last trains ever to reach the city from Central China.

Longtcheou, the first town over the border, was clustered on a knot of cliffs on either side of the Hsi Kiang, the great river of South China, with its two parts joined by a tremendous rusty iron footbridge. It was a bustling town, at that time in the throes of complete reconstruction. Wide automobile roads were being cut through it wholesale, and where

the shops and houses had not yet been provided with new
fronts, their interiors, arbitrarily sliced into, gaped like
rows of dolls' houses. Even in this small provincial backwater stirred the air of industry and change typical of the
two southern provinces of Kwangsi and Kwangtung; oddly
in China the Southerners have always been the aggressive
and radical Yankees, while the North Chinese have been
noted for the placid, conservative, easy-going character
associated with Southerners in other countries.

Next day I went on in an excellent bus of American
make, clattering past more rows of black rock pinnacles,
over plains of shining gray-green grass, empty except for
occasional herds of buffalo grazing among their flocks of
attendant birds. Across these folded plains the course of

the road flirted with a small red river. We crossed it at
least four times in the one day, once on a motorized ferry,
twice on cable ferries, and once on a ferry ingeniously poled
by coolies who dug their long bamboo shafts into the river-
bottom, then fitted them to their shoulders and crouched
down to climb from bow to stern along ladders nailed flat to
the deck. Nanning, reached in the sweltering end of the
afternoon, was a sizable city of whitewashed buildings built
beside the Hsi Kiang at a point where the river made a wide
bend between rounded, grass-covered hills. Until the year
before this had been the capital of Kwangsi, but in the summer of 1936, under the leadership of Generals Pai Chung Hsi
and Li Tsung Ren, Kwangsi and Kwangtung had united in a
revolt against Chiang Kai-Shek and his cautious policy of

politeness to the Japanese. Their armies lined up on the northern borders of the two provinces, but before any shots were fired, Chiang exercised his amazing gift for strategy and liquidated the situation as smoothly and secretly as he was later to dismantle the revolt at Sian. Pai Chung Hsi and Li Tsung Ren swore allegiance to the Central Government — their crack troops and military talents have since played an important part against the Japanese — and as a minor result of the trouble, the capital of Kwangsi was moved from Nanning north to Kweilin, where it would be more accessible to Central Government supervision.

In the early summer of 1937, the abandoned capital still gave evidence of the excitable and kinetic character of the provincial government. The streets were full of anti-Japanese posters and slogans, the most vehement I'd seen. There were also some anti-foreign posters, notably anti-British and anti-French, since those two were the European nations whose pressure, through Hong-Kong and Indo-China, was most strongly felt in this area. One poster, however, accused a dozen other nations of grabbing, since it represented China's proper size as the greatest extent of Genghis Khan's empire, stretching from India to the Arctic Circle and from the Pacific to the Danube.

From Nanning to Yunglin and Yunglin to Wuchow, the bus traveled through a bumpy green country of small mountains and small plains. Gradually the saw-toothed limestone peaks of western Kwangsi gave way to rounded hills, and the grassy slopes were replaced by paddy-fields dotted more and more closely with farms, villages, and towns. Wuchow on the Kwangtung border was a packed city of perhaps a hundred thousand, squatting on a small red hill beside the wide Hsi Kiang. For three days I waited here for a boat in which to continue eastward, and if it hadn't been for the drumming heat I should have enjoyed this first contact with one of the swarming southern coastal towns. As it was, I spent my days in Wuchow lying half naked on the polished

bamboo surface of the bed in my dark room at a Chinese
hotel, drinking tepid German beer I had found in a Chinese
grocery store, reading a volume of modern Russian short
stories in English I'd discovered in a Chinese bookstore,
fanning myself with a fan of white goosefeathers consider-
ately provided by the management of the hotel. My one
daytime expedition was onto the river to see the boat-races
celebrating the mid-June Dragon Festival; these were handsome but rather unexciting contests between long boats
containing fifty oarsmen each, rowing in a frantic din of
gongs and drums.

Such Chinese cities as Wuchow were the ones first visited
by Occidentals in any quantity and many things characteristic only of them have been reported abroad as typical of
the whole country; perhaps if the old idea of China as an
uncomfortable country full of oddly inhuman people derives
from any basis at all, it is founded on these fantastically
overpopulated settlements. To me the South China weather
alone seemed enough to have sent away with prejudices any
early traveler unable to visit more agreeable parts of the
country. Even from the awninged shade of the balcony
before my hotel room Wuchow had an uninhabitable appearance from nine to five. The white-hot sunlight beat
mercilessly down on the street, draining color from the lurid
Oriental signs and banners, laying exaggerated shadows
below all objects and making every scene resemble an over-
exposed photograph. At midday the pavements emptied
except for a few belated pedestrians keeping well under the
arcades before the stores and perhaps a few beggars lying
on papers in the gutter, their bodies gray and contorted
under the burning light, like plaster casts of the creatures
who perished under the ashes of Pompeii.

Late in the afternoon black thunderheads frequently
rolled overhead, wiping out the glare and the acid shadows,
returning color and shape to the buildings of the town and
giving them suddenly in the heat an unreal look of a sharply

realistic actuality, like a lucid moment in a delirium. With
the brief, violent showers, however, came hot winds which
negated their effect and it was not until the sun had disappeared for the night that any breath of cooler air stirred
through the city. But as soon as the dusk turned blue, cool
air began floating up from the river, out of the cellars and
the deep interiors of the shops. Gradually it filled the
streets. Then the electric lights in the arcades were turned
on, illuminating the piles of gaudy merchandise. The
radios in the shops were tuned high and through the streets
the people of Wuchow sauntered in light silk robes, fanning
themselves, chattering, and laughing.

From Wuchow I embarked for Hong-Kong and for two

days and nights sailed deviously down the twisting water-
ways of the Hsi Kiang delta on a stocky old craft, perhaps
half rotten, but painted an immaculate white and impres-
sively armed against river-pirates by barricades of pointed
iron bars and barbed wire. This ship was owned by a
Chinese company, but to enjoy the protection of Britain, it
was registered at Hong-Kong and officered by battered
English seamen too old to get such good jobs elsewhere. I
understood that the actual work of running the ship was
managed by Chinese subordinates; as their ship was steered
for them among the green Chinese islands, the imperially
red-faced and obese old salts spent their days under the
ceiling fans of the salon, drinking prodigious quantities of
beer and recounting endless stories, heroic or obscene.

We came into Hong-Kong during the second night, and
when I went on deck next morning it was electrifying to
find the ship lying in vivid green ocean water before a tree-
covered peak spotted with creamy villas and apartment
houses, even at that distance completely European. When
I went ashore I found that Hong-Kong's foreign streets
lined with great hotels, marble banks, and similar piles were
indeed too overwhelmingly European, or to be specific too
immaculately British, for me. Dressed in wrinkled clothes,
unbathed for two weeks, I stole through the streets feeling
like a White Russian panhandler, and after consuming my
first milkshake in a year and a half at a sterilized dairy lunch,
I fled inland again by the first train to Canton.

In that colossal, sprawling, sunstruck city I stayed three
days, waiting for a north-bound train, but after six months
of intensive travel my sense of curiosity had atrophied. I
stayed in the largest Chinese hotel, and overcome by the
joys of having a foreign toilet all to myself, spent most of the
three days in the bath. Otherwise I sat in the lobby admiring the lovely Cantonese girls going to and fro in chiffon
robes slit halfway up the thigh, and marveling at the American Chinese who chattered among the potted palms — returned immigrants of such completely American manners
and carriage, wearing good American clothes, that after
months with few glimpses of real foreigners I could not
recognize them as Asiatics. Of the sweltering metropolis
outside I remember little. Canton was one of the last great
cities of the world to begin building into the air and,
stretched out as it was on flattish land, it was impossible to
grasp its shape or character in a short time. Though along
the Pearl River a few six- and eight-story office buildings
and hotels overlooked the swarming life on the water and
there was a proper-looking little foreign quarter, on an island just offshore, the rest of Canton was a mass of three-
and four-story buildings cut through by miles and miles of
streets similar to the semi-foreign avenues of the provincial

towns. That legendary Canton which beckoned to so many generations of Occidental sea-captains, the port city similar to one on a willow-pattern plate, had disappeared entirely.

Late on a close, airless evening at the end of June, I climbed into a packed railway carriage in the Canton Station and for seven days thereafter existed uncomfortably as the hills, plains, and cities filed by: Tsingyun, Yingtak, Suichow, Liling, Sinyang, Chengchow, Kaoyihsien, Tingchow, and hundreds more, none with more identity for me than the pattern the letters of their names made on the signs of their station platforms. Up through the small verdant mountains of Kwangtung the train crawled, over a fantastically uneven roadbed. Into the rounded hills of Hunan it wound, along rivers rising for the summer floods and already dotted with floating trees and housetops. Past Changsha it steamed, over flatter country, and out on the swampy plains of Hupeh.

From Wuchang I was ferried to Hankow across the Yangtze, now unrecognizably swollen above its low winter level, and entrained again on the Ping-Han line. More swiftly the new train rattled northward into the dry mountain-dotted flatlands of Honan. It bridged the Yellow River flowing wide and shallow between bluffs of glistening loess and sped over the pink plains of Hopei. Surfeited with the process of such rapid motion up the whole broiling length of the country, I sat bathed in sweat and crusted with dust, anticipating the comforts of a settled life and in particular the pleasures of Peking.

XIV. THE CITY STILL ENCLOSED

ON THE last day of the journey I woke early and in the cool half-light before dawn recognized to the west the line of hills which bound and adorn the Peking plain. Just as the summer sun rose, huge and ruddy, the train reached Lukou-chiao and clicked out on the viaduct over the mist-covered Yung Ting River; a hundred yards to the east lay the pale marble bulk of the Marco Polo Bridge, sunk in the mud of centuries, its carved flanks battered and discolored, but still a splendid sight and even then an eminently historic one, though this present war was not to begin upon it until the end of that week.

The bridge was the first thing I'd seen in eight months that I'd ever laid eyes on before and it made me feel I was coming home. Rapidly the train covered the last few miles to the city, flashing past the race-course at Paomachang, past the big Pagoda, piercing the gray outer walls, coasting by the willow-lined moat, and sliding into the long, shadowy station. After the slatternly sedan-chairs, litters, and carts of the interior, the immaculate and well-oiled rickshaw in which I left the station seemed the quintessence of accustomed comfort. And after the teeming, tumbled alleys of the southern towns and the gigantic landscapes of the west, the ordered gray streets of Peking were like corridors in a familiar house.

In the fresh morning light gangs of half-naked coolies were watering and sweeping the dusty pavements. Along the empty ways farmers wheeled barrows of sleek wet vegetables and past them gardeners trotted with baskets of plants hung from carrying-poles, hurrying to sell their flowers before the day's heat should descend. Riding up the silent avenues I found myself inexpressibly satisfied with my return to this calm unchanging city.

I'd been planning to stay through the summer to paint from sketches I had made in the west and I wanted to find a place of my own in which to do so. In renting Chinese houses it was customary to contract for a year at least, so I was very fortunate in finding within a day or two a small establishment which I could take for three months only. I leased it immediately and, after one day for cleaning, papering, and whitewashing, moved in.

This house was on a by-street, Ta Shih Tso Hutung, in the northern part of the old Imperial city, nearly two miles from the Legation Quarter and the section where most foreigners lived, but in the handsomest part of Peking. It was one of a narrow neck of houses stretching down between the Lake Palaces and the Forbidden City; at one end of its twisting alley rose the scarlet pavilions of Coal Hill, at the other lay the lotus-filled moat of the Purple City, and over it to the west towered the gigantic white dagoba of the Winter Palace. The neighborhood had formerly been used to accommodate the Imperial servants, none of whom were allowed to stay inside the Forbidden City after dark, and even in 1937 the proprietor from whom my landlord sublet was one of the surviving palace eunuchs. Probably because of this Imperial connection, the house had certain elegancies unusual in such small places — in its outer court was a tiny pavilion shading a well with a marble lip carved in a pattern of twining vine leaves, and in the hall of the main house was a panel painted with the panorama of a garden through which ladies in faded white garments wandered, over bric-à-brac bridges and among weeping willows which seemed made of hair.

At my disposal were two courts; a small outer one containing the well, servants' house, and kitchen, and a large

inner one containing one big house with two rooms and a
hall and a smaller house with one room and a storeroom.
For furniture there were two huge built-in brick beds; with
mats for each of these the house was nearly furnished.
From friends I borrowed a desk, a dresser, some odd tables
and chairs, and the house was completely furnished. My
bath was a wooden tub in the court, filled with clear but
slightly smelly water from the well, and my remaining needs
were taken care of in the Chinese style, by a mao-feng
containing a simple hole in the ground. For illumination
candles were sufficient, as there was no impetus to read
during an evening in such satisfactory surroundings.

Into this pleasaunce I settled with a young married couple
for servants, under no obligation but to eat, sleep, paint,
and enjoy the fine summer weather. The only disadvantage
I could find in my arrangements was a total lack of privacy,
for the establishment was but one section of a large house
inhabited by an active and numerous Chinese family; at all
times of the day and night they overflowed into my courts,
but as they lacked privacy as much as I, there were interesting compensations. Next to the tumultuous incursions
of Chinese family life probably the most picturesque aspect
of my existence was the fact that all of it cost me less than
forty-five American dollars a month, including rent, food,
drink, wages, and extras, down to every last cigarette and
rickshaw ride.

In a way my moving in here was the climax of my stay in
China. After a year and a half I had finally become acclimated enough to adopt with very few reservations the Chinese way of life. And perhaps my adjustment to its unhur-
ried regimen has a more than personal interest, since just at
the time I was entering into it, the events which were to
doom it were taking place. On the second day after I settled in at Ta Shih Tso, the war broke out.

In the fourth week of June while I was still jolting northward on the train, it had been reported that Japanese and

Russian border patrols had met and fought on an island in the Amur between Manchukuo and Siberia; in the negotiations which followed, for the first time in years, it was the Russians not the Japanese who backed down. During the first days of July, while I was house-hunting through Peking, hundreds of Japanese and Korean ronins — military plain-clothesmen — filtered into the city, and on July third they attempted riots in several important streets. Serious trouble was averted only by the prompt action of the Chinese police, who arrested three hundred of the rowdies and dispersed the others.

Then on the night of July seventh, during unexplained Japanese maneuvers near the Marco Polo Bridge, far beyond the territory where the Legation soldiers were allowed by treaty, a Japanese patrol came too close to a Chinese garrison and was greeted with a blast of machine-gun fire. Instead of retreating, the Japanese called for aid and spent the rest of the night entrenching themselves. At five-thirty in the morning of July eighth a fairly large and lively battle broke out, continuing through most of the day and spreading to Fengtai, a few miles to the east, when a train full of Japanese reinforcements from Tsientsin was waylaid by Chinese.

Fengtai and Lukouchiao were at least eight miles beyond the southern walls of Peking and perhaps a dozen from the quarter where I lived. The sound of rifle-fire was naturally not audible over such a distance, and isolated as I was, I knew nothing of the trouble until I went downtown in the late afternoon of July eighth. I first heard about it at a cocktail party, where the report that the Japanese and Chinese had begun exchanging bullets was almost lost among bits of Peking gossip.

He performs in the costume of a Louis XIV blackamoor and boasts he's the only man alive who can dance on a kettledrum without breaking it....

With that complexion she certainly does herself no favor by getting tattooed....

The Japanese claim they advanced to rescue a lost soldier, but now they've found that the man in question had just retired into a bush for reasons which were nobody's business but his own....

It was another 'incident,' a comic development in the intricate opera-bouffe relations between China and Japan, and before going off to dinner all agreed that the fighting must soon be replaced by an exchange of ludicrous demands and counter-demands.

When I landed in China I had been chronically excited at the thought of being in a country on the verge of war, but after eighteen months sprinkled with scares, familiarity had taken the edge off my restlessness and I was inclined to concur in belittling this first battle. Since returning to America I've seen some of the newspapers of those early July days and it was a surprise to discover that already they carried the black headlines of war. Certainly the rest of the world was more worried about the trouble than were the Pekinese on whose doorsteps it was taking place.

For days I was interested chiefly by the small events incidental to my settling down at Ta Shih Tso. As the character of my establishment developed, it was becoming evident that it was not to form so much around my own plans as around those of my house-boy and his wife. Like most other foreigners in Peking, I was to be run by my servants, but I had no wish to object, as that made life only the more agreeable.

Both my retainers were really children. The boy, Chou Hwa-Chang, was a lean and simian seventeen-year-old comic, married to a plump little matron a year his senior. He had come up from the country near Tientsin a few years back and until he became my major-domo had served in a minor capacity in the house of some American friends of mine. His wife, to whom he was formally wed at the age of fourteen, had only recently joined him in the city — he was still unused to the married state and frequently in the midst of sweeping or house-cleaning would suddenly look as if he'd remembered something nice and vanish in the direction of his quarters.

I think his country upbringing made Chou more aboveboard than the average Peking boy, and it gave him other virtues I valued. He had a fund of energy and animal spirits which would have been curbed by urban training and he retained the peasant's directness of speech. This last trait might not have been evident if I'd been a person of more years and substance or if I'd discouraged it, but on the contrary it amused me very much. As, for example, my wardrobe had become limited by this time and in order to have a supply of clean things my clothes had to be sent to the laundry several times a week; Chou sometimes forgot the wash, and once when I found myself without a white suit and began scolding him, he howled with laughter and chanted:

> *Mo-yu cou-dzah,*
> *Mo-yu wa-dzah,*
> *Mo-yu chen,*
> *Mo-yu fa-dzah.*

Meaning —

> *He has no pants,*
> *no socks,*
> *no money,*
> *no method.*

At the drudgery of housework Chou was rather lax; the only part of it he enjoyed, and consequently the only part he regularly indulged in, was the dusting of the walls and ceiling with a rooster's tail-feathers tied to a bamboo wand, and the setting to rout with a Flit-gun of the many flies and mosquitoes which swarmed over from the lake in the Winter Palace. Still he cooked and served my meals, shined my shoes, hunted up models, delivered chits, scrubbed my back when I was in the bath (his own idea), and did odd jobs of fetching and carrying. His wife helped with the cooking when guests came, mended my clothes and washed some of them, but her chief duty was to run into the street to find her husband when I required something and he had gone off gossiping. Together they made me comfortable enough, and if there were flaws in their system it was a compensation to know that at any hour of the day or night, like rubbing a lamp, I need only cry, 'Hua-a-a,' and with an answering 'Hua-a-a-a!' a small genie in a white robe would run grinning from the outer court, ready to do my bidding.

Without effort, and with very few thoughts toward what was happening a dozen miles south of the city, I fell into a lazy Peking routine in my house. As I slept on a brick bed with only a cotton pad beneath me, I woke early every morning while the sunlight was still horizontal, clear and liquid as only the North China weather could make it. Undressed for the day to a pair of shorts, I breakfasted under the grape-arbor in the courtyard — though I ate Chinese food for lunch and dinner, I had a foreign breakfast of fruit, toast, and coffee. After reading the paper I worked until twelve, sat in the sun until one or one-thirty, and then had a lunch of mixed meat and vegetables, rice and soup. In this matter of food, incidentally, I had trouble at first, for Chou was not accustomed to marketing for one and would buy each commodity in such quantity that it took me several monotonous days to consume it. When I moved in he purchased nearly a bushel of seaweed, and day after day, noon and night, I ate seaweed boiled, fried, or stewed. It was tasty at first, but I finally refused to eat any more, so Chou went to market and returned with a load of lily-buds, also in such quantity that they became my staple vegetable for the next half-week.

In the afternoons I worked until four and then bathed in the big wooden tub in the center of the court. Chou would primly send his wife out to stand in the street until I had finished, but the Chinese family with whom I shared the house seemed to enjoy watching the foreigner wash — I'd been freed of shyness on the day I moved in when, just as I stepped into the tub, a detachment of local police called to register me as a resident and accompanying them as spectators came half the children and all the loiterers of Ta Shih Tso.

When bathed and dressed, I usually went out calling, for after so many months away from other foreigners I hated to let a day pass without talking to someone in English. Otherwise I had guests in for dinner. On these evenings the house undoubtedly looked its best, the blue twilight in its courts dotted with candles stuck in pewter holders borrowed by Chou from the shopkeeper at the corner, and globular hanging lanterns of white and scarlet gauze borrowed by Chou from the landlord. On evenings when there were guests, Chou and his wife were also at their unique best, joyfully shouting out, 'Kuh-ren lai' (the guest comes), rushing out like puppies and escorting them in from the gate with pocket flashlights, later plunging about with food and drinks rather aimlessly but with the best intentions, affectionately scolding each other in the tiny kitchen as they prepared more and more intricate foods, or gossiping knowingly about their employers with the rickshaw coolies of those who had come.

For entertaining I was handicapped by lack of an icebox, but the cold spring water in the well made a good substitute; Chou kept the bucket at the bottom full of drinks and appropriately enough this well with the carved marble lip flowed not with water but with vodka cocktails.

Perhaps the high point of my entire residence at Ta Shih Tso was a brilliantly moonlit evening in these early days of the war when I had some friends in for dinner and afterward, the pull of the moon being so strong and the landlord having opportunely left a ladder in the corner of the court, we ascended onto the flat roof of the gate-house for the evening.

It was a beautiful night, suave and cloudless, with the moon shining metallic on the tiled walls of the Imperial Palaces on one side and milky white on the great dagoba on the other. Beyond the expanses of curving roofs the city was silent except for the purr of a belated automobile or occasionally a faint breath of music from the roof-garden of the Hôtel de Pékin two miles to the south. As yet no sound of guns, even in the distance; only near at hand a rattling artillery of comments from the Chinese neighbors collected to observe the moonstruck foreigners and a cross-fire of snorts and sarcastic but proprietary explanations from Chou as he crashed up and down the ladder laden with chairs, cushions, trays of coffee, and later beer.

For some time the incipient war did nothing to disturb this sort of life. I could reflect comfortably on my good fortune in having returned to Peking when I did, since from the first the battlefields stretched along the Peking–Hankow railway line and completely disrupted the service. Otherwise the conflict might have been twelve hundred miles away rather than twelve.

After the sharp fighting of July eighth, the Chinese and Japanese officers in the field conferred, and on the ninth, though sporadic firing continued, a truce was declared. On the tenth the informal skirmishing became heavier and for a time disrupted traffic on the Peking–Tientsin as well as the Peking–Hankow railway, but the situation remained officially peaceful.

On the eleventh, claiming the Chinese had been insincere and had not retreated far enough away from them, the Japanese displayed a curious logic and advanced, capturing two villages near the Marco Polo Bridge. Even then, for days the fighting remained quite light; the crux of the matter seemed to be that while neither side was anxious to fight, neither could retreat without losing face. Both Chinese and Japanese troops remained in the same small area. They

could not entirely avoid each other and whenever either side
felt it had been provoked, the firing would begin afresh.

Of course these last are newspaper facts which we in
Peking probably learned slightly later and in slightly more
garbled form than did the news readers of Europe and
America. As to more actual signs of the conflict, there
were none yet in the city. The fine days of early July
slipped by and still there was no appearance of unrest in the
sunny streets, no sound of guns. Only in the evening
newsboys ran through the alleys with Chinese extras on the
war — a shrill 'MAI PAO!' 'MAI PAO!' was the way they
shouted them. Both factions had their military headquarters in the city and it seemed typical of Peking that inside its walls Chinese and Japanese soldiers should pass
peacefully on the streets, while in the fields not far outside
they were attempting to kill one another.

The first time I had reason to understand that this war
was real, a grim presence within a few miles, was on a stifling
night when I wakened at three or four and, unable to get to
sleep again because of the heat, went into the courtyard for a
cigarette. The dawn was turning green in the east, but the
city was still dark and absolutely silent. From the south
west came a faint pulsing of guns, distant but very distinct
in the breezeless air. There was an intermittent crackle of
rifle-fire, drowned occasionally by the thudding boom of
artillery, punctuated by the hasty tattoo of machine-gun-
ning. Standing in the quiet court in the center of the slum-
bering city, it took an effort to understand that in the fields
only twelve miles away these small sounds were shattering
explosions, some of them catastrophes which tore and destroyed human beings.

As I remember, I first heard the guns on the morning of
July twelfth. In the next few days the not-so-distant war
began to have its effect on Peking. The city had been
technically under martial law from the outbreak of fighting;

now its restrictions were felt. The gates in the outer wall were kept shut and guarded all day, opened only at specified times when a certain number of farmers with food to sell were allowed to pass — the price of food began to go up. Increasingly stringent curfew restrictions were also declared. First the time when all had to be off the streets was set at ten, then it was gradually advanced to seven. More alarmingly, barricades began to appear in the big streets. For the rest of July the makeshift fortifications were to be thrown up and torn down as the threat of fighting in the city fluctuated; in typically Pekinese fashion, the largest barricades were those built first when danger was least probable — as the days passed and the possibility of violence grew more real, the indifference of the barricade-builders grew with it and the barricades became smaller and smaller.

Still these developments brought the war close enough to define the attitudes those in the city were to take toward it. Even the imperturbable Chinese were being forced to recognize the possibility that at last, after so many empty alarms, perhaps this was it. Though there was no appearance of panic, the price of food went higher as many began laying in supplies for a siege, and accommodations in the Legation Quarter became scarce as the wealthier Chinese quietly prepared to move in their valuables and families.

We foreigners were in an extremely false position, being in the area of a war and yet not part of it. With all the unpleasantness kept outside the walls and only the excitement filtering in, it was hard to make a tragic thing of it. The war seemed no more than one of those pleasantly novel and exciting group inconveniences, like a small blizzard or a cloudburst, which throw everyone together in more or less comic misfortune and so increase conviviality.

In my own case the early restrictions were perhaps more serious than to the majority; since I lived so far in the north city my movements in the evening were uncomfortably curtailed by martial law. For several days, though, the police enforcing it were lax and riding Chou's bicycle I could generally get downtown and back as long as I returned before midnight — the only real difficulty was in lugging the bicycle over the barricades which were closed at dusk.

Such expeditions were undertaken because even though martial law sometimes made it necessary for dinner guests to stay the night, entertaining continued to be as heavy as was usual in summer-time Peking. Every gathering was stimulated by the thought of war and the newspapermen who had been on the battlefields were becoming the centers of voluble groups. The older residents were still inclined to belittle the whole business and like alumni compared it disparagingly with the old wars of '32, or '27, or '00. The tourists and the more elegantly feathered birds of passage were working themselves into a very satisfactory ferment, however. The colorful and sinister East was proving more picturesque than expected.

'It's like having been at Sarajevo,' was the pleased cry heard frequently in the corridors and bars of the two big hotels.

And day by day, so gradually that there was never cause for special alarm, the sound of the guns grew louder. First they became audible in the comparatively quiet hours of early evening. Later their explosions could be heard over the noise of daytime traffic. Martial law was soon strictly enforced and no one, foreign or Chinese, was allowed on the streets after sunset without a special pass. Unless I spent the night with friends I was imprisoned every evening in my own house. I went downtown in the afternoons, though, for the foreigners still gathered then for a daily stint of gossip and rumors about the fighting.

Although each day came reports that thousands of Japanese soldiers were being freighted down through the Great Wall at Shanhaikwan and other rumors spoke of an army marching north from Central China, it was still a small local war, appropriate to the kind of chit-chat which circulated about it inside the city. Pushed up by a hot rainy spring, the summer crops in the battlefields were already higher than a man's head and in this sea of green stalks small companies of Japanese and Chinese floundered about, firing and slicing at each other when they chanced to meet. The Chinese apparently had no policy except to fight whenever it became necessary; there was no general plan, indeed there couldn't be, since no one in North China yet knew at what point Nanking wished the resistance to hold. The Japanese, on the other hand, reportedly aimed to form a line south and west of Peking, capture the railways to Tientsin and Hankow, and so isolate the city.

Typical of the skirmishing of this period and of the amused attitude foreign Peking was taking toward it were the tales we heard of Chinese prowess with beheading swords. The weapon has always been a favorite of Chinese story-book heroes and many of the tales already had the stature of legend. It was said that every night scores of Japanese sentries were surprised and decapitated by creeping Chinese swordsmen. It was affirmed that the Japanese High Command had hired trucks from the Italian garage and sent them through the lines in the gray hours before dawn to collect the torsos and heads and cart them to a secret place to be cremated before other Japanese could take alarm at the fate of these. Still a party of correspondents visiting the Chinese front reported they had bought a melon from a roadside vendor and borrowed a beheading sword with which to cut it from an obliging soldier. They could hardly dent the fruit with it.

Already, of course, these bush-league battles were superseded in importance by the diplomatic maneuverings in Tokyo and Nanking and of them we could get only the sketchiest idea in Peking. At first Tokyo claimed it would not negotiate with Nanking on the question at all, that North China was the only area involved and consequently the North China military authorities were the only Chinese to be dealt with. This was taken to mean that all the Japanese wanted was one more slice of North China, with a treaty giving them footholds on another slice.

Meanwhile the Nanking Government maintained a fairly belligerent front, but until the last week of July this seemed a pretense to appease the Communist armies and the rabidly anti-Japanese factions of South China. No discernible steps for defense were taken and Chiang Kai-Shek was generally considered too shrewd a man not to realize the odds against him and reconcile himself to another loss of northern territory. With this spirit in the two capitals many felt that the trouble would be settled with only a minor defeat for one side and a minor victory for the other.

On the nineteenth it was even reported that General Sung-Cheh-Yuan, head of the North China garrison, had come to an agreement with the Japanese in Tientsin. It was at the Japanese Officers' Club, over drinks, that the parley was supposed to have taken place and the agreement was characteristic of the old school of Sino-Japanese treaties. The Chinese would not only retreat, but would apologize for not having done so sooner. Clauses for the suppression of anti-Japanism, Communism, and other forms of 'insincerity' would be worked out later.

Though no one could yet hope that the trouble was over, the actual fighting showed no signs of spreading, and during the third week of July Peking began to regain its ordinary composure. Martial law was relaxed, the barricades dismantled and the sandbags emptied of sand. Even the sound of the guns disappeared for a time. The only sinister detail in the placid picture was a stream of reports from Tientsin, Taku, and Shanhaikwan, warning that more thousands of Japanese troops were debouching on the North China plain. They pointed to a fact which nobody wanted to accept then, that a situation was forming which could only be solved by violence on a large scale.

For several days the Pekinese breathed easily. After all the alarm, the trouble had been another 'incident' which would taper off according to schedule in a tragi-comic flourish of diplomacy. No doubt the Japanese would come out of the affair with a stronger hold on Peking, if not complete control. Some of their demands would be aggravating, some humiliating, but it was to be expected; the situation was not a new one. In the foreign colony, the old-China-hands were loud with their 'I-told-you-so's,' secure again in their assurance that as a show nothing could approach the bad old days of '12 or '23. Among the travelers there was a little disappointment and a little relief at the apparent return of peace.

Like the others I accepted these developments with mixed feelings. Having had absolutely no previous experience of it, I could not help but be curious about the nature of war. On the other hand, I was very contentedly fixed and hated the possibility of any change. I was maintaining a precarious financial balance and as I had already paid my rent through October, war in Peking would embarrass me; I could not afford to leave my house as long as it had four walls and a roof.

So far the war affected me only as it affected my plans, but inside Peking there was no way of getting a decent understanding of its character as a catastrophe; from inside, it seemed as small and faraway as any of the lesser events which had failed to affect the calm of the city's thousand courtyards. Actually my painting was less disturbed by the war than the heat, for while I found it comparatively easy to become accustomed to the distant explosions, it was impossible for me to concentrate with drops of sweat rolling slowly down my spine.

July, usually rainy, had developed into a beautiful but uncomfortable month and day and night the weather stayed consistently clear and unbearably hot. And as one tropic day succeeded another I found that in the enclosures of my small house my own special version of the Celestial Never-Never Land was taking shape. The flowers I'd had planted were growing like weeds and the weeds themselves were bursting into bloom. On the grape-arbor over my door, long pale clusters of Persian grapes were ripening, and at the far end of the court a jujube tree also bore a burden of maturing fruit and cast its shadow over the carved spirit-wall on which was inscribed in faded scarlet lacquer 福 the propitious character for happiness.

On one morning of this week Chou came jubilantly back from market with a small mimosa-like plant in an earthen pot. He placed it on my desk and proudly demonstrated that if touched, its leaves would fold up and draw back against the main stalk. For a day or two he even neglected to caper through the house with the Flit-gun and spent almost all his time poking and teasing the little bush, laughing uproariously at its every nervous withdrawal. Still he had noticed my amusement one noon at finding in my soup some cucumber slices nicked into the form of daisies and thereafter for half an hour before lunch and dinner would closet himself in the kitchen to slice cucumbers and laboriously cut the slices into the shape of stars, crosses, swastikas, flowers, or bugs.

With the conservatism of her sex, Chou's wife inclined to disapprove of these japes, but she was too young and amiable to make a stand. One morning Chou tore the knee of his baggy black cotton trousers while sporting on the roof-tiles with the children of the landlord; he took himself off to his wife for repairs and I could hear much talk and laughter coming out of their tiny one-roomed house. At lunch time the boy pranced back like a peacock and showed me that his wife had mended the rent by embroidering over it in silk thread an engagingly pop-eyed centipede with azure and vermilion stripes.

It hardly disturbed my idyllic little pen when over it,

every day in larger quantities, Japanese war planes droned
through the hot blue sky. As yet they dropped no bombs
near the city, but they frequently released bales of scurri-
lous anti-Nanking propaganda over it. Seated at ease in a
flower-decked courtyard it was hard not to regard these
fantastic paper showers aesthetically — the implications
could not matter. When thrown from the planes the bundles of pamphlets would plunge rapidly down for two or
three hundred feet, then rip apart and scatter into descending flights of tiny pages, flickering silver and white as they
turned over and over in the blue air; like butterflies, like
snowflakes, like manna, like anything but what they were.

Then on the twentieth of July something went wrong with
the mending peace. In Peking on the twentieth we could
only learn what the rest of the world was already reading in
its newspapers — that in Tientsin Sung-Cheh-Yuan had
announced the cancellation of his agreement with the Japanese, declaring no Chinese would retreat without direct
orders from Nanking, and at Kuling a little earlier Chiang
Kai-Shek had made an extremely belligerent speech.
On the twenty-first, however, these events bore terrible
fruit, immediately apparent to everyone in Peking without
the aid of newspapers. The fighting south of the city broke
out with redoubled ferocity and all through the day the
noise of bombardment rolled overhead, louder and nearer
than ever before. The barricades in the streets were hurriedly reconstructed and the restrictions of martial law enforced with unprecedented vigor. As was later reported,
on the twenty-first the Japanese shelled Wanpinghsien,
the largest town in the disputed area, and set it afire. A
savage battle began at Fengtai and Peking was again cut
off from the coast. In the fighting on this day big guns were
used in large quantities for the first time; extensive trenches
were dug and a formal line of battle established.

From now on events began happening so rapidly and on

such a scale that the mechanisms of reliable news-dissemination could no longer cope with them and the ordinary people of Peking really knew no more of the approaching war than their own eyes and ears could tell them. The Chinese papers began publishing extras several times a day, full of alarming and contradictory reports, and at all hours the city pulsated with wild rumors spread from mouth to mouth. but the only thing definitely known by all was that while the tide of battle waxed and waned inexplicably, the sound of the guns was generally closer. By cycling downtown, which I now did several times a day, I had access to the more rapid, and usually more feverish, rumors of the foreign colony and I could also read the typewritten bulletins posted in the hotels by the foreign news agencies. This was hardly satisfying, however, for these reports also became more and more peremptory and confused.

On the twenty-second it was reported that General Sung-Cheh-Yuan had had another change of intention, if not allegiance, and ordered his troops to retire. Many refused, notably the Thirty-Seventh Division composed of exiled Manchurians who were implacably anti-Japanese. They entrenched themselves and declared they would fight to the death; in Peking on this day. the boom of the big guns gathered enough volume to vibrate loose window-panes and small bric-à-brac.

But then on the twenty-third the battle began to die down and on the twenty-fourth all was abruptly quiet. The soldiers of both sides were said to be retreating from the front and it was rumored that both Tokyo and Nanking had become amenable to negotiation. It seemed that the recent spat had only been a two-sided attempt to gain last advantages before signing a treaty. On the twenty-fifth, Japanese and Chinese retreated completely from the main battlefield at the Marco Polo Bridge and the firing died down enough for traffic to resume on the Peking-Hankow railway, cut for nearly three weeks.

Arriving on the first train from the south was a General
Hsiung Pen of Chiang Kai-Shek's staff. His first action
was to make a fiery anti-Japanese speech to an assembly of
soldiers and his presence could indicate that China was
finally prepared to fight; on the other hand, the first train
going south from Peking was full of members of the anti-
Japanese Thirty-Seventh Division, banished to Paoting in
accordance with a Japanese suggestion. Whatever these
developments might mean, the opposing troops had not
retreated from each other in territory away from the
Marco Polo Bridge and, as there had not been a formal
front except in that section, both forces were inextricably
mixed together. With all nerves tense to the breaking
point, peace was at the mercy of the slightest accident.

From the twenty-third until the twenty-fifth, Peking
enjoyed its last breathing spell. Though few now believed
that this could be more than a lull, the appearance of the
city was still amazingly as usual. Under the dusty trees in
the avenues the citizens loitered in white summer clothes,
talking anxiously of the war, but also drinking tea, eating
seed-cakes, airing their birds, or playing with their children.
Though most of the barricades were left standing, large
openings were made in them for the passage of traffic.

On the twenty-fourth my landlord approached me anxiously to ask if he might buy an American flag to hang over
our mutual gate. Chou, on the other hand, showed no signs
of worry; when Japanese bombers roaring overhead inter-
rupted his housework he would aim at them with his broom
or duster, click his tongue resoundingly, sketch a tail-spin
and crack-up with one swooping gesture, and go back to
work crowing, 'Ii-ko fei-chi whai-liao!' (One flying-machine
spoiled!)

But the calm in the city was like the pause at the end of
the long slow ascent to the top of a roller-coaster. The foreign Embassies began delivering notices to their nationals

informing them what to do if evacuation should prove necessary. On the twenty-fifth, when I went to the American Chancery to register my residence, I found it milling with tourists asking for trains to Tientsin and old residents straightening out lapsed passports — incidentally when such passports were received, they were found to be cautiously marked, 'Not valid for travel in Spain.' Downtown it appeared that the Occidentals of Peking were in more of a ferment than the Chinese. The fire-eating Thirty-Seventh Division had entrenched itself on the golf-course at Paobashan, digging fortifications which ruined the fairways and greens, and now even the old China hands were beginning to admit that this war was serious. Among the floating populations there were those who had had enough and were turning panicky at the prospect of holding front seats for a war, and those who were curiously excited, delighted to stay on through to 'see all the fun,' as they said.

On July twenty-fifth the expected incident occurred and the lid blew off again, for the last time. On the railway east of Peking a Japanese field-telephone squad engaged in stringing a line from Tientsin came too close to the barracks of the Chinese garrison at Lanfeng. The Chinese attacked, but the Japanese were able to telephone their predicament to Tientsin. Ground reinforcements and a squadron of bombing planes went to their rescue and a furious struggle ensued. Lanfeng was nearly demolished and in the course of the fighting the big railway bridge near-by was damaged, cutting the line to the coast for an indefinite time.

On the twenty-fifth the actual nature of this incident was not known in Peking, but none except the deaf could be ignorant of its effect. From Lanfeng the fighting rapidly spread over all the territory it had previously occupied and into wide stretches of new country. By the twenty-sixth there were battles in progress on all sides of Peking except the northwest. The noise of the explosions rolled back and forth over the sun-baked city and through the groups congregated in its streets flew the rumor that a few stray shots had already begun landing inside the walls.

On the evening of the twenty-sixth a company of Japanese soldiers in trucks attempted to enter through the Southwest Gate to reach the Japanese Legation; it was by no means an attack, as the extraordinary fact of the matter was that the invaders had previously come and gone as they pleased. But this time the Chinese guards trapped the trucks between the double gates and then began tossing hand grenades on them from the walls above. A short, fierce battle ensued before the Japanese could blast their way free. All the southern part of Peking was thrown into a panic, and uneasiness and incredulity spread over the rest of it as the hot night air was jarred by sharp explosions. The impossible was happening; the war had reached the city.

AT NOON on the twenty-seventh I was eating lunch under the grape-arbor in my court when Chou came in with a chit from a friend of mine who lived near the Legation Quarter. The scrawl inside the small folded paper advised me to pack what I could and come down immediately as trouble inside Peking was expected within twenty-four hours.

This was it.

Suddenly and completely all tranquillity was scooped out of the sunlit courtyard. In half an hour I was packed and ready to go. This was excitement; in a sneaking way I had even anticipated it during the past three weeks, but as I left my house not knowing under what conditions I could ever return, I found that all I wanted was to stay there in peace.

Through Ta Shih Tso word had quickly spread that the foreigner was going and there was a crowd to watch me leave. Men, women, and children from up and down the alley stood silently and expressionlessly in the dust, some with their arms folded or their hands clasped behind them, others slowly fanning themselves. My landlord and his numerous family stood at our gate with an odd air of embarrassment on their faces. Chou was the only one who could not ignore the spectacle I made perching in a rickshaw under my clothes and household goods, trying to balance a roll of wet canvases. As I left, he jeered tolerantly until his wife, who at eighteen knew all the proprieties, shushed him by pinching his shoulder-blades.

Out in the big streets flanking the Forbidden City the final barricades were under construction as I passed. At important corners sandbags had been piled waist-high in businesslike lines and semicircles, and between them lay ramshackle walls of boxes, old furniture, broken masonry, lumber, matting, and rubbish — tawdry and fantastic in the white glare of sunlight. In front of all ramparts gangs of sweating coolies were busily tearing up the pavement and digging ditches.

Still none of the barricades yet blocked the way entirely and between them traffic flowed little heavier and no more hurried than usual. There were a few rickshaws piled like my own with disheveled luggage, but most of them swung past, their warning gongs pealing joyously and their wire spokes flashing in the sunlight, ridden only by merchants, ladies, or students as placid and composed as on any other day. Along the gutters milled the usual crowds, gossiping, meditating, now hooting amusedly at the confusion by the barricades. Under the roadside trees vendors meandered and quantities of people bargained, bickered, ate, drank, had their shoes mended, their hair cut, or their fortunes told. Plainly the general conviction was that this could only be a scare, that the ultimate must somehow be averted.

When I reached the house where I was to stay, I found that among the foreigners this comfortable conviction was failing. Instead there was uncertainty, rendered the more irksome by the fact that it was impossible to know accurately even the ambiguities of the position. The meager bits of real news were already dwarfed by rumors of every sort and it was not until days later that we were to learn what had been happening.

But the fact was that by the twenty-eighth the Japanese had been successful enough in the fighting outside the city to make it likely that they would try their luck inside. Their troops were just beyond the gates in the east and north, and they already had a considerable force inside the walls, in barracks at the Japanese Legation.

Outside the Legation Quarter Peking was still entirely held by Chinese. They were concentrated in the northern part of the city, but they kept all the gates in the outer wall strongly guarded. It was expected that street-fighting would begin with the Japanese in the Legation attempting to march to the eastern or northern gates to let in reinforcements from that section, and the Chinese defenses were all calculated to defeat this move. The barricades thrown up that afternoon commanded the strategic avenues leading from the Legation Quarter to the endangered gates.

Late on the twenty-eighth these special streets were closed to general traffic and that night Chinese troops took their positions behind the barricades while machine-gunners and snipers established themselves on the roofs above.

But in the meanwhile we knew nothing of this. It seems ridiculous, for the house to which I had come was less than a hundred feet off Morrison Street, the avenue up which it was most likely that the Japanese would attempt to march, as it led straight north from the Japanese gate of the Lega-tion Quarter. Still, while Morrison Street drained of life and changed into a grim scene for violence, we sat in a pleasant courtyard, in equally pleasant ignorance.

Though technically a refugee, I was finding that in reality I had but moved from one Peking courtyard to an-other equally walled-in — geographically less remote, but perhaps more isolated in spirit from the current urgencies. The friend with whom I had come to stay was a dealer in Chinese curiosities who lived in a large house, thickly ornamented with his wares. His imposing courtyards, full of flowers and pottery figures, and his high painted rooms garnished with porcelain, lacquer, and bronzes, made an elegant and supremely orderly setting in which even the thought of war seemed out of place. Here the telephone could ring, as indeed it did all afternoon and evening, bringing rumors of disaster, but the Celestial Never-Never Land was still intact and in a peculiarly ornate form.

I remember that it was a fine summer's evening; the sunset was salmon pink, flecked with purple clouds. Though the noise of the guns had become a continuous rumble, booming from all sides of the horizon, at dusk the homing doves of the neighborhood circled the sky as usual, the clay whistles on their tails sighing and fluting with piercing sweetness.

We dined very late, with an elegance which even then seemed slightly idiotic, beside a tank of lotus in the courtyard lit by cream and scarlet lanterns. But apparently we were more upset than we realized, for after dinner we sat on and on, talking and listening sometimes to the victrola, sometimes to the reverberation of the guns. It was four in the morning and the sky was getting gray when we finally went to bed. The fine July weather had broken at last; in the dim light the sky showed cloudy and a thin rain was beginning to fall.

I fell asleep immediately. Less than an hour later a squadron of Japanese planes bombed the suburbs of Peking. The noise of the explosions was shattering, driving many to lie in the middle of their courts or stand in doorways, and it is with a little sheepishness and much relief that I recall having slept through it without waking once.

At about eight-thirty, however, I was perfunctorily shaken awake by one of the house coolies. I don't remember now just how it was I first realized that this was the day, perhaps it was the expression on the face of the boy who woke me, but from the first there was no doubt that the time had come.

The Japanese troops were expected to march out of their Legation at any moment. The Chinese behind the barricades were tense to the point of frenzy. Normal traffic had ceased throughout the city; the alleys were full of apprehensive gossips, but the big streets were deserted except for a desperate trickle of refugees aimlessly attempting to find security by exchanging one place for another.

All this we naturally learned by hearsay. Inside the house the courtyards were as insulated and peaceful as ever and it was very hard to understand that scenes of desperation were only a few walls away and violence might be only a few minutes off.

Toward nine o'clock an American marine came to the front gate, delivered a notice, and hurried away. The mimeographed paper advised all Americans to go to their assembly points immediately, prepared for an indefinite stay in the Embassy. Less than a minute after the marine had disappeared, while we were still standing by the gate reading the notice, there came a sudden burst of clattering detonations. The explosions were sharp, abrupt, and deafening — very near, certainly within two hundred feet. My instinctive reaction was a Pekinese one.

'That can't be the guns,' I assured myself. 'It's too close.' In the next split second I hoped that it might be fireworks and only when I saw how it was affecting others did I realize what it had to be. The alley full of idling coolies emptied in a flash. A half-dozen Chinese refugees who had been passing toward Morrison Street in baggage-laden rickshaws rushed into the front court with us. The gate-man slammed shut the gate and locked it.

There was another sharp burst of firing longer than the first, then a frozen hush and this silence so much louder than the explosions, prolonged itself through several telescoping minutes. But at last the gate-man opened the gates again. The refugees departed nervously back in the direction from which they had come. The alley was already full of people crowding in groups as the rumors flew up from the big street; in short order we heard that the firing had been directed at the party of American marines delivering notices and one of the marines had been shot.

This small clash, which resulted in the only injury to an American in all the fighting in the Peking area, was soon superseded by more important calamities and its cause was never completely settled. The marines had been proceeding up Morrison Street on horseback, stopping at the mouths of the side streets inhabited by Americans long enough for a messenger to run in and deliver the notices. Just north of our alley was the first of the Chinese barricades. The Chinese involved subsequently claimed that, as the marines approached, a Japanese ronin stepped into the street in front of them. That was possible but unlikely. It was more probable that the Chinese, for hours tensed to the expectation that a Japanese force would charge down upon them, had mistaken the Americans for Japanese — their uniforms and helmets could look alike to a nervous eye. In any case, they opened fire and the Americans returned it. The mistake of identity was not discovered until several rounds of shot had been exchanged and one of the marines received a slight but bloody wound in the thigh.

Mainly because of this skirmish we decided to try our luck where we were rather than risk a trip to the Embassy. Judging by the experiences of other foreigners moving in, such a journey would have been unpleasant but not dangerous. All day the temper of the streets remained nervous to the verge of panic. Some refugees were nudged with pistols by tense sentries and others were swept about in crowds fleeing from the sound of invisible guns — as there was no fighting in the city that day, the shots must have been fired simply by overwrought soldiers. Still no foreigners were injured except the one marine.

By remaining in the house we avoided even these minor excitements, and when the turmoil over the shooting at our corner died down, we found ourselves marooned in a vacuum, embarked on a marathon of the most stultifying boredom. I know that to be trapped in an Oriental city by the

threat of impending hostilities is a stock situation of melo-
drama, but the consciousness of a picturesqueness in our
position could not occupy us at the time. Actually there
was nothing for us to do but sit and wait for something to
happen, and while a sense of danger may sharpen an experience if it is brief, when prolonged it becomes the most
tiresome factor of all as it hobbles the mind to a single
track.

All day the deadlock in Peking remained unbroken.
The fighting swept up to the walls and the Japanese surrounded the city on all sides except the west, but still the
Chinese showed no intention of relinquishing their position
inside. All day Peking remained tense, its streets empty,
all its ordinary life suspended, and all day we sat in the
house. We sat, we ate, we drank, we sat. Imprisoned
inside the walled courtyards in the center of the walled
city, we enjoyed the unwholesome calm which prevails at
the center of a circular hurricane.

Our knowledge of the invisible battle was approximately
the same as if we had been listening to it by radio and as in
a radio drama the sounds painted the events which produced them with terrible clarity. The curiously soft but
profoundly jarring fu-fu-fu-fu-u-u-mm of the air bombs
presented the slug-shaped missiles streaking down in slanted
groups, the splintering chaos as each hit one split second
after the other, the fat pillar of smoke and dust which billowed up as the echoes faded. The artillery spoke with
a sharper and more concentrated impact of recoiling guns
and shells whistling horizontally across the countryside,
clipping the tops off trees and the corners off houses as they
descended to bury themselves in circular fountains of earth.
The scattered pepperings of rifle-fire clicked rapid snapshots
of men rushing at random through the tall crops, firing as
they ran and sometimes flailing their arms and stumbling
with hot insect-like bites in their elbows, necks, or thighs;
the vicious tittering of machine guns flickered a grotesque

movie of a plane diving low over a marching column and leaving it a black scatter of men hurling themselves into the ditches or lying contorted in the dust.

The courtyards where we sat surrounded by walls and tasteful bric-à-brac constituted a microcosm of the whole museum-city of Peking and even during the explosions it seemed incredible that the ancient honeycomb of tree-shaded enclosures should be jarred by the noises of a modern battle.

My host had lived in Peking for several years, becoming very attached to the city and in particular to the objects he had collected in it; in this crisis which endangered both he expressed a desire to sleep until the trouble was over and did as much as was humanly possible to attain that end. In the next house to the east of his lived another American who had decided not to go into the Embassy. She was one of those resilient expatriate ladies who have spent years living around the world in spots like Mexico, Morocco, Bali, or Majorca; she had no family, but on her travels had accumulated a houseful of handsome things with which she had settled permanently in Peking. On the first morning of the siege friends of hers in the Legation Quarter offered to send a car to fetch her, but she declined to leave her furniture, saying it was really all she had and if anything was to happen to it the same had best happen to her too. In a compound just to the west lived the landlord of both these houses, a perennially cheerful American-educated Chinese. By the use of ladders we could climb from one house to another without going onto the street, and often we four gathered to exchange rumors and speculations, drink, and determinedly assure each other that we were more comfortable than if we had gone into the Legations.

At times the telephone functioned and we were able to hear alarming and contradictory news from the Quarter.

More often, the telephone was dead — the electricity fluctuated, too, but that was not as serious as it would have been in an Occidental city, since we were not dependent on it.

From the stories we heard by telephone and the reports the servants brought in off the streets, we were able to piece together a sketchy idea of what was happening. It was definite that the Japanese, now at the advantage, had commanded the Chinese troops to quit Peking and they threatened to attack if their orders were not obeyed. We heard of various ultimatums and deadlines; the city was to be gassed at noon or bombed at midnight, street-fighting would start at dawn. One after another the rumors arrived, each more unsettling than the last.

Late in the afternoon the anxiety and boredom finally drove my host and myself out of the house. We walked cautiously to the end of the empty alley and looked out on Morrison Street. Either the Chinese soldiers had withdrawn from their barricades or else their tension had relaxed enough to make the street safe. While there was no traffic, not a single automobile, rickshaw, or bicycle, the sidewalks were covered with people. Dressed in white, they milled about anxiously, fanning themselves in the sunless, leaden heat. The clustering groups were static and each person evidently remained within running distance of his own door. With faces greenish-pale and tightly drawn, all were talking hurriedly and worriedly; they were the wires over which the many rumors traveled.

Early that evening the servants came in off the street with jubilant accounts of Chinese victories at Lanfeng, Fengtai, and other strategic points. It seemed too good to be true, but later newsboys ran through the alley screaming extras with the same report. As it proved, this news was indeed false, cruelly false, since it raised the spirits of the Pekinese just at the time when they should have been abandoning hope

Later in the evening came rumors of Japanese successes and it was said that the deadlock inside the city must now be broken. Midnight had been appointed the zero hour and if the Chinese troops did not retreat the city was to be attacked from the air.

But by this time neither my host nor I could any longer convince ourselves that the danger was real. After so many hours of expecting calamity momentarily, it was no longer possible to believe in it. We needed sleep, so we went to bed and slept through until morning, saving ourselves considerable trouble.

As we heard next day, during the first part of the night apprehension had increased to the pitch of panic. The central telephone office even went so far as to call telephone holders advising them of remedies to have on hand in case of gas and of the safest shelter to take from bombs. But midnight came and nothing happened. At two in the morning the Chinese troops quietly marched out the western and northwestern gates. By the time we woke up, it was all over. Though no Japanese had entered the city, every Chinese soldier had left it. Peking had fallen.

XVI. THE CAGE

OF THE slow return to an altered normality, I have the most jumbled recollections. Through the first day after the withdrawal of the Chinese troops, it was considered unsafe to move about the city and we remained seated in the house, hearing much from the telephone and the verbal telegraph of the alleys, but knowing nothing. It was rumored that the Chinese troops had left for strategic reasons and would soon return. At the same time it was said that the Japanese were planning a triumphal entry, after which Peking would be given over for pillage. Many feared that in retreating the Chinese had only prepared a trap for the Japanese and that fierce fighting would break out after the arrival of the invaders. There were reports that the city would then be bombed by Chinese. With no violence to put a clean end to the tension which had been growing during the past weeks, the situation collapsed into a wallow of uncertainty and unbridled rumor. The Pekinese were stunned by the conquest of their city; it was the more incredible that it should have been so peacefully effected.

There were rumors that hundreds of Japanese and Korean ronins had been turned loose to terrorize and pillage and on that first afternoon the servants reported that a Korean on a bicycle had come up the alley examining the numbers on the houses until he reached our gate, then turned and departed. That night the landlord dug out his pistol and the neighbor produced another, pearl-handled, from among her furniture. No more ronins appeared, however, and we heard no reliable reports of depredations anywhere in Peking.

The city's dazed calm was extraordinary because for an interval during the change of control it was without real police protection. When the Chinese troops departed, the police remained in the city, but they gave up their arms and in large part left their posts. It was hours before they accepted the inevitable and went back to work; when they did reappear, incidentally, they had only changed from khaki summer clothes into black-and-white winter uniforms to signalize the change of régimes.

At all hours the noise of guns still resounded from very near, and in the city all peace-time activities were still suspended. The barricades remained across the big streets and the gates in the outer wall were kept shut, guarded by skeleton crews of police; hordes of frightened refugees had collected on both sides of the walls, some anxious to flee the city, others to enter, but the gates were never opened, as it was uncertain what troop movements might yet center on them.

Over the telephone on the second day came the story of how the first gates were opened during this anxious period. Apparently it was the custom of the British Legation guard to wear roses in their lapels to celebrate the anniversary of the battle of Minden, waged between French and Anglo-Hanoverian troops in Westphalia on August 1, 1759. Just before the final trouble in Peking, a messenger on a bicycle had been dispatched to Fengtai where the required flowers were being grown, but, as he was delayed by fighting along his road, he was unable to return before the gates had been closed and fortified. Immediately on his appearance before the walls, the British Legation set its influence crashing against the police and after much telephoning the sandbags and barbed wire at the gate were laboriously removed and the twenty-foot bolts shot back. The great metal-studded portals swung out and the first man to enter the beleaguered city cycled in, laden with roses.

We foreigners were spectators to a war, to something which should under no condition have an audience. It was a puzzling and distressing situation. We had the luxury of not being forced to anger or hate, but at the same time were exposed to events tolerable only to closed minds. As spectators we occupied the same position in relation to the war which women once traditionally held in a combatant country, and indeed the attitudes of most of us seemed womanish — I use the word as a term of reproach but not unfairly, since individuals of either sex placed in the same artificial position go to the same extremes.

As the war receded, many were succumbing to the morbid fascination of sight-seeing, and chased after excitement, or, as it proved to be more usually, after horror. They wanted 'Experiences' — comfortably come by of course. Their aim was to see life, but their achievement was to see, and usually to photograph, the more spectacular aspects of death.

On the other hand, some tried to ignore the whole business. They proceeded with their personal life as if nothing had happened, taking the view that, if people should persist in slashing, mashing, and killing each other in their neighborhood, they would treat it as any other dirty, unmentionable thing and overlook it.

In the middle of one evening — I think it was the third night after the fall of the city — we were sitting stupidly in the house when we heard the faint sound of music coming from overhead. Several blocks south we could see the tall bulk of the Hôtel de Pékin and along one shoulder of it tiny figures were moving about in a flat area of radiance; the roof had reopened for dancing.

Though martial law was still strictly enforced and the streets were absolutely forbidden after dark, we were able to reach the hotel quite easily by the back alleys, and it was indeed an agreeable change to dance and talk in this cool place instead of sitting in a stupor in the sweltering house. The hotel was outside the Legation Quarter, but it stood opposite a gate in the Italian Embassy and was consequently accessible to the refugees; since boredom had become a problem even in the crowded Quarter, quite a number of gentlemen in white mess-jackets and ladies in chiffon gowns were swinging around the polished cement dance-floor to the tootling of the small American band.

From the roof after dark the war was only an occasional flickering of lights on the black horizon, but here for the first time I got some idea of its actual nature, for here gathered the newsmen and cameramen who had been at work beyond the walls. Several parties had just that day managed to get out the South Gate and drive down the road to Nan Yuan — the South Barracks. What they saw was horrifying enough to make quite satisfactory copy, for the ruined country was littered grotesquely with the dead and near-dead, all of them rotting and swelling in the heat.

The carnage was said to be most appalling where a column of Chinese fleeing in trucks and automobiles had run into a nest of Japanese machine guns. The cars still stood in a crazy line, each one packed with corpses. The chef d'oeuvre was a staff car under which a dead horse, inexplicably wedged, was swelling and jacking upward a cargo of dead men. Still all agreed that none of these sights or even the smells were as harrowing as the sounds which hung over the scenes of battle, for the moans and screams of the wounded hidden in the crops were still unceasing.

Around the dance-floor such tales were told and listened to with excitement. The dancers would congregate with glistening eyes, eager to be horrified between dances, and it was edifying to observe the wave of rather wet-lipped flirtatiousness which followed in the wake of any peculiarly gruesome story. But really it was no longer so agreeable to dance or sit drinking cool drinks, conscious that the lights above the tables made an island in the sky to men decaying on the plain, or that with a favorable breeze the wretches might even hear snatches of the dance-music.

Without decision I had embarked on the passive attitude toward the war, but in the next few days I became extremely restless. It was possible for me to return to my house during the day, but I found that I could not climb back into the ivory tower and isolate myself in the life I'd enjoyed during July. It appeared that a war could make most occupations seem futile near it, and painting was of course the first to look useless. For the time being I could not go back to it, and when I found I could borrow an automobile from a Chinese friend, I volunteered with it for Red Cross work.

XVII. OUTSIDE AND INSIDE

THE machinery of relief in Peking was extremely disorganized and it took me several aimless days to find what to do and how to do it. The foreign colony was forming a branch of the Red Cross which concerned itself with supplying and distributing medical equipment inside the city, and at first I worked for this organization, driving doctors and nurses from one hospital to another, delivering batches of bedding, bandages, disinfectants, or mosquito netting. But before long the need for this kind of transportation became known and more than enough private cars, complete with their Chinese chauffeurs, were loaned.

The important job was still the carrying into the city of as many wounded as possible. The foreign newsmen who went outside brought in all those they could load on their cars, and other parties of Occidentals, notably a group of Germans, going out independently brought in dozens on each of their trips. A few sight-seers had also managed to get beyond the gates, and while their main interest was in the use of their cameras and the search for souvenirs, they generally brought in wounded when returning. This took care of only the most accessible sufferers, however, and a multitude still lay in need of help.

The bulk of the work was being handled by the Chinese Red Cross and it was proceeding very slowly. The gates of the city were already under Japanese control and as they were opened only occasionally, without discernible schedule, it was impossible to be certain of getting out except by going to a gate and waiting; many cars spent valuable hours or entire days going from one closed gate to another. Even when they did get out the efficiency of the ambulances was not great, for their crews of hired chauffeurs and student volunteers showed a natural reluctance to go near any Japanese. There were rumors that Red Cross parties had been fired upon and whether they were true or not, they provided an opportunity for a foreigner to be somewhat useful. The Chinese who went out were very eager for the protection the presence of an Occidental was felt to give; at that time foreign prestige was still practically intact.

My first trip out was to the village of Tsing Ho, about twelve miles north of Peking. It was reported that after the battle at Hsi Yuan a company of Chinese fled here; Japanese pursued, several hours of fighting followed, and in the end the village was partially demolished by Japanese bombing planes. Some wounded had reached Peking and they affirmed that there were many more still in the village.

We went to leave the city through Hsi Chih Men (the Northwest Gate). When we arrived at the walls, the great metal-studded portals were shut and barred, fortified with sandbags and guarded by a few Japanese soldiers and a company of sullen Chinese police armed with night-sticks. Along the avenue leading to the gate stood a huge silent crowd, some with bundles and other luggage who were country people caught inside the city by the trouble, and empty-handed hundreds who were the idly curious.

Rather surprisingly the guards immediately agreed to let us go out. They rounded up a dozen of the nearest bystanders and set them to moving the sandbags from in front of the tall vaulted stone passage. Then they had them push back a brass-bound bolt the size of a telegraph pole, and one of the ancient thirty-foot doors was laboriously swung wide enough for a car to pass.

We were jolting into its maw when suddenly the crowd behind surged forward pushing aside the police and ignoring the cries of the Japanese. Thirty or forty scrambling men and women escaped the guards and managed to hurl themselves through the opening ahead of us, while the others jogged behind in a tight-packed phalanx. When we passed under, we confronted another wave of yelling runners clutching luggage and children and pieces of furniture. As soon as the cars cleared the gate, the two tides converged on it from opposite directions and the narrow passage was jammed with a screaming, pushing mob, half of them fighting to get in, half of them fighting to get out.

Into this multitude the police charged, whacking and gouging with their sticks. By main force they began to move the great gate shut again, but still a stream of people flowed in and out the narrowing gap. As the door swung farther in, they pushed through in single file, with those coming out crawling, squeezing, stumbling over those going in. The last one in was a fat and disheveled merchant in a Panama hat and oyster-white silk robe, balancing a patent-leather suitcase over his head. The last one out was an old farm woman stumping along on bound feet with her arms miraculously full of odd bundles, a bird-cage hooked over her elbow. She cackled triumphantly when the great gate ground shut at her heels.

As we drove away from the city on the road to the Summer Palace, I apprehensively expected at every bend to be plunged into scenes of desolation, but on the contrary I had never seen the country looking lovelier. The low clouds which had been drizzling over Peking almost every day since its fall had temporarily broken into sailing cumuli and wide splashes of sunlight and shade moved slowly across the green landscape. After weeks cooped up inside the city, practically restricted to a single house, it was delightful to see again the waving fields of rich crops, the glistening banks of trees, and the line of blue hills in the distance.

But along the willow-shaded highway streamed a dark tide of refugees hurrying in both directions. Those going away from the city were mostly men, empty-handed or swinging a few small possessions twisted in cloths; they were rickshaw boys and other coolie laborers returning to their native villages to be with their relatives in case of emergency. Inbound were whole families traveling in carts or rickshaws, carrying with them piles of clothing, chairs, cooking utensils, scrolls, mirrors, bowls of goldfish, sewing machines, lacquered chests electric fans, and other prized possessions. They were benighted Peking vacationists from the Western Hills and the richer class of village-dwellers, fleeing to the comparative safety of the city.

About five miles out, we passed a patrol of Japanese, a company of tired, dirty men resting on the edge of the road with their rifles piled beside them, morosely smoking, scratching themselves, knocking the mud from their boots, or sprawling on their backs with their eyes shut. Their small square faces, sharp with fatigue and black with several days' stubble of beard, made a startling contrast to the round hairless ones of the Chinese multitude. As the stream of refugees swept ceaselessly past, each nationality stared at the other with hostile curiosity, as at insecurely caged beasts.

Along this main road the territory was indisputably conquered and almost every farmhouse displayed a make-shift Japanese flag. There was something very pathetic about these white rags on which circles had been splashed with red paint or to which disks of red paper were pinned; it was lucky for the peace of mind of the simple farmers that the flag of Nippon was so easy to imitate. Some of the refugees wore red-dotted handkerchiefs fastened to their sleeves and some carried tiny paper flags fastened on long twigs.

Beyond Tsing Hua University, empty and apparently abandoned, we left the paved highway and proceeded cross-country over a network of dusty lanes. In this area there had been fighting three or four days before, but the peaceful appearance of the landscape was hardly marred. Only along the roads the grass and underbrush was trampled flat and occasionally through the crops an erratic swath marked the passage of a tank. There were even a few farmers at work in the fields, but they were timid and vanished at sight of our cars.

We entered Tsing Ho through a gray street empty except for a few dazed peasants. The silent, shuttered houses were scarred by machine-gun fire and at the far end of the village they gave way to a flat field of desolation. An old man standing against a truncated wall explained that the Chinese troops had been concentrated around the police station at this end of the main street and here they had been attacked by planes. By a fluke the police station itself was still standing, minus its front wall, but around it stretched a shapeless confusion of splintered timber, tiles, and adobe bricks, broken crockery and glass, torn paper, straw, and clothing.

Seeping up from under the ruins was a suffocating brassy stench. I dreaded what each glance might disclose, but the sources of the smell were invisible. Only in one valley of débris lay a frightful fly-covered mass of green and red corruption. My stomach twisted at the sight and it was an immense relief when I realized that I was looking not at the remains of a man, but at an exploded pile of watermelons.

We were told that soon after the attack from the air, Tsing Ho had been partially surrounded by Japanese troops, and, although they later abandoned their attack and never did enter the town, the Chinese troops had fled. Inside the police station were several abandoned boxes of potato-masher hand grenades, looking remarkably like cases of ginger ale, and in the street before it was a tangled heap of cast-off uniforms. I was later to find that the whole countryside was dotted with these garments, strewn in the fields, the roads, and the ditches; singly, in dozens, or in great piles like this one. As no rifles ever lay with the clothing, it was possible to believe that each abandoned uniform indicated the evolution of another guerrilla warrior, from then on indistinguishable from China's hundred million farmers.

Through Tsing Ho the Chinese internes in our party went from house to house, inquiring for wounded. We had heard that there were at least a hundred casualties here, and the appearance of the village made that seem an underestimate. In a quarter of an hour we learned the astonishing fact that there was not a single wounded person to be taken to Peking. The injured soldiers had been removed at the approach of the Japanese and the wounded civilians, of whom there were admitted to be a good many, were unwilling to leave home.

It was a tragic situation, as without medical aid many would undoubtedly die. Still there was an unshakable conviction that to go with the Red Cross would cost money. These country folk could not believe that they were being offered something for nothing, and the wounded, or their families, had all decided that a free demise was preferable to an expensive convalescence.

Also as Peking was known to be full of Japanese there was understandable apprehension about going into it. These people were medieval and their idea of war was not complicated by ethics. As the war has developed, their conception of it has proved true only too often and perhaps our efforts were out of place.

Our departure from Tsing Ho was supremely anticlimactic. We had got into our empty trucks and were ready to drive away when a farm woman ran up with her naked little son in her arms. She pointed out that the child had some sort of boil on his penis and asked for medical aid. One of the Chinese internes got down from his place and, after some minutes of probing and pinching, cured the condition. We waited in the devastated street, which was silent except for the screams of the infant, seven men in two trucks, a large party for so small a job.

This fiasco was characteristic of the fumbling, flurried work of those days. False reports sent us hustling all over the countryside. We would hear that there were twenty wounded or fifty wounded in a certain place, but on going there would discover either that there never had been any injured, that they had been removed, or that they were unwilling to come into the city. It was a comedy of disorganization, rendered completely unfunny by the fact that all the time, on all sides, there was desperate need for help if we could but locate it.

Most of my trips at this time were into territory to the west, occupied by Japanese troops recuperating after the battles before Peking. Fortunately in this area the fighting had not been severe nor long drawn out and the men had not been brutalized as those in other parts of China later became. The iron discipline of the Japanese army was still apparently perfect. Though there were rumors of frightfulness I did not encounter evidence of it nor did I hear any reports of it from sources which could be identified as reliable. The worst offenses of the Japanese seemed to be in the line of petty thievery and meannesses which are no doubt the habit of any conquering army.

As a matter of fact, it was during these trips that I first had the slightest sympathy for the Japanese. My previous experiences with them had been limited to the military police, the petty officials, and the ronin class in China — admittedly the scum of the nation. This was my first contact with ordinary citizens.

Most of the soldiers around Peking were very young, obviously fresh from training school, and it was hard to resent as individuals these hordes of grinning children helping themselves to the benefits of the countryside and only incidentally making life miserable for the Chinese they encountered. They sat in the shade drinking tea and beer, which they paid for whenever they felt they could afford to. They ranged through the farms taking eggs, vegetables, and chickens, with grins which showed how fine they thought these stolen goods would taste. They amused themselves by trying to speak Chinese to the local farmers, who naturally accorded their efforts the same welcome they would have given a cobra attempting to make friends.

The dusty North China plain where clear water was a rarity was plainly a disagreeable environment for the islanders and when we went out past the Summer Palace, then the Japanese army headquarters, we found every brook and pond full of naked little Japs scrubbing themselves and rinsing their underwear. They were delighted to be still alive and many would laugh and wave at the Red Cross trucks as we passed. All this would have been jolly if it hadn't been for the sick excitement which tensed the Chinese drivers and internes at sight of them.

One incident in particular destroyed for me the Japanese soldier as an ogre. One morning we were trying to get to the Western Hills following a rumor that there were casualties in a temple there; we already had two wounded Chinese in the back of our truck. Before the Jade Fountain we were hailed by a pair of Japanese sentries who refused to allow us to pass, then very gingerly began searching the cars. Small parties of Japanese were continually being ambushed at this time and as the sentries searched, such an eventuality was obviously in their minds.

We had one Ford sedan and a large truck entirely covered in by a canvas top. First they went over the smaller car carefully, even to looking under the seats; then, after examining the driver's cabin of the truck with equal caution, they went around to its back. Nervously they loaded their rifles and began poking open the rear door with the points of their bayonets.

As the door swung out, their pose and expression showed that the two small Japanese expected to find the truck full of armed Chinese soldiers crouching to spring at them, but of course the opening door only revealed two miserable Chinese boys staring up with alarm from the floor of the truck. It was a memorable tableau; two Japanese in the road, two Chinese in the truck. Not one of the four was more than seventeen and it would have been impossible to tell which pair was more terrified.

Before long it began to appear as if all the urgent relief work had been accomplished. The wounded along the roads open to automobile traffic had been picked up and it was comfortable to assume that the others, in less accessible places, had either taken care of themselves or died. In searching for those in need of aid, we were beginning to find ourselves used by those who did not really need assistance. Several times I helped bring in men who, as I later decided, should under no condition have entered the city. These were Chinese soldiers with only minor wounds; it was feared that the presence in Peking of any number of such able-bodied men might rouse the Japanese to clean the hospitals of the wounded and healed alike.

The slightly wounded soldiers who did choose to come in with us were pathetic figures. It was easy to see why they wanted to come to the relief organizations in Peking, even though it meant putting themselves at the mercy of their enemies. Far from home and cut off from their companies, they faced the prospect of becoming either beggars or bandits.

Their ignorance of the nature of the war and the place they occupied in it as individuals was pitiful. On one trip into the eastern suburbs I helped bring in four soldiers; none of them was injured so badly that he could not walk and all their wounds were healing cleanly, but they were very anxious to enter the city. At the gate as a matter of routine the guard asked what company they belonged in. They were not in uniform and should have denied that they were soldiers at all. Instead they replied that they were Pao-an-tui (militia) from Tungchow.

We were horrified. The Pao-an-tui had been responsible for the massacre of Japanese civilians at Tungchow and since then Japanese patrols had been relentlessly hunting them down with the intention of exterminating every last man. We drove the four poor fools into the city, told them never to say again that they were Pao-an-tui, and delivered them at a different hospital from the one to which we had told the guards at the gate we would take them. I have no idea what finally became of them.

In a military way the Peking area quieted very rapidly. A week after leaving the city the Chinese troops had officially withdrawn on all sides to a distance of at least a dozen miles. In the south they fell back beyond the Liuli River and in the west they retreated into the hills. In the north and east, the territory from which the Japanese advance had first come, there were of course no formal Chinese lines, though the country was said to be infested with small parties of soldiers cut off from their companies, now living off the land and trying to keep out of the way of the Japanese.

And for the time being the invaders did not press their attack. With almost symbolic promptness the weather had turned bad with the fall of the city and this delayed rainy season made the first weeks of August miserable. It also rendered the clay roads of North China impassable to Japan's mechanized troops, so for some time the region was calm except for occasional local 'mopping-up' operations.

By the second week in August, life inside the walls had regained its usual tenor to an amazing extent. All the foreign refugees left the Legation Quarter — it was a popular story that the American authorities had to tear down their tent city in order to get rid of some who were loath to leave such comfortable quarters and luxuriously cheap meals. The foreigners' small world inside the city was disconcertingly settled and almost everyone had reconstructed his or her special variety of calm. While there might not be

quite the spaciously carefree atmosphere of pre-war days,
there was a comfortable feeling of security from violence
and that, for the time being, was enough.

Even socially the city was returning to its accustomed
ways. From a distance it may seem grisly that anyone
should have been bent on entertainment at such a time,
but from the Pekinese point of view the situation was just
bad enough to make distractions welcome and still not so
bad as to make them inappropriate. There were no large
parties yet — martial law made them hardly feasible —
but at six and seven in the afternoon, in courtyards all over
the city, little groups gathered to be stimulated by the flow
of rumors and gin. I continued to live downtown and after
an aimless or harrowing day outside the walls, any relaxa-
tion was pleasant.

It was typical of Peking that by the time reports of
disasters outside filtered through its walls they had somehow lost their element of tragedy. While there were some
subjects which could not possibly be viewed divertingly,
the war was nevertheless productive of anecdotes, and the
minor adjustments necessary between the two races made
rich sources of tittle-tattle.

Much was heard of the difficulty the Japanese had in
keeping clean. It was said that the Chinese farmers in the
occupied territory had two major complaints against their
new lords; they raped their daughters and bathed in their
fresh-water tanks. Some day, it was agreed, they would go
too far.

One tale in particular made a comfortable talisman
against more disquieting rumors of atrocity. It seemed
that when the war broke out a certain Chinese doctor and
his very attractive wife had been vacationing at a hotel in
the Western Hills. They were unable to return to Peking
in time and, after the Chinese retreated, their hotel was
visited by a Japanese patrol. The soldiers lined up all the
women in the hotel and after deliberation selected the

doctor's wife and marched her upstairs at the point of a
bayonet. After an hour or two she came down again
trembling with fury. What the soldiers had wanted of her
was to scrub their backs while they were in the bath, a duty
any Japanese woman would expect to perform but un-
thinkable to a Chinese.

Under Peking's emollient influence even pillage had
whimsical aspects. One lady whose villa in the Western
Hills had been broken into by a roving band of Japanese
managed to visit it a few days later and found it strangely
plundered. All photographs of her three handsome daughters were missing, as were their more frivolous pieces of
underwear. Nothing else of value was gone, and there was
no damage done except to the villa's stock of toilet-paper.
This had been unwound and cut up — not simply slashed,
but with a care which spoke of hours of labor it had been
snipped into lacey streamers and fanciful doilies which
were strewn all over the house.

Of course even to Peking the subject of military occupation could not always be nice and the Japanese whimsicality
was sometimes coupled with a brutality which indicated
what might happen in less favored neighborhoods, should
army discipline break down. At another inn in the Western
Hills a Chinese lady had been trapped with her two small
children and in the course of events a party of Japanese
appeared. When the soldiers came into the inn, the children, both under ten, showed signs of fright. This irritated
the soldiers and to teach him not to be afraid of Japanese,
they picked up the little boy and threw him out the window.

It was a ground-floor window and the child was not
seriously injured, but witnessing this, his infant sister ran
screaming from the house and hid in a near-by cornfield.
When the Japanese had gone, the mother and her friends
ran out calling to the child to come back, but she scuttled in
panic from those who were looking for her and would not
even answer their cries. Although it was raining violently,

she spent the night crouching out in the field and it was late the next day before she dared return to the inn.

On August eighth the Japanese army staged its official entry into Peking. Through all the morning a long column of troops, trucks, and tanks filed into the city through Yung Ting Men (the South Gate), parading up the central avenues before they divided to occupy the barracks vacated by the Chinese. I went out of the city with the Red Cross that day and missed the more spectacular parts of the procession, but I did get back in time to see the tail end of it. Up Hatamen Street was rolling a thundering column of trucks loaded with food and ammunition. All of them were draped with coarse netting in which cornstalks and foliage had been woven for camouflage; even the grim dust-covered drivers wore on their helmets small nets like lettuce bags, into which leaves and grasses, and sometimes flowers, were twisted with an unexpectedly coquettish effect.

By the Legation Quarter the several hundred Japanese and Korean civilians of Peking were massed, waving small Japanese flags with shrill enthusiasm. Near them stood a number of Chinese paid or coerced to wave the same flags; photographs of them were to be subsequently published in Japan and elsewhere as pictures of the oppressed North Chinese welcoming their liberators.

The atmosphere of the rest of the city was characterized by a hostile apathy which contrasted strangely with the vociferations of this organized cheering section; the idlers who usually swarmed to witness the smallest demonstration were nowhere to be seen. Only an ordinary number of passers-by stood at the corners waiting for an opportunity to cross, and some of the householders along the line of march stood in their doorways, holding their small children from running out to play in the road.

For an American the triumphal procession was embarrassing, as it demonstrated that the mechanized Japanese

neat and clean, they made pictures which must have given pleasure to the families in Japan to whom the films were mailed; these were soldiers who had been sent directly to occupy Peking after its fall and none of them had yet seen active service.

Of course the Winter Palace was now shunned by Chinese, though groups of coolies stood by the gate to talk and look in at the sporting conquerors. Like the rest of Peking, all the other streets of my neighborhood, even small alleys like the one where I lived, were dotted with similar groups of idlers, talking endlessly and trying to compensate for such dismal developments by the circulation of hopeful rumors.

Time and again the population was galvanized by tales of a victorious Chinese army appearing at the very gates and such reports were given ground by unaccountable explosions very near the walls. Until the opening of major hostilities at Shanghai, it was believed that the Nanking Government was sending huge forces of men, tanks, and planes to blast the Japanese out of North China. At one time it was claimed that bombers had already been sent North and many thought that the planes seen flying very high over the city were Chinese, not Japanese. The appearance of these ships could always bring large crowds into the streets to stare and speculate.

It was also rumored that the Japanese had sustained fatal losses, that already the war was proving too expensive for them, and so on and on. This sort of wishful thinking went to fantastic and pathetic lengths; at one time it was said that the Japanese were running so short of men that they had been forced to resort to dummies to preserve an effect of military strength. Trucks full of Japanese soldiers were often seen in the streets and it was claimed that only the soldiers around the sides of the trucks were real. Those in the center were inflated imitations, artfully made of rubber.

Chou naturally was an enthusiastic subscriber to such

tales, and one morning while I was eating breakfast he rushed in from the street saying he had just been talking with a man whose uncle's partner knew a girl who had seen such a soldier fall out of a truck.

He had bounced!

The English-language paper of Peking, *The Peking Chronicle*, subsidized by Nanking but run by a British staff and serviced by foreign news agencies, provided a welcome amount of reliable information and each morning erected some small structure of fact in this shifting morass of rumor. Isolated as I was in the northern part of the city, without a telephone and without foreign neighbors, it supplied my only regular contact with the events of the war.

The *Chronicle* had been printed every day of the actual siege even though it could not be delivered until the streets were open to traffic again. Soon after the Japanese entry, however, it failed to appear one morning, and when I sent Chou to see if he could fetch a copy, he returned saying that all the newsboys had been caught by Japanese and impressed for work in the barracks. For a day or two the paper was still printed and was available to all who came to get it, but one morning Chou came back reporting that no papers were to be had. When I went downtown I heard that a company of Japanese had marched into the newspaper office and flatly ordered that publication be suspended; as the controlling stock in the paper was owned by Chinese, the British editors were unable to protest effectively.

Thereafter I was left floating in my elegant retreat, bereft of all regular connection with the outside world. After an intolerably newless day or two I subscribed to the *Journal de Pékin*, a small French-language paper which was run entirely on French capital and could not be interfered with. The war had seemed remote enough before, but when I began reading about it in French it receded beyond all reality. This conflict, described in the elegant phrases and resounding periods of the language of Racine, could not be the grim and dirty business taking place just beyond the walls. It was one of those stately clashes such as are depicted in eighteenth-century prints, waged between mandarins and samurai in embroidered armor.

XVIII. A WET DAY

I T TOOK only one day to destroy entirely my budding complacence. I had decided that the necessary relief work was done and was about to give up going to the Red Cross when by chance I descended into new territory south of the city. Word had come in that a soldier of some importance, the son of a former President of China in fact, was lying wounded in a village about twenty miles southeast of Peking. Friends of his family in foreign diplomatic circles had arranged to send an old French professional soldier, an ex-aviator of Chang Tso Lin's, to fetch him. A truck from the Red Cross was dispatched to drive this man on his way as far as possible and I went along on the truck for whatever assistance my white face might give in getting it back inside Peking, should the Frenchman be unable to return before dark.

The August morning was hot and overcast, and as we reached the Yung Ting Gate in the center of the lower wall of Peking, a tepid drizzle began falling. After only ten minutes of telephoning, the Japanese guard at the gate opened the huge doors and let us out, warning, however, that unless we returned between five and six in the afternoon we would not be allowed in again. Outside it took a good half-hour to go the first two hundred feet because the narrow road leading to the gate and the bridge over the moat were packed with the carts of refugees and the barrows of farmers with produce for the markets inside. The tide of waiting vehicles was desperately jammed from curb to curb and we could make passage for ourselves only by walking to the outermost carts and then urging them back one by one, with pleas and abuse.

But once we had skidded and crashed through this tangle the road south was deserted except for an occasional farmer walking silently under his brown-paper umbrella, between the lines of dripping willows. Less than a mile beyond the walls we found the way cut by a huge winding ditch gouged across it and into the crops on either side. With some difficulty we passed by driving over the spongy wet fields, through a grove in which half the trees were erect and green, and half were slewed sideways at all angles, their trunks splintered by cannon fire, their leaves brown and withered. Back on the motor-track again we drove down the winding avenue past more prostrate trees and fields of rich crops scuffed and broken in winding alleys. Here the trees which had not been felled by cannon had been peppered by bullets and were dotted with dead branches and twigs — brown against green — which hung from partially severed limbs. The crops which were not completely ruined were snipped and twisted as by an eccentric barber. The earth itself was spoiled in many places, torn and gouged into craters now full of stagnant water.

Not far beyond the first trench I noticed a farmer walking on the road about a hundred yards ahead with his hand cupped over his nose. Immediately we also entered the smell. I had known the odor of the long-dead before, but only as a minor unpleasantness attendant on dead rats or dead birds, something to close one's nose against and hurry past. This terrible sweet metallic stink could not be passed. It permeated every square foot of air and tainted every breeze. Like a heavy gas it seemed to coat the countryside, and every breath, however gingerly taken, was almost palpably a gulp of decay.

The road here was understandably empty of the living, but soon after entering the smell, we began passing the dead. It was at least ten days since the battle and the hot rainy weather had made frightful sport with the unburied, having swollen them into an unspeakable race of prostrate monsters. In the distant fields were lumpish figures, half hidden in the crops. their stiff limbs embracing the ground, the grass, or the air in horrible, comic attitudes. From the black water of the ditch beside the road projected pale bloated clots which could be either knees, shoulders, or scalps.

The dead men actually in the road had been removed, but many dead horses were still littered along it, making driving a complicated job. The sprawling carcasses were distended into huge mottled globes from which the legs, ridiculously spindly by contrast, stuck out at unlikely angles. Soon we passed the motor caravan of which so much had been heard on the roof-garden in Peking; the dead passengers were gone, but under the leading car the gored horse, now a shapeless mound festooned with decay, still jacked the shattered front wheels skyward.

About eight miles south of Peking we reached the village of Nan Yuan, desolate and deserted except for a few coolies standing with their arms folded, in doorways or under the eaves of the silent shops. The empty streets were a morass of mud, crackling and hissing under the rain which had now increased to a downpour. Some of the houses had been destroyed by bombing or artillery fire and most of the others were shuttered and locked, apparently deserted. As in the north, from the doorposts flapped pitiful little paper imitations of Japanese flags, streaked and disintegrating in the wet.

Just beyond the village were the South Barracks and the Peking airdrome, the scene of the last fierce fighting before the Chinese troops in this area retreated north to the city. Though the country had been conquered by the Japanese, it had not been occupied. The victorious troops had gone on to the west of Peking, leaving only a small company to hold the barracks. This garrison at that time formed the only Japanese outpost south of the city and beyond it the country was supposed to be empty of soldiers for eight or ten miles to the Chinese lines on the Liuli River.

Driving down the main street of the village we came in sight of the Japanese sentries at the entrance to the barracks, whereupon the Chinese driver of the ambulance became nervous and refused to go farther. As the road the Frenchman had to take led through the barracks, he and I went ahead on foot to see if the car would be allowed to pass. Walking widely around a glum sentry tending a machine gun under a leaking straw shelter, we found a very small and nervous detachment of Japanese soldiers, just then decapitating a chicken and washing a pile of vegetables in the great court surrounded by half-demolished black buildings. Owing to the lack of a common language we were unable to learn whether we would be allowed to drive through or not, but when we walked on down the road to try and see if it were clear, we found a large tree fallen squarely across it, destroying all possibility of driving farther.

We returned to the village and the Frenchman prepared to leave on foot. At the last minute the Chinese who had come from Peking to guide him became panicky and refused to go, being prevailed upon only by the threat that unless he went he would not be taken back into the city.

The rest of us — Chinese driver, mechanic, student volunteer, and myself — were about to start on the return trip to Peking when three men of Nan Yuan came up saying that there were a number of wounded at a farm three li (about a mile) to the southwest. All the roads in that direction were wagon-roads and they were flooded, so to fetch them it would be necessary to walk to the place and carry the injured back on litters.

The student volunteer promptly undertook to hire enough carriers; it may seem shocking that it should be necessary to pay Chinese civilians to help in the rescue of wounded Chinese soldiers, but these wretched country coolies lived from hand to mouth under the best conditions. At that time they were entering a very uncertain period and can hardly be censured for trying to make what they could while they could. Also in the country in China, the participation of a foreigner in any enterprise has always made it a traditional source of easy money.

The extreme youth of the student was a handicap in bargaining with the hard-bitten country folk and after half an hour of haggling, he had come to no possible agreement. In the meanwhile another car had arrived from the city, containing two courageous Chinese ladies who were attempting to ascertain the number of needy refugees in the country around Peking. They vigorously entered into our bargaining and armed with a commanding manner and plenty of cash soon arranged for nearly fifty coolies.

Just before noon, at the head of this small army the Chinese student and I made our way slowly out of Nan Yuan, heading to the south along a road which skirted the high clay wall of the barracks and airdrome. The rains of the past week had put all unsurfaced roads and paths in a condition which made them difficult going even for those on foot, and we struggled through mud inches deep, a soft gluey stew which sucked tenaciously at shoes and made each step difficult. About half a mile from the village the road turned away from the wall and led southwestward through open country. Slipping and stumbling in the mud, we followed it out into what was technically no-man's-land.

This stretch of farmland was all sown with the crop called kao-liang, a cereal plant which resembles corn but grows to a height of fifteen feet or more. The green stalks walled us in completely. The country was dead level and a low ceiling of leaden clouds, from which dropped thick gray curtains of rain, cut off any sight of the hills in the distance. Plodding through the mud at the base of the towering kao-liang, we had no more command of our direction than ants in a hayfield.

I was also inclined to feel like a bug on witnessing the handiwork of my kind as displayed in these dripping fields. Every few yards we passed through deserted scenes of battle. Here the kao-liang was trampled flat in little clearings or cut in twisting swaths down which opened sickening vistas of corruption. Among the puddles the ground was strewn with dead men and horses, for no effort had yet been made to bury those which lay so far from the road. Except for the dull green of wet leaves the prevailing colors in these scenes of recent conflict were brown and dirty gray, spotted only by the phosphorescent blue, purple, and orange, and sickening bloated white of decay. Indeed, in total effect the fields made a frightful travesty of all the heroic battle-scenes ever painted, with their bright flags and weapons and scarlet splashes of blood. The dead men were sprawled awkwardly in the mud, most of them in the impromptu attitudes of a sudden and uncomfortable sleep. There were some horses in the rocking-horse position characteristic of conventionally drawn battle-scenes, but instead of being alive, upright, and mounted by gesticulating riders, they were upside-down and dead, their rigid legs pointing at the sky, their bellies gaping, their necks twisted, broken, and buried in the mud, their riders either vanished or lying at a distance, contorted and stiff.

The fighting in this section had apparently taken place several days before the skirmishes on the main road, for the corpses were in a more advanced state of decay. Here they were no longer swollen, but had burst or deflated into masses of sodden matter. The flesh, now abloom with putrescence, was rapidly melting into the ground and already the shape of the skeletons had begun to emerge.

Because of their greater quantities of decaying matter the dead horses should have been more odious, but the dead men had a horror which revolted more than the eye and the nose. To no matter what inhuman shape their disintegration had brought them, they retained a grotesquely human personality. The gaping jaws, the rotten cheeks, and empty eye-sockets could still suggest the expression of a face. Even to see the corpses at a distance — dark shapes of ripped flesh and matted hair and cloth sunk down among the kao-liang roots — brought a jolt, so hideous and yet so exact a parody did they present of living men.

Also scattered in the ruined crops were rotting pieces of equipment — carts, caissons, harness, and uniforms — but none of quite the style or in quite the condition to suggest the spoils which litter formal paintings of battles. There were tons of rations, little paper-wrapped packages of rice, scattered and trampled into the ground, now covered with blossoms of bright orange mold. There were quantities of torn newspapers and magazines, scattered letters, calling cards, and personal papers of all kinds. There were abandoned manuals of arms, pamphlets on the care and handling of guns, sheets of what seemed to be oiling diagrams for artillery — all of them torn and trampled into the mud. Indeed, there were so many crumpled papers that in spots where no corpses could be seen, the small battlefields faintly but definitely suggested popular and ill-kept picnic grounds. Less festive were the unexploded bombs, shells, and hand grenades which lay about at random in the fields. Both sides had apparently been using inferior equipment, and in wet weather, for there were hundreds of duds lying deep in the mud or partially concealed by grass, making every step one to be considered.

By the time we passed through the first wide fields of kao-liang, we had gone more than the promised mile. Our guides were insistent that the wounded were now very close, only one or two li farther south, but after my previous chases after non-existent casualties, I began to have misgivings and it seemed possible that the whole business was a sham cooked up by these coolies to provide employment for themselves.

The farms we passed seemed empty, but occasionally far

fortitude was a clue to the country's immense resources of resistance. Still the war had flowed over them for weeks and made victims of them and they were not yet part of it.

The attitude of such farmers must be the crucial factor in their country's battle, and while their indifference is the product of centuries of habit, there are persistent reports that it is breaking down and being replaced by the determination to sustain partisan warfare. It is unfortunate that accounts of this metamorphosis have so far come chiefly from those who are passionately anxious to believe in it, for if it is indeed a fact, it is an immensely important one. If it has not really been accomplished, China may by sheer size and weight save itself from too shattering a defeat, but if it has been accomplished even in part, Japan's aims are hopeless.

At about quarter to five the last group of coolies arrived; altogether they had found eleven wounded. Ten were soldiers who had to be carried in litters. The eleventh was an old lady who must have been more than seventy-five, as she was accompanied by a daughter who seemed almost sixty. She could still walk, although her arm and breast had been torn by a machine-gun bullet.

Only three of the soldiers were in a condition in which I would have thought it possible for a man to survive. The others were more hideously wrecked and rotted than the first I had seen. The most serious cases had turned literally into garbage and it was impossible to understand how they still lived. The worst one lay on his side in his litter, staring straight before him, his eyes blurred and unmoving. He neither stirred nor cried out during the whole rough journey to the city and the only sign of persisting life was an occasional convulsive shiver. His flesh was a greenish-mustard color and around his wounds it had dissolved into puddles of dark decay. He had been lying in a very unclean place, for over his clothes swarmed thousands of flies and his stench was much stronger and more sickening than that of the entirely dead. I did not examine him, but the coolies told me that his leg, which had been lying next to the bare ground, was crawling with maggots.

It was shocking that we should have been able to find these men within a dozen miles of Peking, for here the fighting had been comparatively light and in Peking there had been at least some effort made to carry on rescue work. It was unbearable to think of the misery on the battlefields which were beginning to spread out into remote country where not even a pretense of relief work could be made, and I'm afraid that the plight of these ten men multiplied by a hundred thousand would still fall short of the suffering that has since been endured on China's plains.

It was the fag end of the rainy afternoon when we finally approached Nan Yuan through the kao-liang fields, down a path at the end of which we could see armed Japanese sentries standing on the wall of the airdrome. This was my time of usefulness, for it was my job to go ahead with the Red Cross flag and demonstrate that the approaching crowd was not composed of Chinese guerrillas. It was a sheepish moment, as the flag was no larger than a handkerchief, but I was relieved to be approaching Nan Yuan under any circumstances. The car was near and the anxiety of wandering through that wet and stinking landscape was finally finished.

Our ambulance was an old omnibus requisitioned for relief work, with no real accommodations for the wounded, and we could only pack our passengers in like so many sides of spoiled beef. It was after five-thirty when we finally set out for Peking, and despite warnings, pleadings, and threats, the Chinese driver, who was determined not to have to spend the night outside the walls, kept pressing his foot on the accelerator; at every jolt indescribable gurgles and bleatings came out of the back of the bus. We reached the walls a few minutes before six and had less trouble getting up to the gate than we had in leaving it, for the crowds which still jammed the approaches moved back at our smell. We were admitted in a few minutes, and without further ado drove over a terribly rutted road into the eastern part of the city and delivered our load of screaming carrion at a hospital.

On the next day I went out again on the same truck in the same direction, but a few miles out of the Yung-Ting Gate we met the Frenchman we had taken out the day before, returning to Peking with his charge piled into a rickshaw. This soldier, also a boy under twenty, had been very oddly wounded in hand-to-hand fighting; threatened by a Japanese with a bayonet he had lunged aside, but tripped by the bayonet had had to leap to regain his balance. While one leg was flying horizontally through the air a stray bullet entered it through the sole of the foot, piercing up to the knee and hamstringing the whole leg. We took these two back into the city and when we had delivered them it was too late to attempt another trip outside the walls.

For several days now all other Red Cross searching trips from Peking had stopped, since wounded could now be reached only by long blind trips such as we had made, and even then the chance of finding them was slim. We had cleaned out what must be the last unsearched area within a day's trip of the city; to be effective now it would be necessary to go into the country for two or three days at a time, and that was too dangerous to be practical. All the other foreign volunteers had given up the job as hopeless and even the Chinese authorities were convinced that no more effort could sensibly be made. My inclinations were in confusion, for I hated the thought of descending into those desolate fields to the south again, and hated equally the thought of not doing so, since it was quite possible that in other fields just off our former route other men were still waiting to die or be rescued.

On the second day after my long trip, while riding to Ta Shih Tso on my bicycle, I skidded on a patch of mud, fell, and twisted my knee. Two days later, before I could be active again, the Chinese Red Cross was dissolved by order of the Japanese military authorities and that was the end of that.

FROM now on I could only be a spectator, but soon that became almost as uncomfortable as a job.

The second week of August had started quietly, even though heavy movements of Japanese and Chinese troops were incessantly reported and Japanese civilians in the South China and Yangtze ports were being hastily evacuated. Japanese warships and troop transports were said to be massing off Shanghai, but the conquerors in the North rested in Peking and Tientsin and there was no shooting except for occasional skirmishes in the crops along the occupied railways. The Japanese naval authorities at Shanghai, allegedly jealous of the glory gained by the army in the North, had attempted to start a fuss over the disappearance of a marine, but their belligerence collapsed when the missing man turned up and confessed he had run away himself because he feared he'd been seen entering a brothel which was out of bounds to marines; in Peking the chatterers reassuringly prophesied that the comic old days of 'incidents' were returning.

Then on the tenth of August the typewritten news bulletins posted in the Peking hotels began carrying a terrifying and sickening story. On the tenth two Japanese were killed when they came indiscreetly close to the Chinese military airdrome in Hungjao, Shanghai's country-club suburb. For two days passions festered in the midsummer heat while Japanese marines and Chinese soldiers poured into Shanghai by the thousand. On the thirteenth savage fighting broke out in Chapei, the crowded Chinese quarter just north of the International Settlement, and thousands of desperate refugees jammed south into the streets of the Settlement while fires set by the explosions began consuming block after block of their homes, spreading a black pall of smoke over the whole city.

On the fourteenth — Bloody Saturday — the fighting became heavier, and it was demonstrated that even for spectators this war was to be something more than it had been in the North. Foreign sight-seers who went to the roofs of the two big water-front hotels to watch the artillery duel over the river had an unpleasant surprise at cocktail time when a Chinese plane flew over to bomb the Japanese flagship *Idzumo*, docked beside the Bund. The plane flew so high that the pilot's aim was faulty — so high, indeed, that it was some time before the watchers in the hotels realized that instead of falling toward the river, the explosives were plummeting down straight over their own heads. After a few seconds of screaming panic the bombs ricocheted thunderously down the side of one hotel, blasting a crater in the street below and blowing the life and shape out of some two hundred passers-by. A few minutes later, another set of bombs lighted on a corner still deeper in the Settlement, squashing and burning eight hundred more. From the fourteenth on, day and night the big shells screamed over the city and in the lesser confusion of machine-gun and rifle-fire, thousands suffered and died. Partly by accident, perhaps, partly by intention, a major war had started.

In the second week of August, also, the Japanese army in the North began pushing out from the conquered cities, south from Tientsin on the railway to Shanghai, south from Peking on the railway to Hankow, and north from Peking on the railway to Suiyuan. On the eleventh their northern vanguard reached the foot of Nankow Pass, twenty-five miles from Peking, and engaged in a sharp skirmish with strong Chinese forces. On the twelfth their bombing planes set afire the town at Nankow and the Chinese retreated into natural fortifications among the heights by the Great Wall. For more than two weeks a fierce battle raged here, and through all the hot, moist days of August, the noise of its explosions rolled down across the Peking plain. Shortly after the middle of the month another battle, also audible, began on the Hankow railway south of the city, and fierce skirmishing commenced in the mountains to the southwest. But then on the twenty-third it was reported that a Japanese force marching cross-country from Manchukuo had reached the Suiyuan railway north of Nankow, bottling its defenders in the pass. Through the next week they advanced slowly toward Peking; on the twenty-ninth the trapped Chinese exploded half a dozen locomotives in the tunnel by the Wall, blocking the line completely, and then scattered into the mountains. At the same time the Japanese south of Peking gradually fought their front line down out of earshot of the city. Soon the fine autumn weather began and the roads dried, and became passable to mechanized forces. Active troops were no longer quartered inside Peking and often for days at a time there was no sound of guns.

Now the conflict really had passed on, but at last it began to have its effect on Peking. The walls which had been proof against the violence of early summer could not keep out the sadness, ugliness, and monotony of a prolonging war. Peking was the city enclosed no longer. Over it floated a captive balloon tethered to the Chien Men Gate, trailing the names of newly conquered cities — Kalgan, Chochow, Machang, Paoting, Tatung — and in its shadow the Pekinese were ignominiously learning the manners of a government by force.

Throughout the city there were sudden and unwarranted invasions of private houses — searches for Nationalist literature, Kuomintang insignia, or pictures of Chiang Kai-

Shek and Sun-Yat-Sen. There were sudden arrests, without explanation and sometimes without cause. On a less serious but no less aggravating plan were the hundred smaller changes in the accustomed life of the city; the mails were interfered with and every letter was opened and scrutinized for suspicious sentiments. Despite this surveillance, incidentally, the new government could not yet afford to print new stamps and all letters still bore the likenesses of Chiang Kai-Shek or Sun-Yat-Sen. In mid-September the Chinese schools did not open and it was announced that they would remain closed until textbooks quite free of pro-Chinese bias could be procured. At the same time compulsory lessons in Japanese were started for policemen and trolley conductors, while shopkeepers and chauffeurs were rather bluntly advised that it would be convenient if they could learn the new tongue too.

It seemed a special indignity to the logical and humorous Chinese that this should not be a frank conquest, but, in accord with the curious plans of the Japanese military, must be disguised as a spontaneous movement for autonomy. Now that laughter was dangerous it was sickening for them to watch Japanese and Korean ronins swarming over their city tacking up slogans, such as, 'North China for the North Chinese,' and it was abominable for them to be forced to bow politely to the omnipresent Japanese sentries — their friends from across the sea who were helping them to establish a more 'sincere' government.

Though so far no puppets had been found except disgruntled riffraff and anti-Nanking politicians in retirement since the fall of the Empire — so senile that not even the Japanese wanted them — incessant parades and demonstrations were nevertheless arranged to give photographic evidence of this government's existence.

As an example, one afternoon I saw a long line of women and girls in rickshaws parading through the Legation Quarter under the escort of a few Japanese in cutaways.

Each wore a paper peony, and their rickshaws were decorated with banners proclaiming that this was 'The North
China Association of Female College Students,' on its way
to comfort the Japanese soldiers who were defending the
city. Half a dozen of the younger girls might really have
been students; they crouched in their seats, frightened and
embarrassed. Others rode with their hands or handkerchiefs
over their faces so that no one might recognize them. But
the majority of the women, brassy-eyed and painted, were
obviously prostitutes, while some in poor blue clothes were
housewives of the lowest class, who must earn money in
whatever way they could — some of these 'students' were
old peasant women over sixty.

Later in September, at the time of the harvest moon, the
Japanese ordered that the traditional Lantern Festival be
turned into a grand celebration of autonomy. On the night
of the full moon it had been customary for the children and
young people of the city to walk about carrying fantastic
paper lanterns constructed in the form of fish, flowers, birds,
dragons, and so on. The conquerors ordered that as further
celebration lines of red and white paper lamps be strung
down all the big streets — the cost of the lamps, candles,
and ropes to be collected from the householders along the
way.

On the night of the festival the prescribed lamps glowed
in long, regularly aligned rows, but no strollers walked between them brandishing comic or fantastic lanterns. The
streets were almost deserted, and after a while the lines of
untended lights guttered away or flared up, charring the
strings which held them, and fell on the ground to flame
briefly before burning out.

Even in the minor details of its everyday appearance,
Peking was changing sadly, and in the cool September sunlight its streets began to seem like those of another city.
The high-stepping rickshaw boys who had once trotted
proudly down the middle of the avenues, shouting loiterers

out of their path, now dragged their carts slowly along the gutters, for down the center of the streets Japanese trucks and motor-cycles roared incessantly. Every day more of the cautious rickshaws were piled with luggage and furniture as Pekinese families of brothers and cousins began moving in with each other to retrench for the coming winter and the many to follow; with so much of the farmland around the city ruined or inaccessible the price of food was going higher and with most of the coal-mines in the Western Hills entirely cut off, the price of coal was skyrocketing. Already the unsettled conditions of the summer had ruined a large proportion of those thousands who lived from hand to mouth under the best conditions, and at all hours the streets resounded with the cries of an unprecedented number of beggars.

The street-cleaning departments had apparently become disorganized under the stress of events, for the pavement of even the biggest streets was frequently left unwatered and unswept. In the small unpaved streets and alleys the puddles created by the August rains soon thickened into stretches of stagnant mud, dotted with decaying garbage, and the faint persistent stink of these morasses hung over the whole city. Breeding here and, so it was claimed, among the still unburied cadavers beyond the walls, the worst plague of flies in years swarmed over Peking, polluting even the most sheltered courtyards.

Except for the increasing multitude of beggars and the bewildered refugees who from time to time straggled in from the growing areas of untenable farmland, the actual misery of the civilian Chinese was surprisingly little seen, hidden as if was behind private walls and the resigned attitudes of a stoic race. Of course the Chinese soldiers who were occasionally maimed within reach of the city could never appear in it now, since they lay beyond an active military front and must either be rescued from the other side or decay without help.

Conversely, even so soon a certain amount of Japanese distress was becoming evident in Peking, and though their triumphal balloon always trailed the news of fresh conquests overhead, the invaders were beginning to seem almost as much the victims of their own war.

The cheerful young warriors who had swarmed over Peking after its fall were the first to march on, and in the last weeks of August it was reported that they had begun to perish by the hundred, particularly on the slopes of Nankow Pass. Whenever possible their bodies were carted down to the environs of Peking, stacked in heaps, soaked with gasoline, and ignited — the black smoke ascending from such pyres could be seen from the roof of the Hôtel de Pékin. Then the ashes were packed in small white boxes, each inscribed with the name of one of the dead; these were brought to a temporary shrine of straw matting erected in the space outside the Legation Quarter and after the proper military and religious services, were dispatched to Japan. Meanwhile, as Peking was reasonably safe from counter-attack, it was manned by second- and third-rate troops to whom the possibility of being killed was plainly only one of the many disadvantages to a war. These were the older men — small shopkeepers, clerks, and farmers — settled husbands and fathers still surprised at the sudden change in their lives. Sometimes in spasms of bravado they got red-facedly drunk and tried to act as victorious troops are expected to, but more often they tramped rather mournfully about the conquered city, staring apathetically at the lame but recovering bustle of Chinese life or watching with home-sick wistfulness the Chinese children who played in the streets.

That the war was not easy even for the young Japanese who remained alive was demonstrated graphically to me one morning when I saw a company which had just returned from the country and was resting on the street at the end of my alley, waiting to be assigned to one of the barracks; this street was the one which bounds the Forbidden City on the north, separating it from the enclosure of Coal Hill.

Previously the troops I'd seen inside Peking had been well dressed, well equipped, and under perfect discipline. Whatever else they might do, they always observed the smaller proprieties. These troops in the street, however, were too exhausted to think of any rules. For convenience in tethering, some of their horses had been driven up into the Imperial entranceways on either side of the road, and just as they must have during the medieval invasions, the animals stood wearily chewing straw inside the ornate little pavilions, their halters knotted about the red-lacquer columns, their dung fouling the white marble floor. In the street on either side of the gate the other beasts stood patiently under their burdens of guns, tents, and ammunition. All of them were covered with sores and fantastically emaciated. Some were wounded — one had a broken or sprained leg to which was bound the branch of a tree, half splint, half crutch. Among the horses stood impromptu replacements; several donkeys, grotesquely small under their immense loads, even one stolid black ox with a pair of machine guns strapped on its back.

The men were in as sad condition as their animals. Their chins black with unkempt beards, their eyes glazed with exhaustion, they lay with their backs propped against the red walls of the Forbidden City and their muddy legs sprawling across the sidewalks. Some were wounded, their hurts tied up with bandages which had once been properly wound but were now muddy and unraveled, their broken limbs bound with boards or branches. Some turned toward the passing traffic faces of a terrible pasty whiteness, out of which mattered eyes stared with the dull boredom of the diseased. Some few had collapsed entirely and lay either asleep or unconscious on the sidewalk and the roadway itself, their cheeks flat against the dirty pavement.

By the end of September the official front had receded along the railways for more than a hundred miles north and south of Peking and the warfare around the city was taking the form it has held ever since — and will no doubt hold for a good many years to come. The Japanese had the use of the railways and the few highways; their activity already lay less in fighting out from these communications than in establishing garrisons, cutting down crops, evacuating farmers, and so on, to make these lanes of conquered country safer.

The Chinese held the hills and the inaccessible sections of flatland, or, to put it specifically, the Chinese held all the land not actively surveyed by Japanese soldiers. That they were not passively occupying it was demonstrated two or three times a week, when the sound of explosions could be heard in the city and Japanese bombing planes could be seen flying out from the Peking airdrome to drop their loads on the hills or the farther stretches of flatland. According to the Japanese press representatives this was only bombing practice, but the targets often became mobile enough to cut the railways and highways and once or twice those in the Western Hills managed to take over the power station twelve miles from Peking, temporarily depriving the city of electricity. Also, as the weeks passed, more and more Japanese soldiers, venturing into the target country to mop up, either returned to Peking in the spent condition I had seen, or returned only to be packed in the small white boxes for their return to Japan.

As a matter of interest to anyone other than myself, my story really ends with my last trip for the Red Cross. After that I went back to Ta Shih Tso and tried to paint until my lease should expire, when I would have to start for America. I was still upset by what I'd seen, heard, and smelled outside — until the rains cleared up in early September all the houses of Peking were moldy and this faint but penetrating odor of decay kept returning me to the stinking fields of Nan Yuan. However, I repaired the paintings I'd smudged when I refugeed and did a few more; in the last week of September I had an exhibition of them at the Peking Institute of Fine Arts, whose committee was then casting about for any kind of show to put in their gallery, to demonstrate to the Japanese that they would continue as usual.

In the clear, cool September weather the big courtyard of my house was more than ever an ideally comfortable living-room. It was full of yellow and white chrysanthemums now, brought in and planted in full bloom for the equivalent of a penny a bush. As I was to leave soon, Chou's wife was very busy these days, making under her husband's supervision a fancy farewell present for me. This was a pair of black cloth bedroom slippers with their toe-ends embroidered in the semblance of stylized pigs' faces, the pig being an animal of auspicious meaning; the slippers had round cross-eyes of white cloth, embroidered scarlet nostrils, and loose scarlet-lined ears built to flap with every step.

Simply writing about such things here makes me realize again how out of place I and those like me had become. It is unimportant when considered in relation to the real miseries of war, but for the self-devoted foreigners in China, and for those Chinese who by position instead of race were similarly released from the press of circumstances, the beginning of the fighting meant that the individual life, pleasant and unconstrained, had become painfully inappropriate, really impossible.

At the time I was vaguely aware of this — I knew of course that the kind of life I'd led and the agreeable travels I'd taken were for an indefinite time out of the question, if only for reasons of mechanics. I felt, but vaguely too, that a catastrophe on such a scale imposed a problem requiring more than a negative response, more than a decently averted eye. I wanted to go to Shanghai to see if I couldn't help again, but my somewhat shapeless impulses were controlled by one very concrete fact. My money was gone and my conscience could not prompt me to do anything unless it was profitable enough to support me; indeed, I must start back to America immediately or be stranded.

Just before I left Peking I made one more trip outside the walls to chauffeur a friend of mine, a correspondent, on his way to interview a company of Chinese, officially called bandits, who had kidnaped half a dozen French priests from a monastery in the hills behind the Summer Palace and were demanding as ransom enough money to outfit themselves completely with arms and ammunition. My friend wanted to find just what sort of men these kidnapers were and how their captives were being treated. My part in the trip was a simple one; I drove him to the abandoned spa about fifteen miles from the city and left him there to walk the three or four remaining miles between the automobile road and the camp where the priests were held. Not a Chinese soldier — regular or irregular — did I see, though on the road out we passed several trucks of heavily armed Japanese off for their daily mopping-up.

In two days my friend returned with a strange account of the outlaws. They were a company of several hundred men, some refugee farmers, some soldiers from companies which had been scattered at Nankow. They were led by a few officers from Nankow and a sprinkling of students from the Peking colleges. They were organized as a military unit and were completely under military discipline. Besides rifles they had several salvaged machine guns and even a few pieces of artillery, all of it located less than twenty miles from Peking and well behind the Japanese frontier. That they were not conventional bandits even in their treatment of prisoners was shown by a set of snapshots the correspondent brought back; these were in the style of school group pictures and showed the captive priests seated in dignity in a line of carved blackwood chairs, smiling broadly, with several of their young captors in a row behind them, smiling and leaning on the backs of the chairs like so many fond nephews. The priests, incidentally, were later returned in good condition, though still unransomed, when the Japanese surrounded this area and the Chinese were forced to retreat into the hills.

These were very odd bandits, but at that time it seemed that their unusual character might only be the product of a fortunate set of local circumstances — they were one of the first large bands of guerrillas to develop and it was some time before their organization was to become a typical one. Since then, they and the thousands like them have proved to be China's most effective weapon for ridding herself of her attackers, but then their presence so near Peking seemed only another mildly surprising accident in a war which was full of freakish and unexpected events. As I had not seen them and had only heard of them at second hand, I could not even suspect the possible implications of their activity. The incident did nothing to mitigate the slack horror I felt toward this war, and when I left I still carried a picture of it as a terrible inert disease, like cancer or gangrene, spreading out through the healthy body of the countryside, leaving behind it only dead areas of empty farms, flooded and blasted roads, and ruined crops full of the cloying stink of unburied corpses.

And when I left Peking in mid-October the disease was beginning to spread with fatal rapidity. In the North the front was steadily pushing up the railway toward Kweihwa. The provinces of Shantung and Shansi had been invaded and their capitals, Tsinan and Taiyuan, were threatened. Though among the ruined suburbs of Shanghai, savage hand-to-hand fighting still flowed constantly without advantage to either side, the Chinese forces there were plainly weakening under the punishment of the Japanese big guns. When I left Harbin in early November the fighting at

Shanghai had at last swept west of the International Settlement and for thousands the long trek into the interior had begun; Tsinan had fallen and Japanese cannon were near enough Taiyuan to land shells inside its walls. As I was moved slowly across Siberia and Russia, then more rapidly across Europe, Taiyuan fell, Kweihwa was taken, Soochow west of Shanghai was captured, and Hangchow south of it was conceded lost. Before I could reach America in December, the capital at Nanking was brutally invaded by conquerors who thought they had won the war.

But the news which followed me on that rapid trip halfway round the world was only one of the things which made the journey disheartening. At the Manchukuan-Siberian border the frontier was a mile-wide no-man's-land, striped with barbed-wire entanglements and guarded as grimly as if war here were also a fact. The week's trip from the border to Moscow was lengthened to eight days because at almost every station the passenger cars had to wait in sidings while troop trains for the Mongolian frontier filed by. On the westbound train with me were young Russian aviators and tank-drivers plainly on their way to another front as they amused themselves in the dining-car by speaking to each other in halting textbook Spanish.

Even after the warring Orient, the trip across Europe had a medieval flavor; I passed the Russo-Polish, Polish-German, and German-French frontiers after nothing but savage questioning but for some of my temporary fellow passengers each border was a barrier beyond which they could not venture without appalling risks. Across the Atlantic I sailed on a boat full of refugee German Jews. It was a sick world, and it was dismal to speculate how soon the more virulent disease might break out in other parts of its surface.

Just as a personal footnote, out of the string of disasters in China whose reverberations reached me through radios and papers on that headlong westward journey, there came news which was to change entirely the direction of my plans.

Early in December, when the Japanese were advancing dangerously close to Nanking, the Chinese Government began its flight inland. The executive branch re-established itself at Hankow, but already many of the administrative bureaus, as well as the colleges and some of the refugee factories, were pushing into the extreme southwestern provinces, Szechuan, Yunnan, and Kweichow. In perspective it still seems to me that this first moving of the capital was the most dangerous period for China's resistance, the most serious trial of Chiang Kai-Shek as a national leader and his Government as a national government; when through the garbled dispatches of those tense December days it appeared that the move had been successfully effected, I was confident that, whatever its outcome, this war would be a long one.

From what I had seen of the geography of central and western China, and what I knew of the tremendous advantage enjoyed by Japan's mechanized troops when operating on flatlands, I felt that sooner or later the Government must also abandon Hankow and the other cities on the plain, retreating beyond the mountains for the long fight.

But once entrenched in the inaccessible western half of their country, I was certain — and still am — that the Chinese would be in territory which could never be invaded. And soon, war or no war, it was inevitable that the rich but incredibly backward West would become a boom country, rushing through centuries of development in as many years, growing even more rapidly and spectacularly than our American West because it was so much richer to begin with, and its changes would be forced on it as an emergency.

My painting in the West had led me into a rather desultory pursuit of tribal subjects, mainly because their appearance was a novelty after the uniform masses of Chinese, but now suddenly this work took on a meaning I had never considered before. With the changes in the West, the tribes must be assimilated and their peculiar cultures would disappear as irrevocably as those of the American aborigines had; among the invincibly prolific Chinese who had crowded out or swallowed so many other peoples in their long history, the process should take still less time than it had in America. If any record of the tribes in their native condition was to be made, it must be started immediately. In many ways I was not qualified to try even a pictorial record, but for that at least I had had some experience. Before I reached America I knew that if I could possibly manage it and if there still be time, I would go back.

THE END